MONTGOMERY COLLEGE LIBRARY
ROCKVILLE CAMPUS

FIFTY ESSAYS

FIFTY ESSAYS

EDITED BY

BERGEN EVANS

Essay Index Reprint Series

 BOOKS FOR LIBRARIES PRESS
FREEPORT, NEW YORK

First Published 1936
Reprinted 1972

Library of Congress Cataloging in Publication Data

Evans, Bergen, 1904- comp.
   Fifty essays.

   (Essay index reprint series)
   1. English essays.
PR1363.E8 1972   824'.008   72-5798
ISBN 0-8369-2988-8

PRINTED IN THE UNITED STATES OF AMERICA

FOREWORD

THE essays that compose this collection were selected for their intrinsic merits. They are not meant to illustrate types of the essay or the development of English prose style; the chronological arrangement is merely a matter of convenience.

They include great variety. There are narrative essays, biographical, humorous, ironical, critical, familiar, and scientific. Some are short. Some are long. Some are so simple that they may be read for pure pleasure and need not be discussed in class. Others, difficult but not obscure, will challenge the fullest efforts of the best students. Bacon's essays in particular, demanding the closest attention if their subtle and concentrated thoughts are to be untwined, offer excellent discipline. It is for this reason that so many of them have been included. A lighter but no less valuable exercise is offered by the brilliant series of metaphors in the seventeenth-century "Characters."

Quite a number of the essays in this volume have been chosen with the idea that perhaps the way to stimulate thought on contemporary events is to let the student view some aspect of a current issue which is sufficiently remote or disguised for him not to perceive immediately that it *is* a current issue; and then, his prejudices having been thus thrown off the scent, when he has dispassionately formed an opinion — well, let *him* find out that Utgard-Loki's cat is the Midgard serpent!

To give a specific example, the student who is outraged by "A Modest Proposal" will find his own indignant way (equally surely, whether he plunge forward or backward) to the "current" problem of unemployment. And he who has read Bacon's "Of Judicature" with care, and arrived, almost disinterested, at a conclusion, will suddenly find that he has committed himself to an opinion on some of the most burning of present-day issues.

This essay, incidentally, illustrates rather strikingly the value of an anthology which draws its material from a considerable range of literature rather than from contemporary periodicals. Ten years ago it would have been regarded as quaint, embodying a conception of the relation of the judiciary to the sovereignty that was outmoded in the seventeenth century. To-day it would be hard to find any treatment of the subject more timely, more "advanced," more "radical." And if the student perceived that, it might awaken in him a realization of the fact that some of the great "problems of the day" have been with us for quite a while and, what is more, a great deal of very good thought has long been given to them.

It is hoped, however, that the numerous nineteenth-century and contemporary essays will convey the complementary idea that if thinking did not begin yesterday it also did not stop the day before.

The five brief biographical sketches have been carefully chosen for their intrinsic biographical worth, not for their historical value. They serve as excellent commentaries, by the way, on Bacon's "Of Simulation,"

FOREWORD vii

"Of Great Place," and "Of Negotiating," and they also illustrate the sixtieth *Rambler,* which André Maurois and Harold Nicolson have declared to be one of the best things on the art of biography ever written. The most delightful of them all, that of Ralph Kettell, is a beautiful exemplification of Johnson's assertion that the merit of a biography has no relation to the importance of its subject.

That various of the essays here presented so illustrate and develop each other was a considerable factor in determining their selection. There are several such related groups: Bacon's "Of Simulation" (practically "A Home Manual of Lying") defines his "Of Truth," and Johnson's account of Marvel's journey illustrates them both; Johnson and Bacon both treat of friendship, but they approach it from opposite poles; Bacon, Steele, Johnson, and Beerbohm discuss conversation; "On the Feeling of Immortality in Youth" and "Aes Triplex" are supplementary; and many other of the essays are reflected in each other's facets.

Although essays dealing with literary subjects have been, for the most part, omitted, it would have been bending over backwards to have ruled them out entirely. And so from the least pedantic of all the great critical essays, Johnson's Preface to his edition of Shakespeare, the best part has been selected.

Since such volumes as this are frequently used in courses that include composition as a part of the regular work, it might not be amiss to point out that many of the essays suggest topics for writing. I have had very good results with the "Directions to Servants"; the students write "Directions" for weeks after to anyone who has annoyed them. The seventeenth-century "Characters" evoke some amusing modern counterparts. Johnson's account of Will Marvel suggests a host of parallels. And so on.

My obligations are many. Certainly the first of them is to the authors from whose works I have so freely drawn, and the second to those publishers who have permitted the use of copyrighted material. A due statement of this particular indebtedness has been made before each essay so included. But that does not cover all obligations. Although the biographical sketches, for instance, are taken from the indicated sources, no one can enter that field without being indebted to Professor Nichol Smith's *Characters of the Seventeenth Century*. And although Aubrey's vignette of Ralph Kettell is taken from the manuscript in the Bodleian, I am directly indebted, as are all lovers of that "roving and maggotieheaded" gossip, to the *Brief Lives* as edited by Dr. Andrew Clark. Both of these books are from the Clarendon Press, and it is to be hoped that many students will be led to them by these brief samples.

To thank my colleagues for their assistance is almost impertinent. So many of their ideas are embodied in the book that it would be no great exaggeration to regard myself as their secretary. I am particularly grateful to Professor Bryan, Professor Prior, and Professor Lawrence Wright for their suggestions, encouragement, and patience.

BERGEN EVANS

CONTENTS

FOREWORD v

SIR WALTER RALEIGH (1552–1618)
   THE LAST FIGHT OF THE "REVENGE" . . 3

FRANCIS BACON (1561–1626)
   OF TRUTH 12
   OF DEATH 15
   OF SIMULATION AND DISSIMULATION . . 17
   OF MARRIAGE AND SINGLE LIFE . . . 21
   OF GREAT PLACE 23
   OF WISDOM FOR A MAN'S SELF . . . 27
   OF FRIENDSHIP 29
   OF REGIMEN OF HEALTH 37
   OF DISCOURSE 39
   OF YOUTH AND AGE 41
   OF NEGOTIATING 43
   OF STUDIES 45
   OF JUDICATURE 47

SIR THOMAS OVERBURY (1581–1613)
   AN IGNORANT GLORY-HUNTER . . . 53

JOHN EARLE (1601?–1665)
   A MERE EMPTY WIT 54
   A DETRACTOR 55

CONTENTS

SAMUEL BUTLER (1612–1680)
The Rude Man 57
A Flatterer 58

EDWARD HYDE, EARL OF CLARENDON (1609–1674)
The Earl of Arundel 60
John Hampden 62

SIR PHILIP WARWICK (1609–1683)
The Earl of Strafford 67

JOHN AUBREY (1626–1697)
Ralph Kettell 71

GILBERT BURNET, BISHOP OF SALISBURY (1643–1715)
Charles II 78

JONATHAN SWIFT (1667–1745)
A Modest Proposal 83
Directions to Servants 94
   Rules that Concern All Servants in General — Directions to the Butler — Directions to the House-Maid

JOSEPH ADDISON (1672–1719)
Ned Softly 105
Signor Nicolini and the Lions . . . 109
On News-Writers and Readers . . . 114

SIR RICHARD STEELE (1672–1729)
On Conversation 119

CONTENTS

SAMUEL JOHNSON (1709–1784)
- BIOGRAPHY 124
- FRIENDSHIP 129
- POPULARITY 134
- WILL MARVEL'S JOURNEY 139
- MARVEL PARALLELED 143
- SHAKESPEARE 146

CHARLES LAMB (1775–1834)
- POOR RELATIONS 161

WILLIAM HAZLITT (1778–1830)
- VULGARITY AND AFFECTATION . . . 171
- ON THE FEELING OF IMMORTALITY IN YOUTH 184

THOMAS CARLYLE (1795–1881)
- DEMOCRACY 198

HENRY DAVID THOREAU (1817–1862)
- LIFE WITHOUT PRINCIPLE 214

JOHN RUSKIN (1819–1900)
- THE CROWN OF WILD OLIVE: INTRODUCTION 232

MATTHEW ARNOLD (1822–1888)
- SWEETNESS AND LIGHT 247

THOMAS HENRY HUXLEY (1825–1895)
- ON A PIECE OF CHALK 265

ROBERT LOUIS STEVENSON (1850–1894)
- AES TRIPLEX 294
- THE LANTERN-BEARERS 305

BERTRAND RUSSELL (1872–   )
  A FREE MAN'S WORSHIP 320

MAX BEERBOHM (1872–   )
  LAUGHTER 332

G. K. CHESTERTON (1874–   )
  SCIENCE AND THE SAVAGES 347

J. B. S. HALDANE (1892–   )
  ON BEING THE RIGHT SIZE 355

FIFTY ESSAYS

THE LAST FIGHT OF THE *REVENGE*[1]

SIR WALTER RALEIGH (1552–1618)

THE Lord Thomas Howard, with six of her majesty's ships, six victuallers of London, the bark *Ralegh,* and two or three other pinnaces, riding at anchor near unto Flores, one of the westerly islands of the Azores, the last of August in the afternoon, had intelligence by one Captain Middleton of the approach of the Spanish armada. Which Middleton, being in a very good sailer, had kept them company three days before, of good purpose both to discover their forces the more, as also to give advice to my Lord Thomas of their approach. He had no sooner delivered the news but the fleet was in sight: many of our ships' companies were on shore in the island, some providing ballast for their ships; others filling of water and refreshing themselves from the land with such things as they could either for money or by force recover. By reason whereof our ships being all pestered and rummaging everything out of order, very light for want of ballast, and that which was most to our disadvantage, the one half part of the men of every ship sick and utterly unserviceable; for in the *Revenge* there were ninety diseased; in the *Bonaventure* not so many in health as could handle her mainsail. For had not twenty men

[1] From *A Report of the Truth of the Fight about the Isles of the Azores, the last of August 1591, etc.*

been taken out of a bark of Sir George Carey's, his being commanded to be sunk, and those appointed to her, she had hardly ever recovered England. The rest, for the most part, were in little better state. The names of her majesty's ships were these, as followeth: the *Defiance,* which was admiral, the *Revenge* vice-admiral, the *Bonaventure,* commanded by Captain Crosse, the *Lion* by George Fenner, the *Foresight* by Mr. Thomas Vavasour, and the *Crane* by Duffild. The *Foresight* and the *Crane* being but small ships, only the other were of the middle size; the rest, besides the bark *Ralegh,* commanded by Captain Thin, were victuallers and were of small force or none. The Spanish fleet having shrouded their approach by reason of the island, were now so soon at hand as our ships had scarce time to weigh their anchors, but some of them were driven to let slip their cables and set sail. Sir Richard Grenvill was the last that weighed, to recover the men that were upon the island, which otherwise had been lost. The Lord Thomas with the rest very hardly recovered the wind, which Sir Richard Grenvill not being able to do was persuaded by the master [2] and others to cut his mainsail and cast about and to trust to the sailing of the ship, for the squadron of Seville were on his weather-bow. But Sir Richard utterly refused to turn from the enemy, alleging that he would rather choose to die than to dishonor himself, his country and her majesty's ship, persuading his company that he would pass through the two squadrons in despite of them and enforce those of Seville to give him way.

[2] What we to-day should call the captain. In Elizabethan times the captain, or commander, often had no knowledge of navigation; that was the province of his subordinate, the master. Sir Richard, second in command of the entire force, has both a captain and a master under him.

Which he performed upon divers of the foremost, who, as the mariners term it, sprang their luff and fell under the lee of the *Revenge*. But the other course had been the better, and might right well have been answered in so great an impossibility of prevailing. Notwithstanding, out of the greatness of his mind he could not be persuaded. In the meanwhile as he attended those which were nearest him, the great *San Philip,* being in the wind of him and coming towards him, becalmed his sails in such sort as the ship could neither make way nor feel the helm; so huge and high carged [3] was the Spanish ship — being of a thousand and five hundred tons — who after laid the *Revenge* aboard. When he was thus bereft of his sails, the ships that were under his lee, luffing up, also laid him aboard; of which the next [4] was the admiral of the Biscayans, a very mighty and puissant ship, commanded by Brittandona. The said *Philip* carried three tier of ordnance on a side and eleven pieces in every tier. She shot eight forth right out of her chase,[5] besides those of her stern ports.

After the *Revenge* was entangled with this *Philip* four others boarded her, two on her larboard [6] and two on her starboard. The fight thus beginning at three o'clock in the afternoon continued very terrible all that evening. But the great *San Philip* having received the lower tier of the *Revenge,* discharged with cross-bar shot, shifted herself with all diligence from her sides, utterly misliking her first entertainment. Some say the ship foundered, but we cannot report it for truth unless we were assured. The Spanish ships were

[3] built so high above the water
[4] nearest
[5] bow
[6] port (left side, facing from stem to bow)

filled with companies of soldiers, in some two hundred, besides the mariners; in some five, in others eight hundred. In ours there were none at all besides the mariners, but the servants of the commanders and some few voluntary gentlemen only. After many interchanged volleys of great ordnance and small shot, the Spaniards deliberated to enter the *Revenge* and made divers attempts, hoping to force her by the multitudes of their armed soldiers and musketeers, but were still repulsed again and again and at all times beaten back into their own ships or into the seas. In the beginning of the fight the *George Noble* of London, having received some shot through her by the armadas, fell under the lee of the *Revenge* and asked Sir Richard what he would command him, being but one of the victuallers and of small force. Sir Richard bid him save himself and leave him to his fortune. After the fight had thus, without intermission, continued while the day lasted and some hours of the night, many of our men were slain and hurt and one of the great galleons of the armada and the admiral of the hulks both sunk, and in many other of the Spanish ships great slaughter was made. Some write that Sir Richard was very dangerously hurt almost in the beginning of the fight and lay speechless for a time ere he recovered. But two of the *Revenge's* own company, brought home in a ship of Lyme [7] from the islands, examined by some of the lords and others, affirmed that he was never so wounded as that he forsook the upper deck till an hour before midnight, and then, being shot in the body with a musket, as he was a-dressing [8] was again shot into the head and withal his surgeon wounded

[7] an English seaport
[8] having his wound dressed

to death. This agreeth also with an examination taken by Sir Francis Godolphin of four other mariners of the same ship being returned, which examination the said Sir Francis sent unto Master William Killegrew of her majesty's privy chamber.

But to return to the fight, the Spanish ships which attempted to board the *Revenge,* as they were wounded and beaten off, so always others came in their places, she having never less than two mighty galleons by her sides and aboard her; so that ere the morning, from three of the clock the day before, there had fifteen several armadas assailed her, and all so ill approved their entertainment as they were by the break of day far more willing to harken to a composition than hastily to make any more assaults or entries. But as the day increased, so our men decreased; and as the light grew more and more, by so much more grew our discomforts, for none appeared in sight but enemies — saving one small ship called the *Pilgrim,* commanded by Jacob Whiddon, who hovered all night to see the success,[9] but in the morning, bearing with the *Revenge,* was hunted like a hare amongst many ravenous hounds, but escaped.

All the powder of the *Revenge,* to the last barrel, was now spent, all her pikes broken, forty of her best men slain and the most part of the rest hurt. In the beginning of the fight she had but one hundred free from sickness, and four score and ten sick laid in hold upon the ballast. A small troop to man such a ship, and a weak garrison to resist so mighty an army. By those hundred all was sustained: the volleys, boardings and enterings of fifteen ships of war, besides those which beat her at large. On the contrary, the Spanish were

[9] outcome, issue

always supplied with soldiers brought from every squadron, all manner of arms and powder at will. Unto ours there remained no comfort at all, no hope, no supply either of ships, men or weapons; the masts all beaten overboard, all her tackle cut asunder, her upper work altogether razed, and in effect evened she was with the water, but the very foundation or bottom of a ship, nothing being left overhead either for flight or defence. Sir Richard finding himself in this distress and unable any longer to make resistance, having endured in this fifteen hours' fight the assault of fifteen several armadas, all by turns aboard him, and by estimation eight hundred shot of great artillery, besides many assaults and entries; and that the ship and himself must needs be possessed by the enemy, who were now all cast in a ring round about him (the *Revenge* not able to move one way or other but as she was moved with the waves and billows of the sea) commanded the master gunner, whom he knew to be a most resolute man, to split and sink the ship, that thereby nothing might remain of glory or victory to the Spaniards; seeing that in so many hours' fight, and with so great a navy, they were not able to take her, having had fifteen hours time, above ten thousand men and fifty and three sail of men of war to perform it withal; and persuaded the company, or as many as he could induce, to yield themselves unto God and to the mercy of none else, but, as they had like valiant resolute men repulsed so many enemies, they should not now shorten the honor of their nation by prolonging their lives for a few hours or a few days. The master gunner readily condescended, and divers others, but the captain and the master were of another opinion and besought Sir Richard to have care of them, alleging that the Spaniard would be as ready to entertain a composition [10] as they were willing to offer the same; and that there being divers sufficient and valiant men yet living, and whose wounds were not mortal, they might do their country and prince acceptable service hereafter. And whereas Sir Richard had alleged that the Spaniards should never glory to have taken one ship of her majesty, seeing they had so long and so notably defended themselves, they answered that the ship had six feet of water in hold, three shot under water, which were so weakly stopped as with the first working of the sea she must needs sink, and was besides so crushed and bruised as she could never be removed out of the place.

And as the matter was thus in dispute, and Sir Richard refusing to harken to any of those reasons, the master of the *Revenge* (while the captain won unto him the greater party) was conveyed aboard the General Don Alfonso Baçan, who (finding none over hasty to enter the *Revenge* again, doubting lest [11] Sir Richard would have blown them up and himself and perceiving by the report of the master of the *Revenge* his dangerous disposition [12]) yielded that all their lives should be saved, the company sent for England, and the better sort to pay such reasonable ransom as their estate would bear, and in the mean season to be free from galley or imprisonment. To this he so much the rather condescended as well, as I have said, for fear of further loss and mischief to themselves, as also for the desire he had to recover Sir Richard Grenvill, whom for his notable valor he seemed greatly to honor and admire.

[10] come to terms
[11] fearing that
[12] inclination, desire

When this answer was returned, and that safety of life was promised, the common sort being now at the end of their peril, the most drew back from Sir Richard and the master gunner, being no hard matter to dissuade men from death to life. The master gunner, finding himself and Sir Richard thus prevented and mastered by the greater number, would have slain himself with a sword had he not been by force withheld and locked into his cabin. Then the general sent many boats aboard the *Revenge* and divers of our men, fearing Sir Richard's disposition, stole away aboard the General and other ships. Sir Richard thus overmatched was sent unto by Alfonso Baçan to remove out of the *Revenge,* the ship being marvellous unsavory, filled with blood and bodies of dead and wounded men like a slaughter house. Sir Richard answered that he might do with his body what he list, for he esteemed it not, and as he was carried out of the ship he swooned, and, reviving again, desired the company to pray for him. The general used Sir Richard with all humanity and left nothing unattempted that tended to his recovery, highly commending his valor and worthiness and greatly bewailing the danger wherein he was, being unto them a rare spectacle and a resolution seldom approved [13] to see one ship turn towards so many enemies, to endure the charge and boarding of so many huge armadas and to resist and repel the assaults and entries of so many soldiers. All which and more is confirmed by a Spanish captain of the same armada, and a present actor in the fight, who being severed from the rest in a storm, was by the *Lion* of London, a small ship, taken, and is now a prisoner in London.

[13] a courage, or steadfastness, rarely demonstrated

THE LAST FIGHT OF THE *REVENGE* 11

The general commander of the armada was Don Alfonso Baçan, brother to the Marquis of Santa Cruz. The admiral of the Biscayan squadron was Brittandona. Of the squadron of Seville, the Marquis of Arumburch. The hulks and fly-boats were commanded by Luis Coutinho. There were slain and drowned in this fight well near one thousand of the enemies and two special commanders, Don Luis de Sant John and Don George de Prunaria de Mallaga, as the Spanish captain confesseth, besides divers others of special account whereof as yet report is not made.

The admiral of the hulks and the *Ascension* of Seville were both sunk by the side of the *Revenge;* one other recovered the road of St. Michael and sunk also there; a fourth ran herself with the shore to save her men. Sir Richard died, as it is said, the second or third day aboard the General, and was by them greatly bewailed. What became of his body, whether it was buried in the sea or on the land, we know not; the comfort that remaineth to his friends is that he hath ended his life honorably in respect of the reputation won to his nation and country, and of the same to his posterity, and that, being dead, he hath not outlived his own honor. . . .

OF TRUTH

FRANCIS BACON (1561–1626)

WHAT is truth? said jesting Pilate;[1] and would not stay for an answer. Certainly there be that delight in giddiness, and count it a bondage to fix a belief; affecting free-will in thinking, as well as in acting. And though the sects of philosophers of that kind[2] be gone, yet there remain certain discoursing[3] wits, which are of the same veins, though there be not so much blood in them as was in those of the ancients. But it is not only the difficulty and labour which men take in finding out of truth; nor again, that when it is found, it imposeth upon men's thoughts, that doth bring lies in favour; but a natural though corrupt love of the lie itself. One of the later schools of the Grecians examineth the matter, and is at a stand to think what should be in it, that men should love lies; where neither they make for pleasure, as with poets; nor for advantage, as with the merchant; but for the lie's sake. But I cannot tell: this same truth is a naked and open daylight, that doth not show the masks, and mummeries, and triumphs[4] of the world, half so stately and daintily as candle-lights. Truth may perhaps come to the price

---

[1] John xviii. 38. Whether Pilate was actually *jesting* is of no importance; he is used here as a typical skeptic.
[2] the Skeptics
[3] rambling
[4] triumphal processions

of a pearl, that showeth best by day, but it will not rise to the price of a diamond or carbuncle, that showeth best in varied lights. A mixture of a lie doth ever add pleasure. Doth any man doubt that if there were taken out of men's minds vain opinions, flattering hopes, false valuations, imaginations as one would,[5] and the like, but it would leave the minds of a number of men poor shrunken things, full of melancholy and indisposition, and unpleasing to themselves? One of the fathers, in great severity, called poesy "vinum daemonum," because it filleth the imagination, and yet it is but with the shadow of a lie. But it is not the lie that passeth through the mind, but the lie that sinketh in, and settleth in it, that doth the hurt, such as we spake of before. But howsoever these things are thus in men's depraved judgments and affections, yet truth, which only doth judge itself, teacheth that the inquiry of truth, which is the love-making or wooing of it, the knowledge of truth, which is the presence of it, and the belief of truth, which is the enjoying of it, is the sovereign good of human nature. The first creature of God, in the works of the days, was the light of the sense: the last was the light of reason: and his sabbath work ever since is the illumination of his Spirit. First, he breathed light upon the face of the matter, or chaos; then he breathed light into the face of man; and still he breatheth and inspireth light into the face of his chosen. The poet that beautified the sect [6] that was otherwise inferior to the rest, saith yet excellently well: — *It is a pleasure to stand upon the shore, and to see ships tossed upon the sea: a pleasure to stand in the*

[5] An interesting question: are "imaginations as one would" lies?
[6] Lucretius, who beautified, or was the ornament of, the Epicureans

window of a castle, and to see a battle and the adventures thereof below: but no pleasure is comparable to the standing upon the vantage ground of truth (a hill not to be commanded, and where the air is always clear and serene), *and to see the errors, and wanderings, and mists, and tempests, in the vale below:* so always that this prospect be with pity, and not with swelling or pride. Certainly, it is heaven upon earth, to have a man's mind move in charity, rest in providence, and turn upon the poles of truth.

To pass from theological and philosophical truth to the truth of civil business; it will be acknowledged, even by those that practice it not, that clear and round dealing is the honour of man's nature, and that mixture of falsehood is like alloy in coin of gold and silver, which may make the metal work the better, but it embaseth it. For these winding and crooked courses are the goings of the serpent; which goeth basely upon the belly, and not upon the feet. There is no vice that doth so cover a man with shame as to be found false and perfidious; and therefore Montaigne saith prettily, when he inquired the reason why the word of the lie should be such a disgrace, and such an odious charge. Saith he, *If it be well weighed, to say that a man lieth, is as much to say as that he is brave towards God and a coward towards men. For a lie faces God, and shrinks from man.* Surely the wickedness of falsehood and breach of faith cannot possibly be so highly expressed, as in that it shall be the last peal to call the judgments of God upon the generations of men: it being foretold that, when Christ cometh, *he shall not find faith upon the earth.*[7]

---

[7] Luke xviii. 8, where, however, "faith" seems rather to mean "trust in God" than "truthfulness."

OF DEATH

MEN fear death as children fear to go in the dark; and as that natural fear in children is increased with tales, so is the other. Certainly, the contemplation of death, as the wages of sin, and passage to another world, is holy and religious; but the fear of it, as a tribute due unto nature, is weak. Yet in religious meditations there is sometimes mixture of vanity and superstition. You shall read, in some of the friars' books of mortification, that a man should think with himself what the pain is if he have but his finger's end pressed or tortured, and thereby imagine what the pains of death are, when the whole body is corrupted and dissolved; when many times death passeth with less pain than the torture of a limb; for the most vital parts are not the quickest of sense. And by him that spake only as a philosopher, and natural man,[1] it was well said, *Pompa mortis magis terret quam mors ipsa.*[2] ❲Groans and convulsions, and a discolored face, and friends weeping, and blacks[3] and obsequies, and the like, show death terrible. It is worthy the observing, that there is no passion in the mind of man so weak, but it mates[4] and masters the fear of death; and therefore death is no such terrible enemy when a man hath so many attendants about him that can win the combat of him.❳ Revenge triumphs over death; love slights it; honor aspireth to it; grief flieth to it; fear pre-occupateth[5] it; nay, we read, after Otho the emperor had slain himself, pity (which is the

---

[1] *i.e.*, not from the religious point of view
[2] The pageantry of death is more terrible than death itself.
[3] mourning garments
[4] overpowers
[5] anticipates

tenderest of affections) provoked many to die out of mere compassion to their sovereign, and as the truest sort of followers. Nay, Seneca adds, niceness [6] and satiety: *Cogita quamdiu eadem feceris; mori velle, non tantum fortis, aut miser, sed etiam fastidiosus potest.*[7] A man would die, though he were neither valiant nor miserable, only upon a weariness to do the same thing so oft over and over. It is no less worthy to observe, how little alteration in good spirits [8] the approaches of death make: for they appear to be the same men till the last instant. Augustus Caesar died in a compliment; *Livia, conjugii nostri memor, vive et vale.*[9] Tiberius in dissimulation, as Tacitus saith of him, *Jam Tiberium vires et corpus, non dissimulatio, deserebant:* [10] Vespasian in a jest, sitting upon the stool, *Ut puto Deus fio:* [11] Galba with a sentence, *Feri, si ex re sit populi Romani,*[12] holding forth his neck; Septimius Severus in dispatch, *Adeste, si quid mihi restat agendum;* [13] and the like. Certainly the Stoics bestowed too much cost upon death, and by their great preparations made it appear more fearful. Better saith he, *qui finem vitae extremum inter munera ponat naturae.*[14] It is as natural to die as to be born; and to a little infant, perhaps, the one is as painful as the other. He that dies in an earnest pursuit is like one that is wounded in hot blood, who, for the time, scarce feels the hurt; and therefore a mind fixed and bent upon

[6] fastidiousness
[7] This is loosely translated in the next sentence.
[8] *i.e.,* good or noble natures
[9] Farewell, Livia, remember our married life.
[10] Tiberius was now losing his vigor and vitality, but not his power of dissimulation.
[11] As I suppose, I am becoming a god.
[12] Strike, if it be for the good of the Roman people.
[13] Be ready, if anything remains for me to do.
[14] who counts the close of life as one of nature's blessings.

somewhat that is good doth avert the dolours of death; but, above all, believe it, the sweetest canticle is *Nunc dimittis*,[15] when a man hath obtained worthy ends and expectations. Death hath this also, that it openeth the gate to good fame, and extinguisheth envy: *Extinctus amabitur idem.*[16]

OF SIMULATION AND DISSIMULATION

DISSIMULATION is but a faint kind of policy, or wisdom; for it asketh a strong wit[1] and a strong heart to know when to tell truth, and to do it: therefore it is the weaker sort of politics[2] that are the great dissemblers.

Tacitus saith, *Livia sorted well with the arts of her husband, and dissimulation of her son;* attributing arts or policy to Augustus, and dissimulation to Tiberius: and again, when Mucianus encourageth Vespasian to take arms against Vitellius, he saith, *We rise not against the piercing judgment of Augustus, nor the extreme caution or closeness of Tiberius.* These properties of arts or policy, and dissimulation or closeness, are indeed habits and faculties several,[3] and to be distinguished; for if a man have that penetration of judgment as he can discern what things are to be laid open, and what to be secretted, and what to be shown at half-lights, and to whom and when (which indeed are arts of state, and arts of life, as Tacitus well calleth them), to him a habit of dissimulation is a hinderance and

---

[15] "Now lettest thou thy servant depart in peace." — Luke ii. 29
[16] Dead the same one will be loved.
[1] It requires a strong understanding.
[2] politicians
[3] separate, distinct

a poorness. But if a man cannot obtain to that judgment, then it is left to him generally to be close, and a dissembler: for where a man cannot choose or vary in particulars, there it is good to take the safest and wariest way in general, like the going softly by one that cannot well see. Certainly, the ablest men that ever were, have had all an openness and frankness of dealing, and a name of certainty and veracity: but then they were like horses well managed,[4] for they could tell passing well when to stop or turn; and at such times when they thought the case indeed required dissimulation, if then they used it it came to pass that the former opinion, spread abroad, of their good faith and clearness of dealing, made them almost invisible.

There be three degrees of this hiding and veiling of a man's self: the first, closeness, reservation, and secrecy; when a man leaveth himself without observation, or without hold to be taken, what he is: the second, dissimulation in the negative; when a man lets fall signs and arguments that he is not that[5] he is: and the third, simulation in the affirmative; when a man industriously[6] and expressly feigns and pretends to be that he is not.

For the first of these, secrecy, it is indeed the virtue of a confessor; and assuredly the secret man heareth many confessions; for who will open himself to a blab or a babbler? But if a man be thought secret, it inviteth discovery;[7] as the more close air sucketh in the more open; and, as in confession the revealing is not for worldly use, but for the ease of a man's heart, so

---

[4] well trained (as well as well controlled)
[5] that which. (The bearing of this in mind will make many passages in Bacon clear.)
[6] purposely (not diligently)
[7] confessions

secret men come to the knowledge of many things in that kind; while men rather discharge their minds than impart their minds. In few words, mysteries are due to secrecy. Besides (to say truth), nakedness is uncomely, as well in mind as body; and it addeth no small reverence to men's manners and actions if they be not altogether open. As for talkers and futile [8] persons, they are commonly vain and credulous withal: for he that talketh what he knoweth, will also talk what he knoweth not. Therefore set it down, that a habit of secrecy is both politic and moral: and in this part it is good that a man's face give his tongue leave to speak; for the discovery of a man's self by the tracts [9] of his countenance is a great weakness and betraying, by how much it is many times more marked and believed than a man's words.

For the second, which is dissimulation. It followeth many times upon secrecy by a necessity; so that he that will be secret must be a dissembler in some degree; for men are too cunning to suffer a man to keep an indifferent carriage between both, and to be secret, without swaying the balance on either side. They will so beset a man with questions, and draw him on, and pick it out of him, that without an absurd silence, he must show an inclination one way; or if he do not, they will gather as much by his silence as by his speech. As for equivocations, or oraculous speeches, they cannot hold out long: so that no man can be secret, except he give himself a little scope of dissimulation, which is, as it were, but the skirts or train of secrecy.

But for the third degree, which is simulation and false profession, that I hold more culpable, and less politic,

[8] leaky
[9] movements

except it be in great and rare matters: and, therefore, a general custom of simulation (which is this last degree) is a vice rising either of a natural falseness or fearfulness, or of a mind that hath some main faults; which because a man must needs disguise, it maketh him practise simulation in other things, lest his hand should be out of ure.[10]

The great advantages of simulation and dissimulation are three: first, to lay asleep opposition, and to surprise; for where a man's intentions are published, it is an alarum to call up all that are against them. The second is, to reserve to a man's self a fair retreat; for if a man engage himself by a manifest declaration, he must go through, or take a fall. The third is, the better to discover the mind of another; for to him that opens himself men will hardly show themselves adverse; but will (fair)[11] let him go on, and turn their freedom of speech to freedom of thought; and therefore it is a good shrewd proverb of the Spaniard, *Tell a lie and find a truth;* as if there were no way of discovery but by simulation. There be also three disadvantages to set it even. The first, that simulation and dissimulation commonly carry with them a show of fearfulness, which in any business doth spoil the feathers of round flying up to the mark.[12] The second, that it puzzleth and perplexeth the conceits[13] of many, that perhaps would otherwise co-operate with him, and makes a man walk almost alone to his own ends. The third and greatest is, that it depriveth a man of one of the most principal instruments for action,

[10] practice
[11] simply
[12] which . . . doth *deprive* (the arrow of) the feathers (which ensure) *neat or direct* flying up to the mark
[13] thoughts, opinions

which is trust and belief. The best composition and temperature [14] is, to have openness in fame and opinion; [15] secrecy in habit; dissimulation in seasonable use; and a power to feign if there be no remedy.

OF MARRIAGE AND SINGLE LIFE

He that hath wife and children hath given hostages to fortune; for they are impediments to great enterprises, either of virtue or mischief. Certainly the best works, and of greatest merit for the public, have proceeded from the unmarried or childless men, which both in affection and means have married and endowed the public. Yet it were great reason that those that have children should have greatest care of future times, unto which they know they must transmit their dearest pledges. Some there are who, though they lead a single life, yet their thoughts do end with themselves, and account future times impertinences.[1] Nay, there are some others that account wife and children but as bills of charges. Nay more, there are some foolish rich covetous men that take a pride in having no children, because they may be thought so much the richer; for, perhaps they have heard some talk, *Such an one is a great rich man,* and another except to it, *Yea, but he hath a great charge of children;* as if it were an abatement to his riches. But the most ordinary cause of a single life is liberty, especially in certain self-pleasing and humorous [2] minds, which are so sensible [3] of every

[14] blending
[15] public opinion
[1] not pertinent (to them)
[2] eccentric
[3] sensitive

restraint as they will go near to think their girdles and garters to be bonds and shackles. Unmarried men are best friends, best masters, best servants; but not always best subjects, for they are light to run away, and almost all fugitives are of that condition. A single life doth well with churchmen, for charity will hardly water the ground where it must first fill a pool. It is indifferent for judges and magistrates; for if they be facile and corrupt, you shall have a servant five times worse than a wife. For soldiers, I find the generals commonly, in their hortatives, put men in mind of their wives and children; and I think the despising of marriage amongst the Turks maketh the vulgar soldier more base. Certainly, wife and children are a kind of discipline of [4] humanity; and single men, though they be many times more charitable because their means are less exhaust, yet, on the other side, they are more cruel and hard-hearted (good to make severe inquisitors), because their tenderness is not so oft called upon. Grave natures, led by custom, and therefore constant, are commonly loving husbands; as was said of Ulysses, *Vetulam suam praetulit immortalitati.*[5] Chaste women are often proud and froward, as presuming upon the merit of their chastity. It is one of the best bonds, both of chastity and obedience, in the wife, if she think her husband wise, which she will never do if she find him jealous. Wives are young men's mistresses, companions for middle age, and old men's nurses; so as a man may have a quarrel to marry when he will. But yet he was reputed one of the wise men that made answer to the question when a man should marry? *A young man not yet, an elder man not at*

[4] training in
[5] He preferred his old wife to immortality.

all. It is often seen that bad husbands have very good wives; whether it be that it raiseth the price of their husbands' kindness when it comes, or that the wives take a pride in their patience; but this never fails if the bad husbands were of their own choosing, against their friends' consent, for then they will be sure to make good their own folly.

OF GREAT PLACE

MEN in great place are thrice servants: servants of the sovereign or state, servants of fame, and servants of business; so as they have no freedom, neither in their persons, nor in their actions, nor in their times. It is a strange desire to seek power and to lose liberty; or to seek power over others, and to lose power over a man's self. The rising unto place is laborious, and by pains men come to greater pains; and it is sometimes base, and by indignities men come to dignities. The standing is slippery, and the regress is either a downfall, or at least an eclipse, which is a melancholy thing: *Cum non sis qui fueris, non esse cur velis vivere.*[1] Nay, retire men cannot when they would, neither will they when it were reason; but are impatient of privateness even in age and sickness, which require the shadow; like old townsmen, that will be still sitting at their street-door, though thereby they offer age to scorn. Certainly great persons had need to borrow other men's opinions to think themselves happy; for if they judge by their own feeling they cannot find it: but if they think with themselves what other men

[1] When you are no longer what you have been, there is no longer reason for wishing to live.

think of them, and that other men would fain be as
they are, then they are happy as it were by report, when,
perhaps, they find the contrary within; for they are the
first that find their own griefs, though they be the last
that find their own faults. Certainly, men in great
fortunes are strangers to themselves, and while they
are in the puzzle of business they have no time to tend
their health either of body or mind. *Illi mors gravis
incubat, qui notus nimis omnibus, ignotus moritur sibi.*[2]
In place there is license to do good and evil; whereof the
latter is a curse: for in evil the best condition is not to
will, the second not to can.[3] But power to do good is
the true and lawful end of aspiring; for good thoughts
(though God accept them) yet towards men are little
better than good dreams, except they be put in act;
and that cannot be without power and place, as the
vantage and commanding ground. Merit and good
works is the end of man's motion; and conscience[4] of
the same is the accomplishment of man's rest: for if a
man can be partaker of God's theatre,[5] he shall likewise
be partaker of God's rest. *Et conversus Deus, ut
aspiceret opera quae fecerunt manus suae, vidit quod
omnia essent bona nimis;*[6] and then the Sabbath.

In the discharge of thy place set before thee the best
examples; for imitation is a globe of precepts; and
after a time set before thee thine own example; and examine thyself strictly whether thou didst not best at
first. Neglect not also the examples of those that have
carried themselves ill in the same place; not to set off

[2] Death presses heavily upon him who dies well known to all (but) unknown to himself.
[3] to be able
[4] consciousness
[5] spectacle — *i.e.*, can look back on good works accomplished
[6] Gen. i. 31: "And God saw every thing that he had made: and behold, it was very good."

thyself by taxing their memory, but to direct thyself what to avoid. Reform, therefore, without bravery [7] or scandal of former times and persons; but yet set it down to thyself, as well to create good precedents as to follow them. Reduce things to the first institution, and observe wherein and how they have degenerated; but yet ask counsel of both times; of the ancient time what is best, and of the latter time what is fittest. Seek to make thy course regular, that men may know beforehand what they may expect; but be not too positive and peremptory; and express thyself well when thou digressest from thy rule. Preserve the right of thy place, but stir not questions of jurisdiction; and rather assume thy right in silence and *de facto,* than voice it with claims and challenges. Preserve likewise the rights of inferior places; and think it more honour to direct in chief than to be busy in all. Embrace and invite helps and advices touching the execution of thy place; and do not drive away such as bring thee information as meddlers, but accept of them in good part.

The vices of authority are chiefly four: delays, corruption, roughness, and facility.[8] For delays, give easy access; keep times appointed; go through with that which is in hand, and interlace not business but of necessity. For corruption, do not only bind thine own hands or thy servants' hands from taking, but bind the hands of suitors also from offering; for integrity used doth the one; but integrity professed, and with a manifest detestation of bribery, doth the other; and avoid not only the fault, but the suspicion. Whosoever is found variable, and changeth manifestly without manifest cause, giveth suspicion of corruption:

[7] great show
[8] overreadiness to yield; amiable weakness

therefore, always when thou changest thine opinion or course, profess it plainly, and declare it, together with the reasons that move thee to change, and do not think to steal it.[9] A servant or a favorite, if he be inward, and no other apparent cause of esteem, is commonly thought but a by-way to close corruption. For roughness, it is a needless cause of discontent: severity breedeth fear, but roughness breedeth hate. Even reproofs from authority ought to be grave, and not taunting. As for facility, it is worse than bribery; for bribes come but now and then; but if importunity or idle respects lead a man, he shall never be without; as Salomon saith, *To respect persons is not good; for such a man will transgress for a piece of bread.*[10]

It is most true that was anciently spoken; *A place showeth the man;* and it showeth some to the better and some to the worse: *Omnium consensu capax imperii, nisi imperasset,*[11] saith Tacitus of Galba; but of Vespasian he saith, *Solus imperantium Vespasianus mutatus in melius;*[12] though the one was meant of sufficiency, the other of manners and affection. It is an assured sign of a worthy and generous spirit, whom honour amends; for honour is or should be the place of virtue; and as in nature things move violently to their place and calmly in their place, so virtue in ambition is violent, in authority settled and calm. All rising to great place is by a winding stair; and if there be factions, it is good to side a man's self whilst he is in the rising, and to balance himself when he is placed. Use the memory of thy predecessor fairly and tenderly; for if thou dost not, it is a debt will sure be paid when thou art gone.

[9] to do it stealthily
[10] Prov. xxviii. 21
[11] By general consent fit to rule — if only he had not ruled.
[12] Alone of the emperors, Vespasian changed for the better.

If thou have colleagues, respect them; and rather call them when they look not for it, than exclude them when they have reason to look to be called. Be not too sensible [13] or too remembering of thy place in conversation and private answers to suitors; but let it rather be said, *When he sits in place, he is another man.*

OF WISDOM FOR A MAN'S SELF

An ant is a wise creature for itself, but it is a shrewd [1] thing in an orchard or garden: and certainly men that are great lovers of themselves waste the public. Divide with reason between self-love and society; and be so true to thyself as thou be not false to others, specially to thy king and country. It is a poor centre of a man's actions, himself. It is right earth; for that only stands fast upon his own centre; whereas all things that have affinity with the heavens move upon the centre of another, which they benefit. The referring of all to a man's self is more tolerable in a sovereign prince, because themselves are not only themselves, but their good and evil is at the peril of the public fortune; but it is a desperate evil in a servant to a prince, or a citizen in a republic; for whatsoever affairs pass such a man's hands, he crooketh them to his own ends, which must needs be often eccentric to the ends of his master or state: therefore let princes or states choose such servants as have not this mark; except they mean their service should be made but the accessary. That which maketh the effect more pernicious is, that all proportion

[13] sensitive
[1] cursed, pernicious

is lost; it were disproportion enough for the servant's good to be preferred before the master's; but yet it is a greater extreme, when a little good of the servant shall carry things against a great good of the master's: and yet that is the case of bad officers, treasurers, ambassadors, generals, and other false and corrupt servants; which set a bias upon their bowl of their own petty ends and envies, to the overthrow of their master's great and important affairs: and for the most part the good such servants receive is after the model [2] of their own fortune; but the hurt they sell for that good is after the model of their master's fortune: and certainly it is the nature of extreme self-lovers, as they will set a house on fire, and it were [3] but to roast their eggs; and yet these men many times hold credit with their masters because their study is but to please them, and profit themselves; and for either respect they will abandon the good of their affairs.

Wisdom for a man's self is, in many branches thereof, a depraved thing: it is the wisdom of rats, that will be sure to leave a house somewhat before it fall: it is the wisdom of the fox, that thrusts out the badger who digged and made room for him: it is the wisdom of crocodiles, that shed tears when they would devour. But that which is specially to be noted is that those which (as Cicero says of Pompey) are *sui amantes, sine rivali,*[4] are many times unfortunate; and whereas they have all their time sacrificed to themselves, they become in the end themselves sacrifices to the inconstancy of fortune, whose wings they thought by their self-wisdom to have pinioned.

[2] scale, proportion
[3] even were it
[4] their own lovers, without rival

OF FRIENDSHIP

It had been hard for him that spake it to have put more truth and untruth together in few words than in that speech, *Whosoever is delighted in solitude, is either a wild beast or a god:* for it is most true, that a natural and secret hatred and aversion towards society in any man hath somewhat of the savage beast; but it is most untrue that it should have any character at all of the divine nature, except it proceed, not out of a pleasure in solitude, but out of a love and desire to sequester a man's self for a higher conversation:[1] such as is found to have been falsely and feignedly in some of the heathen; as Epimenides, the Candian; Numa, the Roman; Empedocles, the Sicilian; and Apollonius of Tyana; and truly and really in divers of the ancient hermits and holy fathers of the Church. But little do men perceive what solitude is, and how far it extendeth; for a crowd is not company, and faces are but a gallery of pictures, and talk but a tinkling cymbal, where there is no love. The Latin adage meeteth with it a little, *Magna civitas, magna solitudo;*[2] because in a great town friends are scattered, so that there is not that fellowship, for the most part, which is in less neighbourhoods: but we may go further, and affirm most truly, that it is a mere[3] and miserable solitude to want true friends, without which the world is but a wilderness; and even in this sense also of solitude, whosoever in the frame of his nature and affections is unfit for friendship, he taketh it of the beast, and not from humanity.

[1] intercourse, or way of life
[2] a great city (is) a great solitude
[3] entire

A principal fruit of friendship is the ease and discharge of the fullness and swellings of the heart, which passions of all kinds do cause and induce. We know diseases of stoppings and suffocations are the most dangerous in the body; and it is not much otherwise in the mind; you may take sarza [4] to open the liver, steel to open the spleen, flowers of sulphur for the lungs, castoreum for the brain; but no receipt openeth the heart but a true friend, to whom you may impart griefs, joys, fears, hopes, suspicions, counsels, and whatsoever lieth upon the heart to oppress it, in a kind of civil shrift or confession.

It is a strange thing to observe how high a rate great kings and monarchs do set upon this fruit of friendship whereof we speak; so great, as they purchase it many times at the hazard of their own safety and greatness: for princes, in regard of the distance of their fortune from that of their subjects and servants, cannot gather this fruit, except (to make themselves capable thereof) they raise some persons to be as it were companions, and almost equals to themselves, which many times sorteth to inconvenience. The modern languages give unto such persons the name of favourites or privadoes, as if it were matter of grace or conversation; but the Roman name attaineth the true use and cause thereof, naming them *participes curarum;* [5] for it is that which tieth the knot. And we see plainly that this hath been done not by weak and passionate princes only, but by the wisest and most politic that ever reigned, who have oftentimes joined to themselves some of their servants, whom both themselves have called friends, and allowed others likewise to call them in the same manner, us-

---

[4] sarsaparilla
[5] partners in cares

ing the word which is received between private men.

L. Sylla, when he commanded Rome, raised Pompey (after surnamed the Great) to that height that Pompey vaunted himself for Sylla's overmatch; for when he had carried the consulship for a friend of his, against the pursuit of Sylla, and that Sylla did a little resent thereat, and began to speak great, Pompey turned upon him again, and in effect bade him be quiet; *for that more men adored the sun rising than the sun setting.* With Julius Caesar, Decimus Brutus had obtained that interest, as he set him down in his testament for heir in remainder after his nephew; and this was the man that had power with him to draw him forth to his death: for when Caesar would have discharged the senate, in regard of some ill presages and specially a dream of Calpurnia, this man lifted him gently by the arm out of his chair, telling him he hoped he would not dismiss the senate till his wife had dreamt a better dream; and it seemeth his favour was so great, as Antonius, in a letter which is recited verbatim in one of Cicero's Philippics, calleth him *venefica — witch;* as if he had enchanted Caesar. Augustus raised Agrippa (though of mean birth) to that height, as, when he consulted with Maecenas about the marriage of his daughter Julia, Maecenas took the liberty to tell him, *that he must either marry his daughter to Agrippa, or take away his life: there was no third way, he had made him so great.* With Tiberius Caesar, Sejanus had ascended to that height as they two were termed and reckoned as a pair of friends. Tiberius, in a letter to him, saith, *Haec pro amicitia nostra non occultavi;* [6] and the whole senate dedicated an altar to Friendship, as to a goddess, in respect of the great dearness

[6] Because of our friendship, I have not hidden these things.

of friendship between them two. The like, or more, was between Septimius Severus and Plautianus; for he forced his eldest son to marry the daughter of Plautianus, and would often maintain Plautianus in doing affronts to his son; and did write also in a letter to the senate by these words: *I love the man so well as I wish he may over-live me.* Now, if these princes had been as a Trajan, or a Marcus Aurelius, a man might have thought that this had proceeded of an abundant goodness of nature; but being men so wise, of such strength and severity of mind, and so extreme lovers of themselves, as all these were, it proveth most plainly that they found their own felicity (though as great as ever happened to mortal men) but as an half-piece, except they might have a friend to make it entire; and yet, which is more, they were princes that had wives, sons, nephews; and yet all these could not supply the comfort of friendship.

It is not to be forgotten what Comineus observeth of his first master, Duke Charles the Hardy; namely, that he would communicate his secrets with none; and least of all those secrets which troubled him most. Whereupon he goeth on and saith that towards his latter time *that closeness did impair and a little perish his understanding.* Surely Comineus might have made the same judgment also, if it had pleased him, of his second master, Lewis the Eleventh, whose closeness was indeed his tormentor. The parable of Pythagoras is dark but true, *Cor ne edito,* — *eat not the heart.* Certainly, if a man would give it a hard phrase, those that want friends to open themselves unto are cannibals of their own hearts. But one thing is most admirable (wherewith I will conclude this first fruit of friendship), which is, that this communicating of a man's self to his friend works two contrary effects; for it redoubleth joys, and cutteth griefs in halves: for there is no man that imparteth his joys to his friend, but he joyeth the more; and no man that imparteth his griefs to his friend, but he grieveth the less. So that it is, in truth of operation upon a man's mind, of like virtue as the alchymists used to attribute to their stone for man's body, that it worketh all contrary effects, but still to the good and benefit of nature: but yet, without praying in aid of alchymists, there is a manifest image of this in the ordinary course of nature; for, in bodies, union strengtheneth and cherisheth any natural action; and, on the other side, weakeneth and dulleth any violent impression; and even so is it of minds.

The second fruit of friendship is healthful and sovereign for the understanding, as the first is for the affections; for friendship maketh indeed a fair day in the affections from storm and tempests, but it maketh daylight in the understanding, out of darkness and confusion of thoughts: neither is this to be understood only of faithful counsel, which a man receiveth from his friend; but before you come to that, certain it is that whosoever hath his mind fraught with many thoughts, his wits and understanding do clarify and break up in the communicating and discoursing with another; he tosseth his thoughts more easily; he marshalleth them more orderly; he seeth how they look when they are turned into words: finally, he waxeth wiser than himself; and that more by an hour's discourse than by a day's meditation. It was well said by Themistocles to the king of Persia, *That speech was like cloth of Arras opened and put abroad; whereby the imagery doth appear in figure; whereas in thoughts they lie but as in packs.* Neither is this second fruit of friendship, in opening the understanding, restrained only to such friends as are able to give a man counsel; (they indeed are best); but even without that a man learneth of himself, and bringeth his own thoughts to light, and whetteth his wits as against a stone which itself cuts not. In a word, a man were better relate himself to a statua or picture, than to suffer his thoughts to pass in smother.

Add now, to make this second fruit of friendship complete, that other point which lieth more open, and falleth within vulgar observation: which is faithful counsel from a friend. Heraclitus saith well in one of his enigmas, *Dry light is ever the best:* and certain it is that the light that a man receiveth by counsel from another is drier and purer than that which cometh from his own understanding and judgment; which is ever infused and drenched in his affections and customs. So as there is as much difference between the counsel that a friend giveth, and that a man giveth himself, as there is between the counsel of a friend and of a flatterer; for there is no such flatterer as is a man's self, and there is no such remedy against flattery of a man's self as the liberty of a friend. Counsel is of two sorts; the one concerning manners, the other concerning business: for the first, the best preservative to keep the mind in health is the faithful admonition of a friend. The calling of a man's self to a strict account is a medicine sometimes too piercing and corrosive; reading good books of morality is a little flat and dead; observing our faults in others is sometimes unproper for our case; but the best receipt (best (I say) to work and best to take) is the admonition of a friend. It is a strange thing to behold what gross errors and extreme absurdities many (especially of the greater sort)

OF FRIENDSHIP

do commit for want of a friend to tell them of them, to the great damage both of their Fame and Fortune: for, as St. James saith, *they are as men that look sometimes into a glass, and presently[7] forget their own shape and favour.*[8] As for business, a man may think, if he will, that two eyes see no more than one; or that a gamester seeth always more than a looker-on; or that a man in anger is as wise as he that hath said over the four and twenty letters;[9] or that a musket may be shot off as well upon the arm as upon a rest;[10] and such other fond[11] and high imaginations, to think himself all in all. But when all is done, the help of good counsel is that which setteth business straight: and if any man think that he will take counsel, but it shall be by pieces, asking counsel in one business of one man, and in another business of another man, it is well (that is to say, better perhaps than if he asked none at all); but he runneth two dangers; one, that he shall not be faithfully counseled; for it is a rare thing, except it be from a perfect and entire friend, to have counsel given but such as shall be bowed and crooked to some ends which he hath that giveth it: the other, that he shall have counsel given hurtful and unsafe (though with good meaning), and mixed partly of mischief and partly of remedy; even as if you would call a physician, that is thought good for the cure of the disease you complain of, but is unacquainted with your body; and therefore may put you in a way for a present cure, but overthroweth your health in some other kind, and so cure

[7] immediately
[8] features
[9] *J* and *w* were added to the alphabet after Bacon's time.
[10] The musket rest was discarded at the invention of the firelock, about 1635.
[11] foolish

the disease and kill the patient: but a friend that is wholly acquainted with a man's estate, will beware, by furthering any present business, how he dasheth upon other inconvenience; and therefore rest not upon scattered counsels; they will rather distract and mislead than settle and direct.

After these two noble fruits of friendship (peace in the affections, and support of the judgment), followeth the last fruit, which is like the pomegranate, full of many kernels; I mean aid, and bearing a part in all actions and occasions. Here the best way to represent to life the manifold use of friendship is to cast [12] and see how many things there are which a man cannot do himself; and then it will appear that it was a sparing speech of the ancients to say, *that a friend is another himself:* for that a friend is far more than himself. Men have their time, and die many times in desire of some things which they principally take to heart; the bestowing of a child, the finishing of a work, or the like. If a man have a true friend, he may rest almost secure that the care of those things will continue after him; so that a man hath, as it were, two lives in his desires. A man hath a body, and that body is confined to a place: but where friendship is, all offices of life are as it were granted to him and his deputy; for he may exercise them by his friend. How many things are there which a man cannot, with any face or comeliness, say or do himself? A man can scarce allege his own merits with modesty, much less extol them: a man cannot sometimes brook to supplicate or beg, and a number of the like: but all these things are graceful in a friend's mouth, which are blushing in a man's own. So again, a man's person hath many proper relations which he

[12] cast up, reckon

cannot put off.¹³ A man cannot speak to his son but as a father; to his wife but as a husband; to his enemy but upon terms:¹⁴ whereas a friend may speak as the case requires, and not as it sorteth with the person. But to enumerate these things were endless; I have given the rule where a man cannot fitly play his own part; if he have not a friend, he may quit the stage.

OF REGIMEN OF HEALTH

THERE is a wisdom in this beyond the rules of physic: a man's own observation what he finds good of and what he finds hurt of is the best physic to preserve health; but it is a safer conclusion to say, *This agreeth not well with me, therefore I will not continue it;* than this, *I find no offence of this, therefore I may use it:* for strength of nature in youth passeth over many excesses which are owing a man till his age. Discern of the coming on of years, and think not to do the same things still; for age will not be defied. Beware of sudden change in any great point of diet,¹ and, if necessity enforce it, fit the rest to it; for it is a secret both in nature and state, that it is safer to change many things than one. Examine thy customs of diet, sleep, exercise, apparel, and the like; and try, in anything thou shalt judge hurtful, to discontinue it by little and little; but so as if thou dost find any inconvenience by the change, thou come back to it again: for it is hard to

---

¹³ *I.e.*, a man's character in society has many peculiar relationships which he cannot discard. The sentence following illustrates clearly what is meant.
¹⁴ formalities
¹ L. *diaeta*, manner of living. Bacon seems to use the word in this instance in its original sense.

distinguish that which is generally held good and wholesome from that which is good particularly and fit for thine own body. To be free minded and cheerfully disposed at hours of meat and of sleep and of exercise is one of the best precepts of long lasting. As for the passions and studies of the mind, avoid envy, anxious fears, anger fretting inwards, subtile and knotty inquisitions, joys and exhilarations in excess, sadness not communicated. Entertain hopes, mirth rather than joy, variety of delights rather than surfeit of them; wonder and admiration, and therefore novelties; studies that fill the mind with splendid and illustrious objects; as histories, fables, and contemplations of nature. If you fly physic in health altogether it will be too strange for your body when you shall need it; if you make it too familiar it will work no extraordinary effect when sickness cometh. I commend rather some diet for certain seasons than frequent use of physic, except it be grown into a custom; for those diets alter the body more and trouble it less. Despise no new accident in your body, but ask opinion of it. In sickness, respect health principally; and in health, action: for those that put their bodies to endure in health may, in most sicknesses which are not very sharp, be cured only with diet and tendering.[2] Celsus could never have spoken it as a physician, had he not been a wise man withal, when he giveth it for one of the great precepts of health and lasting, that a man do vary and interchange contraries, but with an inclination to the more benign extreme: use fasting and full eating, but rather full eating; watching and sleep, but rather sleep; sitting and exercise, but rather exercise, and the like: so shall nature be cherished, and yet taught mas-

[2] treating with more than ordinary care

teries. Physicians are some of them so pleasing and conformable to the humour of the patient as they press not the true cure of the disease; and some other are so regular in proceeding according to art for the disease as they respect not sufficiently the condition of the patient. Take one of a middle temper; or, if it may not be found in one man, combine two of either sort; and forget not to call as well the best acquainted with your body as the best reputed of for his faculty.

OF DISCOURSE

SOME in their discourse desire rather commendation of wit, in being able to hold all arguments, than of judgment, in discerning what is true; as if it were a praise to know what might be said, and not what should be thought. Some have certain common-places and themes wherein they are good, and want variety; which kind of poverty is for the most part tedious, and when it is once perceived, ridiculous. The honourablest part of talk is to give the occasion; and again to moderate and pass to somewhat else; for then a man leads the dance. It is good in discourse and speech of conversation, to vary and intermingle speech of the present occasion with arguments, tales with reasons, asking of questions with telling of opinions, and jest with earnest; for it is a dull thing to tire, and as we say now to jade anything too far. As for jest, there be certain things which ought to be privileged from it; namely, religion, matters of state, great persons, any man's present business of importance, and any case that deserveth pity; yet there be some that think their wits have been asleep, except they dart out somewhat that is piquant, and to the quick; that is a vein which would [1] be bridled;

Parce puer stimulis, et fortius utere loris.[2]

And generally, men ought to find the difference between saltness and bitterness. Certainly, he that hath a satirical vein, as he maketh others afraid of his wit, so he had need be afraid of others' memory. He that questioneth much shall learn much, and content much; but especially if he apply his questions to the skill of the persons whom he asketh; for he shall give them occasion to please themselves in speaking, and himself shall continually gather knowledge; but let his questions not be troublesome, for that is fit for a poser; and let him be sure to leave other men their turns to speak; nay, if there be any that would reign and take up all the time, let him find means to take them off, and to bring others on, as musicians use to do with those that dance too long galliards. If you dissemble sometimes your knowledge of that you are thought to know, you shall be thought another time to know that you know not. Speech of a man's self ought to be seldom, and well chosen. I knew one was wont to say in scorn, *He must needs be a wise man, he speaks so much of himself:* and there is but one case wherein a man may commend himself with good grace, and that is in commending virtue in another, especially if it be such a virtue whereunto himself pretendeth. Speech of touch [3] towards others should be sparingly used; for discourse ought to be as a field, without coming home to any man. I knew two noblemen of the west part of

---
[1] ought to be
[2] Spare the whip, boy, and pull harder at the reins.
[3] *i.e.*, touching upon delicate subjects or referring directly to someone present or to his known affairs

England, whereof the one was given to scoff, but kept ever royal cheer in his house; the other would ask of those that had been at the other's table, *Tell truly, was there never a flout or dry*[4] *blow given?* To which the guest would answer, *Such and such a thing passed.* The lord would say *I thought he would mar a good dinner.* Discretion of speech is more than eloquence; and to speak agreably to him with whom we deal is more than to speak in good words, or in good order. A good continued speech, without a good speech of interlocution, shows slowness; and a good reply or second speech, without a good settled speech, showeth shallowness and weakness. As we see in beasts, that those that are weakest in the course are yet nimblest in the turn; as it is betwixt the greyhound and the hare. To use too many circumstances ere one come to the matter is wearisome; to use none at all is blunt.

OF YOUTH AND AGE

A MAN that is young in years may be old in hours, if he have lost no time; but that happeneth rarely. Generally, youth is like the first cogitations, not so wise as the second: for there is a youth in thoughts as well as in ages; and yet the invention of young men is more lively than that of old, and imaginations stream into their minds better, and as it were more divinely. Natures that have much heat, and great and violent desires and perturbations, are not ripe for action till they have passed the meridian of their years: as it was with Julius Caesar and Septimius Severus; of the latter of whom it is said, *Juventutem egit erroribus, imo furoribus*

---

[4] severe, scornful

plenam;[1] and yet he was the ablest emperor, almost, of all the list; but reposed natures may do well in youth, as it is seen in Augustus Caesar, Cosmus duke of Florence, Gaston de Foix, and others. On the other side, heat and vivacity in age is an excellent composition for business. Young men are fitter to invent than to judge, fitter for execution than for counsel, and fitter for new projects than for settled business; for the experience of age,[2] in things that fall within the compass of it, directeth them; but in new things abuseth[3] them. The errors of young men are the ruin of business; but the errors of aged men amount but to this, that more might have been done or sooner.

Young men, in the conduct and manage of actions, embrace more than they can hold; stir more than they can quiet; fly to the end without consideration of the means and degrees; pursue some few principles which they have chanced upon absurdly;[4] care not to innovate,[5] which draws unknown inconveniences; use extreme remedies at first; and, that which doubleth all errors, will not acknowledge or retract them, like an unready[6] horse, that will neither stop nor turn. Men of age object too much, consult too long, adventure too little, repent too soon, and seldom drive business home to the full period, but content themselves with a mediocrity of success. Certainly it is good to compound employments of both; for that will be good for the present, because the virtues of either age may correct the defects of both; and good for succession, that young

---

[1] He passed his youth in error, even in madness.
[2] the aged
[3] deceives, misleads
[4] The adverb qualifies "pursue," not "chanced upon."
[5] *i.e.*, innovate without care (a procedure) which draws, etc.
[6] ill-controlled

men may be learners while men in age are actors; and lastly, good for externe accidents, because authority followeth old men, and favour and popularity youth: but for the moral part, perhaps youth will have the pre-eminence, as age hath for the politic. A certain rabbin, upon the text,[7] *Your young men shall see visions, and your old men shall dream dreams,* inferreth that young men are admitted nearer to God than old, because vision is a clearer revelation than a dream; and certainly, the more a man drinketh of the world the more it intoxicateth: and age doth profit rather in the powers of understanding than in the virtues of the will and affections. There be some have an over-early ripeness in their years, which fadeth betimes: these are, first, such as have brittle wits, the edge whereof is soon turned: such as was Hermogenes the rhetorician, whose books are exceedingly subtile, who afterwards waxed stupid: a second sort is of those that have some natural dispositions which have better grace in youth than in age; such as is a fluent and luxuriant speech, which becomes youth well but not age: so Tully saith of Hortensius, *Idem manebat, neque idem decebat:*[8] the third is of such as take too high a strain at the first, and are magnanimous more than tract of years can uphold; as was Scipio Africanus, of whom Livy saith in effect, *Ultima primis cedebant.*[9]

OF NEGOTIATING

IT is generally better to deal by speech than by letter; and by the mediation of a third than by a man's self.

[7] Joel ii. 28
[8] He remained the same (and) the same was not suitable.
[9] His last (days) were not equal to his former (days).

Letters are good when a man would draw an answer by letter back again; or when it may serve for a man's justification afterwards to produce his own letter; or where it may be danger to be interrupted, or heard by pieces. To deal in person is good when a man's face breedeth regard, as commonly with inferiors; or in tender cases where a man's eye upon the countenance of him with whom he speaketh may give him a direction how far to go: and generally where a man will reserve to himself liberty either to disavow or to expound. In choice of instruments, it is better to choose men of a plainer sort, that are like to do that that is committed to them and to report back again faithfully the success,[1] than those that are cunning to contrive out of other men's business somewhat to grace themselves, and will help the matter in report, for satisfaction sake. Use also such persons as affect[2] the business wherein they are employed, for that quickeneth much; and such as are fit for the matter, as bold men for expostulation, fair-spoken men for persuasion, crafty men for inquiry and observation, froward and absurd men for business that doth not well bear out itself. Use also such as have been lucky and prevailed before in things wherein you have employed them; for that breeds confidence, and they will strive to maintain their prescription. It is better to sound a person with whom one deals afar off than to fall upon the point at first, except you mean to surprise him by some short question. It is better dealing with men in appetite than with those that are where they would be. If a man deal with another upon conditions, the start or first performance is all: which a man cannot reasonably demand, except

[1] result
[2] like, or wish success to

either the nature of the thing be such which must go before: or else a man can persuade the other party that he shall still need him in some other thing; or else that he be counted the honester man. All practice[3] is to discover or to work. Men discover themselves in trust, in passion, at unawares, and of necessity, when they would have somewhat done and cannot find an apt pretext. If you would work any man, you must either know his nature and fashions, and so lead him; or his ends, and so persuade him; or his weakness and disadvantages, and so awe him; or those that have interest in him, and so govern him. In dealing with cunning persons, we must ever consider their ends to interpret their speeches; and it is good to say little to them, and that which they least look for. In all negotiations of difficulty, a man may not look to sow and reap at once; but must prepare business and so ripen it by degrees.

OF STUDIES

STUDIES serve for delight, for ornament, and for ability. Their chief use for delight is in privateness and retiring; for ornament is in discourse; and for ability is in the judgment and disposition of business; for expert men can execute, and perhaps judge of particulars, one by one: but the general counsels, and the plots and marshalling of affairs come best from those that are learned. To spend too much time in studies is sloth; to use them too much for ornament is affectation; to make judgment wholly by their rules is the humour[1]

---

[3] negotiation, with a sense of trickery
[1] eccentricity, dominant tendency

of a scholar: they perfect nature, and are perfected by experience: for natural abilities are like natural plants, that need pruning by study; and studies themselves do give forth directions too much at large, except they be bounded in by experience. Crafty men contemn studies, simple men admire them, and wise men use them; for they teach not their own use; but that is a wisdom without [2] them and above them, won by observation. Read not to contradict and confute, nor to believe and take for granted, nor to find talk and discourse, but to weigh and consider. Some books are to be tasted, others to be swallowed, and some few to be chewed and digested; that is, some books are to be read only in parts; others to be read but not curiously,[3] and some few to be read wholly, and with diligence and attention. Some books also may be read by deputy, and extracts made of them by others; but that would be only in the less important arguments and the meaner sort of books; else distilled books are like common distilled waters, flashy things. Reading maketh a full man; conference a ready man; and writing an exact man; and therefore, if a man write little he had need have a great memory; if he confer little he had need have a present wit; and if he read little he had need have much cunning, to seem to know that he doth not. Histories make men wise; poets, witty;[4] the mathematics, subtile; natural philosophy, deep; moral, grave; logic and rhetoric, able to contend: *Abeunt studia in mores;*[5] nay, there is no stond or impediment in the wit but may be wrought out by fit studies: like as diseases of the body may have appropriate exercises; bowl-

[2] outside of
[3] not with great care
[4] ingenious, full of thoughts and images
[5] (One's) studies enter (one's very) nature.

ing is good for the stone and reins,[6] shooting [7] for the lungs and breast, gentle walking for the stomach, riding for the head, and the like; so if a man's wit be wandering, let him study the mathematics; for in demonstrations, if his wit be called away never so little, he must begin again; if his wit be not apt to distinguish or find differences let him study the schoolmen; for they are *Cymini sectores*.[8] If he be not apt to beat over matters, and to call up one thing to prove and illustrate another, let him study the lawyers' cases: so every defect of the mind may have a special receipt.

OF JUDICATURE

JUDGES ought to remember that their office is *jus dicere* and not *jus dare; to interpret law,* and not to *make law* or *give law.* . . . Judges ought to be more learned than witty, more reverend than plausible, and more advised than confident. Above all things, integrity is their portion and proper virtue. *Cursed* (saith the law) *is he that removeth the landmark!*[1] The mislayer of a meere [2] stone is to blame; but it is the unjust judge that is the capital remover of landmarks, when he defineth amiss of lands and property. One foul sentence doth more hurt than many foul examples; for these do but corrupt the stream, the other corrupteth the fountain: so saith Salomon, *Fons turbatus et vena corrupta est justus cadens in causa sua*

[6] kidneys
[7] archery
[8] dividers of cummin-seed (or, we should say, "hair-splitters")
[1] Deut. xxvii. 17
[2] boundary stone

coram adversario.[3] The office of judges may have reference unto the parties that sue, unto the advocates that plead, unto the clerks and ministers of justice underneath them, and to the sovereign[4] or state above them.

First, for the causes or parties that sue. *There be* (saith the Scripture) *that turn judgment into wormwood;*[5] and surely there be also that turn it into vinegar; for injustice maketh it bitter, and delays make it sour. The principal duty of a judge is to suppress force and fraud; whereof force is the more pernicious when it is open, and fraud when it is close and disguised. Add thereto contentious suits, which ought to be spewed out as the surfeit of courts. A judge ought to prepare his way to a just sentence as God useth to prepare his way, by raising valleys and taking down hills:[6] so when there appeareth on either side a high hand, violent prosecution, cunning advantages taken, combination, power, great counsel, then is the virtue of a judge seen to make inequality equal; that he may plant his judgment as upon an even ground. *Qui fortiter emungit elicit sanguinem;*[7] and where the wine-press is hard wrought, it yields a harsh wine that tastes of the grape-stone. Judges must beware of hard constructions and strained inferences; for there is no worse torture[8] than the torture of laws: especially in case of laws penal they ought to have care that that

---

[3] Prov. xxv. 26: "A righteous man falling down before the wicked is as a troubled fountain, and a corrupt spring."

[4] The essay will be more fully understood if it is borne in mind that to Bacon the sovereign was the personification of (and the throne the symbol of) the sovereignty.

[5] Amos v. 7

[6] Luke iii. 5

[7] He who wipes his nose (too) vigorously draws blood.

[8] twisting, distortion

which was meant for terror be not turned into rigour;
and that they bring not upon the people that shower
whereof the Scripture speaketh, *Pluet super eos laqueos;* ⁹ for penal laws pressed are a shower of snares
upon the people: therefore let penal laws, if they have
been sleepers of long or if they be grown unfit for the
present time, be by wise judges confined in the execution: *Judicis officium est, ut res, ita tempora rerum,
&c.*¹⁰ In causes of life and death, judges ought (as
far as the law permitteth) in justice to remember mercy,
and to cast a severe eye upon the example but a merciful eye upon the person.

Secondly, for the advocates and counsel that plead.
Patience and gravity of hearing is an essential part
of justice; and an overspeaking judge is no *well-tuned
cymbal*. It is no grace to a judge first to find that
which he might have heard in due time from the bar,
or to show quickness of conceit ¹¹ in cutting off evidence
or counsel too short, or to prevent ¹² information by
questions though pertinent. The parts of a judge in
hearing are four: to direct the evidence; to moderate
length, repetition, or impertinency of speech; to recapitulate, select, and collate the material points of that
which hath been said; and to give the rule or sentence.
Whatsoever is above these is too much, and proceedeth
either of glory and willingness to speak, or of impatience to hear, or of shortness of memory, or of
want of a staid and equal attention. It is a strange
thing to see that the boldness of advocates should prevail with judges; whereas they should imitate God, in

[9] Psalm xi. 6: "He shall rain snares upon them."
[10] It is a judge's office (to note) not only the facts, but the circumstances of the facts.
[11] conception, understanding
[12] anticipate

whose seat they sit, who represseth the presumptuous and giveth grace to the modest: but it is more strange that judges should have noted favourites, which cannot but cause multiplication of fees and suspicion of by-ways. There is due from the judge to the advocate some commendation and gracing, where causes are well handled and fair pleaded, especially towards the side which obtaineth not; for that upholds in the client the reputation of his counsel, and beats down in him the conceit of his cause. There is likewise due to the public a civil [13] reprehension of advocates, where there appeareth cunning counsel, gross neglect, slight information, indiscreet pressing, or an over-bold defence; and let not the counsel at the bar chop [14] with the judge, nor wind himself into the handling of the cause anew after the judge hath declared his sentence; but, on the other side, let not the judge meet the cause half-way, nor give occasion to the party to say, his counsel or proofs were not heard.

Thirdly, for that that concerns clerks and ministers. The place of justice is a hallowed place; and therefore not only the bench but the foot-pace [15] and precincts and purprise [16] thereof ought to be preserved without scandal and corruption; for certainly *Grapes* (as the Scripture saith) *will not be gathered of thorns or thistles;* [17] neither can justice yield her fruit with sweetness amongst the briars and brambles of catching and polling [18] clerks and ministers. The attendance of

[13] used here in the modern sense
[14] bandy words with
[15] a mat, here a carpet or raised floor on which the seat of justice is placed
[16] border
[17] Matt. vii. 16
[18] plundering

courts is subject to four bad instruments: first, certain persons that are sowers of suits, which make the court swell and the country pine: the second sort is of those that engage courts in quarrels of jurisdiction, and are not truly *amici curiae,* but *parasiti curiae,*[19] in puffing a court up beyond her bounds for their own scraps and advantage: the third sort is of those that may be accounted the left hands of courts; persons that are full of nimble and sinister tricks and shifts, whereby they pervert the plain and direct courses of courts, and bring justice into oblique lines and labyrinths: and the fourth is the poller and exacter of fees: which justifies the common resemblance of the courts of justice to the bush, whereunto while the sheep flies for defence in weather he is sure to lose part of his fleece. On the other side, an ancient clerk, skilful in precedents, wary in proceeding, and understanding in the business of the court, is an excellent finger of a court, and doth many times point the way to the judge himself.

Fourthly, for that which may concern the sovereign and estate. Judges ought above all to remember the conclusion of the Roman Twelve Tables, *Salus populi suprema lex;*[20] and to know that laws, except they be in order to that end, are but things captious and oracles not well inspired: therefore it is a happy thing in a state when kings and states do often consult with judges; and again, when judges do often consult with the king and state: the one when there is matter of law intervenient in business of state; the other when there is some consideration of state intervenient in matter of law; for many times the things deduced to

---

[19] not friends of the court, but parasites of the court
[20] The welfare of the people is the supreme law.

judgment may be *meum* and *tuum*,[21] when the reason [22] and consequence thereof may trench to point of estate: I call matter of estate not only the parts of sovereignty, but whatsoever introduceth any great alteration or dangerous precedent, or concerneth manifestly any great portion of people: and let no man weakly conceive that just laws and true policy have any antipathy; for they are like the spirits and sinews, that one moves with the other. Let judges also remember that Salomon's throne was supported by lions on both sides: let them be lions, but yet lions under the throne; being circumspect that they do not check or oppose any points of sovereignty. Let not judges also be so ignorant of their own right as to think there is not left to them, as a principal part of their office, a wise use and application of laws; for they may remember what the apostle saith of a greater law than theirs; *Nos scimus quia lex bona est, modo quis ea utatur legitime.*[23]

[21] mine and thine — that is, a private concern

[22] "Reason" seems to be used here in the sense of the L. *ratio* ("reckoning"), whence it is derived.

[23] I Tim. i. 8: "But we know that the law is good, if a man use it lawfully."

AN IGNORANT GLORY-HUNTER

SIR THOMAS OVERBURY (1581–1613)

AN IGNORANT GLORY-HUNTER is an *insectum animal*, for he is the maggot of opinion; his behavior is another thing from himself and is glued and but set on. He entertains men with repetitions, and returns them their own words. He is ignorant of nothing, no not of those things where ignorance is the lesser shame. He gets the names of good wits and utters them for his companions. He confesses vices that he is guiltless of, if they be in fashion, and dare not salute a man in old clothes or out of fashion. There is not a public assembly without him and he will take any pains for an acquaintance there. In any show he will be one, though he be but a whiffler [1] or a torch-bearer, and bears down strangers with the story of his actions. He handles nothing that is not rare and defends his wardrobe, diet, and all customs, with entitling their beginning from princes, great soldiers and strange nations. He dares speak more than he understands and adventures his words without the relief of any seconds. He relates battles and skirmishes, as from an eye-witness, when his eyes thievishly beguiled a ballad of them. In a word, to make sure of admiration he will not let himself understand himself but hopes fame and opinion will be the readers of his riddles.

[1] An officer who goes at the head of a procession to clear the way.

A MERE EMPTY WIT[1]

JOHN EARLE (1601?–1665)

A MERE EMPTY WIT is like one that spends on the stock without any revenues coming in, and will shortly be no wit at all; for learning is the fuel to the fire of wit which, if it wants this feeding, eats out itself. A good conceit[2] or two abates of such a man, and makes a sensible[3] weakening in him, and his brain recovers from it not a year after. The rest of him is bubbles and flashes, darted out on a sudden, which, if you take them while they are warm, may be laughed at; if they are cool, are nothing. He speaks best on the present[4] apprehension, for meditation stupefies him, and the more he is in travail the less he brings forth. His things come off then as in a nauseating stomach where there is nothing to cast up — strains and convulsions and some astonishing bombast which men, only till they understand, are scared with. A verse or some such work he may sometimes get up to, but seldom above the stature of an epigram — and that with some relief out of Martial,[5] which is the ordinary companion of his pocket, and he reads him as he were inspired. Such men are commonly the trifling things of the world, good to make merry the company, and whom only

[1] From *Microcosmographie*, 1628.
[2] a witty thought or turn of expression
[3] apparent (a pun may be intended)
[4] immediate
[5] the Latin author of a famous volume of epigrams

men have to do withal when they have nothing to do, and none are less their friends than who are most their company. Here they vent themselves over a cup somewhat more lastingly; all their words go for jests, and all their jests for nothing. They are nimble in the fancy of some ridiculous thing, and reasonable good in the expression. Nothing stops a jest when it's coming, neither friends nor danger, but it must out howsoever, though their blood come out after, and then they emphatically rail, and are emphatically beaten, and commonly are men reasonable familiar to this. Briefly they are such whose life is but to laugh and be laughed at; and only wits in jest, and fools in earnest.

A DETRACTOR

A DETRACTOR is one of a more cunning and active envy, wherewith he gnaws not foolishly himself but throws it abroad and would have it blister others. He is commonly some weak-parted fellow, and worse minded, yet is strangely ambitious to match others, not by mounting to their worth but by bringing them down with his tongue to his own poorness. He is indeed like the red dragon that pursued the woman, for when he cannot over-reach another, he opens his mouth and throws a flood after to drown him. You cannot anger him worse than to do well, and he hates you more bitterly for this than if you had cheated him of his patrimony with your own discredit. He is always slighting the general opinion and wondering why such and such men should be applauded. Commend a good divine, he cries postilling;[1] a philologer, pedantry; a poet, rim-

[1] mere commenting upon a text, annotating, glossing

ing; a schoolman, dull wrangling; a sharp conceit, boyishness; an honest man, plausibility.[2] He comes to public things not to learn but to catch, and if there be but one solecism, that's all he carries away. He looks on all things with a prepared sourness, and is always furnished with a "pish" beforehand or some musty proverb that disrelishes all things whatsoever. If fear of the company make him second a commendation, it is like a law-writ, always with a clause of exception, or to smooth his way to some greater scandal. He will grant you something and abate more; and this abatement shall in conclusion take away all he granted. His speech concludes always with an "Oh but" and "I could wish one thing amended," and this one thing shall be enough to deface all his former commendations. He will be very inward with a man to fish some bad out of him and make his slanders hereafter more authentic, when it is said a friend reported it. He will inveigle you to naughtiness to get your good name into his clutches, and make you drunk to show you reeling. He passes the more plausibly because all men have a smack of his humor and that is thought freeness which is malice. If he can say nothing of a man, he will seem to speak riddles, as if he could tell strange stories if he would, and when he has racked his invention to the utmost, he ends, "But I wish him well, and therefore must hold my peace." He is always listening and enquiring after men and suffers not a cloak to pass by him unexamined. In brief, he is one that has lost all good himself and is loth to find it in another.

[2] speciousness, only the appearance of honesty

THE RUDE MAN[1]

SAMUEL BUTLER (1612–1680)

THE RUDE MAN is an Ostrogoth, or northern Hun, that wheresoever he comes, invades and all the world does overrun, without distinction of age, sex or quality. He has no regard to anything but his own humor,[2] and that he expects should pass every where without asking leave or being asked wherefore, as if he had a safe-conduct for his rudeness. He rolls himself up, like a hedgehog, in his prickles, and is as untractable to all that come near him. He is an ill-designed piece, built after the rustic order; and all his parts look too big for their height. He is so ill contrived that that which should be the top in all regular structures — *i.e.*, confidence — is his foundation. He has neither doctrine nor discipline in him, like a fanatic church, but is guided by the very same spirit that dipped the herd of swine in the sea. He was not bred, but reared; not brought up to hand, but suffered to run wild and take after his kind as other people of the pasture do. He takes that freedom in all places, as if he were not at liberty but had broken loose and expected to be tied up again. He does not eat, but feed; and when he drinks, goes to water. The old Romans beat the barbarous part of the world into civility, but if he had lived in those

---

[1] From *The Genuine Remains of Samuel Butler*, pub. 1759.
[2] whim, eccentricity, peculiar nature

times he had been invincible to all attempts of that nature and harder to be subdued and governed than a province. He eats his bread, according to the curse,[3] with the sweat of his brows, and takes as much pains at a meal as if he earned it — puffs and blows like a horse that eats provender, and crams his throat like a screwed gun with a bullet bigger than the bore. His tongue runs perpetually over every thing that comes in its way, without regard of what, where, or to whom, and nothing but a greater rudeness than his own can stand before it; and he uses it to as slovenly purposes as a dog does that licks his sores and the dirt off his feet. He is the best instance of the truth of Pythagoras's doctrine, for his soul passed through all sorts of brute beasts before it came to him and still retains something of the nature of every one.

A FLATTERER

A FLATTERER is a dog that fawns when he bites. He hangs bells in a man's ears, as a carman does by his horse, while he lays a heavy load upon his back. His insinuations are like strong wines that please a man's palate until they have got within him and then deprive him of his reason and overthrow him. His business is to render a man a stranger to himself and get between him and home, and then he carries him whither he pleases. He is a spirit that conveys away a man for himself, undertakes great matters for him, and after sells him for a slave. He makes division not only between a man and his friends but between a man

---

[3] Gen. iii. 19

A FLATTERER

and himself, raises a faction within him, and after takes part with the strongest side and ruins both. He steals him away from himself (as the fairies are said to do children in the cradle) and after changes him for a fool. He whistles to him as a carter does to his horse, while he whips out his eyes and makes him draw what he pleases. He finds out his humor and feeds it till it will come to his hand, and then he leads him whither he pleases. He tickles him, as they do trout, until he lays hold on him, and then devours and feeds upon him. He tickles his ears with a straw, and while he is pleased with scratching it, picks his pocket. He embraces him and hugs him in his arms and lifts him above ground, as wrestlers do, to throw him down again and fall upon him. He possesses him with his own praises like an evil spirit that makes him swell and appear stronger than he was, talk what he does not understand and do things that he knows nothing of when he comes to himself. He *gives* good words, as doctors are said to *give* physic when they are paid for it and lawyers advice when they are fee'd beforehand. He is a poisoned perfume that infects the brain and murders those it pleases. He undermines a man, and blows him up with his own praises to throw him down. He commends a man out of design, that he may be presented with him and have him for his pains, according to the mode.[1]

---

[1] To beg a man for a fool was to sue to be made the legal guardian of his person and property on the grounds that he was mentally incompetent.

THE EARL OF ARUNDEL[1]

EDWARD HYDE, EARL OF CLARENDON (1609–1674)

The Earl of Arundel was the next officer of state, who, in his own right and quality, preceded the rest of the council. He was generally thought to be a proud man, who lived always within himself and to himself, conversing little with any who were in common conversation; so that he seemed to live as it were in another nation, his house being a place to which all people resorted who resorted to no other place; strangers, or such who affected to look like strangers and dressed themselves accordingly. He resorted sometimes to the court, because there only was a greater man than himself; and went thither the seldomer, because there was a greater man than himself. He lived towards all favorites and great officers without any kind of condescension;[2] and rather suffered himself to be ill-treated by their power and authority (for he was often in disgrace, and once or twice prisoner in the Tower) than to descend in making any application to them.

And upon these occasions he spent a great interval of his time in several journeys into foreign parts, and, with his wife and family, had lived some years in Italy, the humor[3] and manners of which nation he

---

[1] From *The History of the Rebellion.*
[2] concession
[3] nature, peculiarities

seemed most to like and approve and affected to imitate. He had a good fortune by descent and a much greater from his wife, who was the sole daughter upon the matter (for neither of the two sisters left any issue) of the great house of Shrewsbury: but his expenses were without any measure and always exceeded very much his revenue. He was willing to be thought a scholar and to understand the most mysterious parts of antiquity, because he made a wonderful and costly purchase of excellent statues whilst he was in Italy and in Rome (some whereof he could never obtain permission to remove from Rome, though he had paid for them), and had a rare collection of the most curious medals; whereas in truth he was only able to buy them, never to understand them. As to all parts of learning he was almost illiterate, and thought no other part of history so considerable as what related to his own family; in which, no doubt, there had been some very memorable persons. It cannot be denied that he had in his person, in his aspect, and countenance, the appearance of a great man, which he preserved in his gait and motion. He wore and affected a habit very different from that of the time, such as men had only beheld in the pictures of the most considerable men; all which drew the eyes of most, and the reverence of many, towards him, as the image and representative of the primitive nobility and native gravity of the nobles when they had been most venerable: but this was only his outside, his nature and true humor being much disposed to levity and delights, which indeed were very despicable and childish.

He was never suspected to love anybody, nor to have the least propensity to justice, charity, or compassion, so that though he got all he could, and by all the ways he could, and spent much more than he got or had; he was never known to give anything, nor in all his employments (for he had employments, of great profit as well as honor, being sent ambassador extraordinary into Germany, for the treaty of that general peace, for which he had great appointments, and in which he did nothing of the least importance, and which is more wonderful, he was afterwards made general of the army raised for Scotland, and received full pay as such; and in his own office of earl marshal, more money was drawn from the people by his avidity and pretense of jurisdiction than had ever been extorted by all the officers preceding), yet, I say, in all his offices and employments, no man used or employed by him ever got any fortune under him, nor did ever any man acknowledge any obligation to him.

He was rather thought not to be much concerned for religion than to incline to this or that party of any; and had little other affection for the nation or the kingdom than as he had a great share in it, in which, like the great leviathan, he might sport himself; from which he withdrew as soon as he discerned the repose thereof was like to be disturbed,[4] and died in Italy, under the same doubtful character of religion in which he lived.

JOHN HAMPDEN[1]

HE was a gentleman of a good family in Buckinghamshire, and born to a fair fortune, and of a most civil

[4] by the English Civil Wars between King Charles I and the Parliament

[1] From *The History of the Rebellion*. This character sketch is the more remarkable in that Hampden and Clarendon were enemies.

and affable deportment. In his entrance into the world, he indulged to himself all the license in sports and exercises and company which were used by men of the most jolly conversation.[2] Afterwards he retired to a more reserved and melancholy society, yet preserving his own natural cheerfulness and vivacity and, above all, a flowing courtesy to all men; though they who conversed nearly with him found him growing into a dislike of the ecclesiastical government of the church, yet most believed it rather a dislike of some churchmen and of some introducements of theirs which he apprehended might disquiet the public peace. He was rather of reputation in his own country[3] than of public discourse or fame in the kingdom before the business of ship-money;[4] but then he grew the argument of all tongues, every man inquiring who and what he was that durst, at his own charge, support the liberty and property of the kingdom and rescue his country, as he thought, from being made a prey to the court. His carriage throughout this agitation was with that rare temper and modesty that they who watched him narrowly to find some advantage against his person, to make him less resolute in his cause, were compelled to give him a just testimony. And the judgment that was given against him infinitely more advanced him than the service for which it was given. When this parliament begun (being knight of the shire for the county where he lived), the eyes of all men were fixed upon him, as their *patriae pater* and the pilot that must steer the vessel through the tempests and rocks which threatened it. And I am persuaded his

[2] social deportment as a whole
[3] *i.e.*, his own part of the country
[4] a tax which Hampden regarded as unjust and which he therefore refused to pay

power and interest at that time was greater to do good or hurt than any man's in the kingdom, or than any man of his rank hath had in any time, for his reputation of honesty was universal and his affections [5] seemed so publicly guided that no corrupt or private ends could bias them.

He was of that rare affability and temper in debate, and of that seeming humility and submission of judgment, as if he brought no opinion of his own with him, but a desire of information and instruction; yet he had so subtle a way of interrogating and, under the notion of doubts, insinuating his objections that he infused his own opinions into those from whom he pretended to learn and receive them. And even with them who were able to preserve themselves from his infusions, and discerned those opinions to be fixed in him with which they could not comply, he always left the character of an ingenious and conscientious person. He was indeed a very wise man and of great parts, and possessed with the most absolute spirit of popularity and the most absolute faculties to govern the people of any man I ever knew. For the first year of the parliament he seemed rather to moderate and soften the violent and distempered humors than to inflame them. But wise and dispassioned men plainly discerned that that moderation proceeded from prudence and observation that the season was not ripe, rather than that he approved of the moderation; and that he begot many opinions and motions, the education [6] whereof he committed to other men, so far disguising his own designs that he seemed seldom to wish more than was concluded; and in many gross conclu-

[5] inclinations, acts
[6] fostering, bringing out

sions, which would hereafter contribute to designs not yet set on foot, when he found them sufficiently backed by majority of voices, he would withdraw himself before the question,[7] that he might seem not to consent to so much visible unreasonableness; which produced as great a doubt in some, as it did approbation in others, of his integrity. What combination soever had been originally with the Scots for the invasion of England,[8] and what farther was entered into afterwards in favor of them and to advance any alteration of the government in parliament, no man doubts was at least with the privity of this gentleman.

After he was among those members accused by the king of high treason, he was much altered, his nature and carriage seeming much fiercer than it did before. And without question, when he first drew his sword he threw away the scabbard; for he passionately opposed the overture made by the king for a treaty from Nottingham, and as eminently all expedients that might have produced any accommodations in this that was at Oxford; and was principally relied on to prevent any infusions which might be made into the Earl of Essex[9] towards peace, or to render them ineffectual if they were made; and was indeed much more relied on by that party than the general himself. In the first entrance into the troubles he undertook the command of a regiment of foot, and performed the duty of a colonel upon all occasions most punctually. He was very temperate in diet and a supreme governor over all his passions and affections, and had thereby a great power over other men's. He was of an industry and

---

[7] *i.e.*, before the vote was taken
[8] The invasion of the Scots, in 1640, was the first of many events that finally broke the power of the king.
[9] Essex was the parliamentary general.

vigilance not to be tired out or wearied by the most laborious; and of parts [10] not to be imposed upon by the most subtle or sharp; and of a personal courage equal to his best parts; so that he was an enemy not to be wished wherever he might have been made a friend, and as much to be apprehended where he was so as any man could deserve to be. And therefore his death [11] was no less pleasing to the one party than it was condoled in the other. In a word, what was said of Cinna might well be applied to him: "He had a head to contrive, and a tongue to persuade, and a hand to execute, any mischief." His death therefore seemed to be a great deliverance to the nation.

[10] mental abilities
[11] at Chalgrove field (1643), an early skirmish in the Civil Wars

THE EARL OF STRAFFORD[1]
SIR PHILIP WARWICK (1609–1683)

THE Lord Viscount Wentworth, Lord President of the North, whom the Lord Treasurer Portland had brought into his majesty's affairs, from his ability and activity had wrought himself much into his majesty's confidence; and about the year 1632 was appointed by the King to be Lord Deputy of Ireland, where the state of affairs was in no very good posture, the revenue of the crown not defraying the standing army there, nor the ordinary expenses; and the deportment of the Romanists being there also very insolent, and the Scots plantations in the northern parts of that realm looking upon themselves as if they had been a distinct body. So as here was subject matter enough for this great man to work on; and, considering his hardiness, it may well be supposed that the difficulties of his employment, being means to show his abilities, were grateful to him. For he was every way qualified for business, his natural faculties being very strong and pregnant; his understanding, aided by a good fancy, made him quick in discerning the nature of any business, and through a cold brain he became

[1] From *Memoires of the reigne of King Charles I,* ed. 1701. Thomas Wentworth (1593–1641) was a vigorous, stern, and able disciplinarian, who urged Charles the First to establish his personal rule by force, offering himself to be the instrument thereto. He was executed under a bill of attainder, 1641.

deliberate and of a sound judgment. His memory was great, and he made it greater by confiding in it. His elocution was very fluent, and it was a great part of his talent readily to reply or freely to harangue upon any subject. And all this was lodged in a sour and haughty temper; so, as it may probably be believed, he expected to have more observance paid to him than he was willing to pay to others, though they were of his own quality;[2] and then he was not like to conciliate the good will of men of the lesser station.

His acquired parts, both in university and inns-of-court learning,[3] as likewise his foreign travels, made him an eminent man before he was a conspicuous, so as when he came to show himself first in public affairs, which was in the House of Commons, he was soon a bell-wether[4] in that flock. As he had these parts he knew how to set a price on them, if not to overvalue them; and he too soon discovered[5] a roughness in his nature which a man no more obliged by him than I was would have called an injustice, though many of his confidents (who were my good friends, when I like a little worm being trod on would turn and laugh, and under that disguise say as piquant words as my little wit would help me with) were wont to swear to me that he endeavoured to be just to all but was resolved to be gracious to none but to those whom he thought inwardly affected[6] him; which never bowed me till his broken fortune and, as I thought, very unjustifiable prosecution made me one of the

[2] social station
[3] *i.e.*, liberal and legal knowledge
[4] a leader
[5] revealed
[6] favored

THE EARL OF STRAFFORD

fifty-six who gave a negative to that fatal bill which cut the thread of his life.

He gave an early specimen of the roughness of his nature when, in the eager pursuit of the House of Commons after the Duke of Buckingham, he advised or gave a counsel against another which was afterwards taken up and pursued against himself. Thus pressing [7] upon another man's case, he awakened his own fate. For when that House was in consultation how to frame the particular charge against that great duke, he advised to make a general one and to accuse him of treason and to let him afterwards get off as he could, which befell himself at last. I believe he should make no irrational conjecture who determined [8] that his very eminent parts to support a crown and his very rugged nature to contest disloyalty, or withstand change of government, made his enemies implacable to him. It was a great infirmity in him that he seemed to overlook so many as he did, since everywhere, much more in court, the numerous or lesser sort of attendants can obstruct, create jealousies, spread ill reports and do harm; for as it is impossible that any power or deportment should satisfy all persons, so there a little friendliness and openness of carriage begets hope and lessens envy.

In his person he was of a tall stature, but stooped much in the neck. His countenance was cloudy, whilst he moved or sat thinking, but when he spake, either seriously or facetiously, he had a lightsome and a very pleasant air; and indeed whatever he then did he performed very gracefully. The greatness of the envy that attended him made many in their prognostics to

[7] urging
[8] who should determine

bode him an ill end; and there went current a story of the dream of his father who, being both by his wife, nighest friends and physicians, thought to be at the point of his death, fell suddenly into so profound a sleep and lay quietly so long that his wife, uncertain of his condition, drew nigh his bed to observe whether she could hear him breathe, and gently touching him, he awaked with great disturbance and told her the reason was she had interrupted him in a dream which most passionately he desired to have known the end of. For, said he, I dreamed one appeared to me, assuring me that *I should have a son* (for until then he had none) *who should be a very great and eminent man: but — and in this instant thou didst awake me, whereby I am bereaved of the knowledge of the further fortune of the child.* This I heard when this lord was but in the ascent of his greatness and long before his fall, and afterwards, conferring with some of his nighest relations, I found the tradition was not disowned. Sure I am, that his station was like those turfs of earth or sea-banks which by the storm swept away left all the inland to be drowned by popular tumult.

RALPH KETTELL [1]

JOHN AUBREY (1626–1697)

RALPH KETTELL, D.D., president of Trinity College, Oxford, was born in Hertfordshire. The lady Elizabeth Pope brought him in to be a scholar of the house at eleven years of age, as I have heard Dr. Ralph Bathurst say.

I have heard Dr. Whistler say that he wrote good Latin, and Dr. Ralph Bathurst (whose grandmother he married), that he scolded the best in Latin of any one that ever he knew. He was of an admirable healthy constitution.

He died a year and more after I came to the college,[2] and he was then a good deal above eighty, and he had then a fresh ruddy complexion. He was a very tall well grown man. His gown and surplice and hood being on, he had a terrible gigantic aspect, with his sharp gray eyes. The ordinary gown that he wore was a russet cloth gown.

He was, they say, white very soon. He had a very venerable presence, and was an excellent governor. One of his maxims of governing was to keep down the *juvenilis impetus*.[3] He was chosen President [in 1598], the second after the foundation of the college.

[1] From MS. Aubrey 6, Folios 57r–59v in the Bodleian Library, with the kind permission of the Librarian. See Foreword.
[2] *i.e.*, in 1643
[3] the violence of youth

He was a right Church of England man, and every Tuesday in term time in the morning the undergraduates were to come into the chapel to hear him expound on the thirty-six articles of the Church of England. I remember he was wont to talk much of the rood-loft and of the wafers: he remembered those times.[4] On these days, if anyone had committed a fault, he would be sure to hear of it in the chapel before his fellow collegiates.

On these days he would be sure to have at him that had a white cap on, for he concluded him to have been drunk and his head to ache. Sir John Denham had borrowed money of Mr. Whistler, the recorder, and after a great while the recorder asked him for it again. Mr. Denham laughed at it, and told him he never intended that. The recorder acquainted the President, who, at a lecture in the chapel, rattled him and told him, "Thy father has hanged many an honester man."[5] . . .

One of the fellows (in Mr. Francis Potter's time) was wont to say that Dr. Kettell's brain was like a hasty-pudding, where there was memory, judgment, and fancy all stirred together. He had all these faculties in great measure, but they were all just so jumbled together. If you had to do with him, taking him for a fool, you would have found in him great subtlety and reach: *e contra,* if you treated with him as a wise man, you would have mistaken him for a fool.

A neighbour of mine (Mr. Lawrence St. Low) told me he heard him preach once in St. Mary's Church at Oxford. He began thus: "Being my turn to preach in this place, I went into my study to prepare myself

---

[4] *i.e.,* the times when England was a Catholic country
[5] Denham's father was a judge.

for my sermon, and I took down a book that had blue strings [6] and looked in it, and 't was sweet Saint Bernard. I chanced to read such a part of it, on such a subject, which has made me choose this text —." I know not whether this was the only time or no that he used this following way of conclusion: — "But now I see it is time for me to shut up my book, for I see the doctors' men come in wiping off their beards from the ale-house." — (He could from the pulpit plainly see them, and 't was their custom in sermon to go there and about the end of sermon to return to wait on their masters.)

He had two wives, if not three, but no child. His second wife was a widow who had two beautiful daughters, co-heiresses. The eldest, whom several of good estate would gladly have wedded, he would needs dispose of himself, and he thought nobody so fit a husband for this angelic creature as one Mr. Bathurst of the college, a second brother and of about three hundred pounds per annum, but an indifferent scholar, red faced, not at all handsome. But the Doctor's fashion was to go up and down the college and peep in at the keyholes to see whether the boys did follow their books or no. He seldom found Bathurst minding of his book but mending of his old doublet or breeches. He was very thrifty and penurious, and upon this reason he carried away this curious creature. But she was very happy in her issue; all her children were ingenious and prosperous in the world and most of them beautiful.

Near seventy years since, I suppose, one Mr. Isham

---

[6] Books were formerly placed on shelves with their backs against the wall, and the open edges of the covers were tied together with thongs.

(elder brother to Sir Justinian Isham), a gentleman-commoner of this house, died of the smallpox. He was a very fine gentleman and very well beloved by all the college, and several of the fellows would have preached his funeral sermon, but Dr. Kettell would not permit it, but would do it himself — which the fellows were sorry for, for they knew he would make a ridiculous piece of work of it. But preach the Doctor did: takes a text and preaches on it a little while; and then takes another text, for the satisfaction of the young gentleman's mother; and anon he takes another text, for the satisfaction of the young gentleman's grandmother. When he came to the panegyric, said he, "He was the finest, sweet young gentleman; it did do my heart good to see him walk along the quadrangle.[7] We have an old proverb that *Hungry dogs will eat dirty puddings,* but I must needs say for this young gentleman that he always loved *sweet"* — he spake it with a squeaking voice — "things," — and there was an end.

He observed that the houses that had the smallest[8] beer had most drunkards, for it forced them to go into the town to comfort their stomachs; wherefore Dr. Kettell always had in his college excellent beer, not better to be had in Oxford, so that we could not go to any other place but for the worse, and we had the fewest drunkards of any house in Oxford. . . .

He was irreconcilable to long hair — called them hairy scalps. And as for periwigs[9] (which were then very rarely worn) he believed them to be the scalps of men cut off after they were hanged, and so tanned

[7] the college yard
[8] weakest
[9] wigs, which came later to be universally worn

and dressed for use. When he observed the scholars' hair longer than ordinary he would bring a pair of scissors in his muff (which he commonly wore) and woe be to them that sat on the outside [10] of the table. I remember he cut Mr. Radford's hair with the knife that chips the bread on the buttery-hatch, and then he sang (this is in the old play of *Gammer Gurton's Needle*)

"And was not Grim the collier finely trimmed?
Tonedi, Tonedi."

"Mr. Lydall," said he, "how do you decline *tondeo?* [11] Tondeo, tondes, tonedi?"

One time walking by the table where the Logic lecture was read, where the reader was telling the boys that a syllogism might be true *quoad formam,* but not *quoad materiam;* [12] said the President (who would put in sometimes), "There was a fox had spied a crow upon a tree, and he had a great mind to have him, and so gets under the tree in a hope, and lays out his tail crooked like a horn, thinking the crow might come and peck at it and then he would seize him. Now come we" (this was his word), "I say the fox's tail is a horn: is this a true proposition or no?" (to one of the boys). "Yes," said he (the Doctor expected he should have said No; for it put him out his design); "Why then," said he, "take him and toot him"; and away he went.

He dragged with one foot a little, by which he gave warning (like the rattlesnake) of his coming. Will Egerton (Major-General Egerton's younger brother),

---

[10] *i.e.,* those who did not sit against the wall, but in the open where he could come up behind them
[11] the Latin verb meaning "to shear, clip, crop, or shave"
[12] in appearance but not in substance

a good wit and mimic, would go so like him that sometimes he would make the whole chapel rise up, imagining that he had been entering in. . . .

He preached every Sunday at his parsonage at Garsington, about five miles off. He rode on his bay gelding, with his boy Ralph before him, with a leg of mutton (commonly) and some college bread. He did not care for the country revels because they tended to debauchery. Said he, at Garsington revel, "Here is Hey for Garsington! and Hey for Cuddesdon! and Hey Hockly! but here's nobody cries, Hey for God Almighty!". . .

He was a person of great charity. In his college, where he observed diligent boys that he guessed had but a slender exhibition [13] from their friends, he would many times put money in at their windows; [in such a manner] that his right hand did not know what his left hand did. Servitors that wrote good hands he would set on work to transcribe for him and reward them generously and give them good advice. Mrs. Howe, of Grendon, sent him a present of hippocris [14] and some fine cheese-cakes by a plain country fellow, her servant. The Doctor tastes the wine: — "What," said he, "didst thou take this drink out of a ditch?" and when he saw the cheese-cakes: — "What have we here, *crinkum, crankum?*" The poor fellow stared on him, and wondered at such a rough reception of such a handsome present; but he shortly made him amends with a good dinner and a half-a-crown . . . When one of his parish, that was an honest industrious man, happened by any accident to be in decay and low in the world, [he] would let his parsonage to him for a

---

[13] allowance
[14] a sort of wine

year or two or three, forty pounds a year under value. . . .

He sang in a shrill high treble, but there was one J. Hoskyns who had a higher and would play the wag with the Doctor to make him strain his voice up to his. . . .

When he scolded at the idle young boys of his college, he used these names, *viz.* . . . *Tarrarags* (these were the worst sort, rude rakehells), *Rascal-Jacks, Blindcinques, Scobberlotchers* (these did no hurt, were sober, but went idling about the grove with their hands in their pockets and telling [15] the number of trees there, or so). . . .

'T is probable this venerable Doctor might have lived some years longer, and finished his century, had not those civil wars come on, which much grieved him, that was wont to be absolute in the college, to be affronted and disrespected by rude soldiers.[16] I remember being at the Rhetoric lecture in the hall, a foot soldier came in and brake his hour-glass. . . .

The dissoluteness of the times, as I have said, grieving the good old Doctor, his days were shortened and he died, anno Domini 1643, and was buried at Garsington.

[15] counting (out of sheer idleness)
[16] Oxford was the royalist headquarters during the civil war.

CHARLES II [1]

GILBERT BURNET, BISHOP OF SALISBURY (1643–1715)

THUS lived and died King Charles the Second. He was the greatest instance in history of the various revolutions of which any one man seemed capable. He was bred up, the first twelve years of his life, with the splendor that became the heir of so great a crown. After that he passed through eighteen years in great inequalities, unhappy in the war, in the loss of his father and of the crown of England. Scotland did not only receive him, though upon terms hard of digestion, but made an attempt upon England for him, though a feeble one. He lost the battle of Worcester with too much indifference: and then he showed more care of his person than became one who had so much at stake. He wandered about England for ten weeks after that, hiding from place to place, but, under all the apprehensions he had then upon him, he showed a temper [2] so careless and so much turned to levity that he was then diverting himself with little household sports, in as unconcerned a manner as if he had made no loss and had been in no danger at all. He got at last out of England, but he had been obliged to so many, who had been faithful to him and careful of him, that he seemed afterwards to resolve to make

[1] From Burnet's *History of His Own Times*.
[2] temperament

CHARLES II

an equal return to them all; and finding it not easy to reward them all as they deserved, he forgot them all alike. Most princes seem to have this pretty deep in them, and to think that they ought never to remember past services, but that their acceptance of them is a full reward. He, of all in our age, exerted this piece of prerogative in the amplest manner, for he never seemed to charge his memory, or to trouble his thoughts, with the sense of any of the services that had been done him. While he was abroad at Paris, Cologne, or Brussels, he never seemed to lay anything to heart. He pursued all his diversions and irregular pleasures in a free career, and seemed to be as serene under the loss of a crown as the greatest philosopher could have been. Nor did he willingly harken to any of those projects with which he often complained that his chancellor persecuted him. That in which he seemed most concerned was to find money for supporting his expense. And it was often said that if Cromwell would have compounded the matter and have given him a good round pension, that he might have been induced to resign his title to him. During his exile he delivered himself so entirely to his pleasures that he became incapable of application. He spent little of his time in reading or study, and yet less in thinking; and, in the state his affairs were then in, he accustomed himself to say to every person, and upon all occasions, that which he thought would please most: so that words or promises went very easily from him. And he had so ill an opinion of mankind that he thought the great art of living and governing was to manage all things and all persons with a depth of craft and dissimulation; and in that few men in the world could put on the appearance of sincerity better than he could, under which so much artifice was usually hid that in conclusion he could deceive none, for all were become mistrustful of him. He had great vices, but scarce any virtues to correct them; he had in him some vices that were less hurtful, which corrected his more hurtful ones. He was, during the active part of his life, given up to sloth and lewdness to such a degree that he hated business and could not bear the engaging in any thing that gave him much trouble or put him under any constraint; and though he desired to become absolute and to overturn both our religion and our laws, yet he would neither run the risk nor give himself the trouble which so great a design required. He had an appearance of gentleness in his outward deportment, but he seemed to have no bowels nor tenderness in his nature, and in the end of his life he became cruel. He was apt to forgive all crimes, even blood itself; yet he never forgave anything that was done against himself, after his first and general act of indemnity, which was to be reckoned as done rather upon maxims of state than inclinations of mercy. He delivered himself up to a most enormous course of vice without any sort of restraint, even from the consideration of the nearest relations; the most studied extravagances that way seemed, to the very last, to be much delighted in and pursued by him. He had the art of making all people grow fond of him at first by a softness in his whole way of conversation, as he was certainly the best bred man of the age; but when it appeared how little could be built on his promise, they were cured of the fondness that he was apt to raise in them. When he saw young men of quality who had something more than ordinary in them, he drew them about him and set himself to corrupt them both in religion and morality; in which he proved so unhappily successful that he left England much changed at his death from what he had found it at his restoration. He loved to talk over all the stories of his life to every new man that came about him. His stay in Scotland and the share he had in the war of Paris, in carrying messages from the one side to the other, were his common topics. He went over these in a very graceful manner, but so often and so copiously that all those who had been long accustomed to them grew weary of them, and when he entered on those stories they usually withdrew; so that he often began them in a full audience, and before he had done there were not above four or five left about him; which drew a severe jest from Wilmot, Earl of Rochester. He said he wondered to see a man have so good a memory as to repeat the same story without losing the least circumstance, and yet not remember that he had told it to the same persons the very day before. This made him very fond of strangers, for they harkened to all his often-repeated stories and went away as in a rapture at such an uncommon condescension in a king.

His person and temper, his vices as well as his fortunes, resemble the character that we have given us of Tiberius so much that it were easy to draw the parallel between them. Tiberius's banishment and his coming afterwards to reign makes the comparison in that respect come pretty near. His hating of business and his love of pleasures, his raising of favorites and trusting them entirely, and his pulling them down and hating them excessively, his art of covering deep designs, particularly of revenge, with an appearance of softness, brings them so near a likeness that I did not wonder much to observe the resemblance of their face and person. At Rome I saw one of the last statues made for Tiberius, after he had lost his teeth; but, bating the alteration which that made, it was so like King Charles that Prince Borghese, and Signor Dominico, to whom it belonged, did agree with me in thinking that it looked like a statue made for him.

Few things ever went near his heart. The Duke of Gloucester's [3] death seemed to touch him much. But those who knew him best thought it was because he had lost him by whom only he could have balanced the surviving brother [4] whom he hated and yet embroiled all his [5] affairs to preserve the succession to him.

[3] a younger brother
[4] James II
[5] The antecedent is Charles.

A MODEST PROPOSAL

For Preventing the Children of Poor People in Ireland from Being a Burden to Their Parents or Country, and for Making Them Beneficial to the Public

JONATHAN SWIFT (1667–1745)

It is a melancholy object to those who walk through this great town [1] or travel in the country, when they see the streets, the roads, and cabin doors crowded with beggars of the female sex, followed by three, four, or six children, all in rags and importuning every passenger for an alms. These mothers, instead of being able to work for their honest livelihood, are forced to employ all their time in strolling to beg sustenance for their helpless infants: who, as they grow up, either turn thieves for want of work, or leave their dear native country to fight for the Pretender in Spain, or sell themselves to the Barbadoes.

I think it is agreed by all parties that this prodigious number of children in the arms, or on the backs, or at the heels of their mothers, and frequently of their fathers, is in the present deplorable state of the kingdom a very great additional grievance; and, therefore, whoever could find out a fair, cheap, and easy method of making these children sound, useful members of

[1] Dublin

the commonwealth, would deserve so well of the public as to have his statue set up for a preserver of the nation.

But my intention is very far from being confined to provide only for the children of professed beggars; it is of a much greater extent, and shall take in the whole number of infants at a certain age who are born of parents in effect as little able to support them as those who demand our charity in the streets.

As to my own part, having turned my thoughts for many years upon this important subject, and maturely weighed the several schemes of our projectors, I have always found them grossly mistaken in their computation. It is true, a child just dropped from its dam may be supported by her milk for a solar year, with little other nourishment; at most not above the value of two shillings, which the mother may certainly get, or the value in scraps, by her lawful occupation of begging; and it is exactly at one year old that I propose to provide for them in such a manner as instead of being a charge upon their parents or the parish, or wanting food and raiment for the rest of their lives, they shall, on the contrary, contribute to the feeding and partly to the clothing of many thousands.

There is likewise another great advantage in my scheme, that it will prevent those voluntary abortions, and that horrid practice of women murdering their bastard children, alas! too frequent among us! sacrificing the poor innocent babes, I doubt, more to avoid the expense than the shame, which would move tears and pity in the most savage and inhuman breast.

The number of souls in this kingdom being usually reckoned one million and a half, of these, I calculate there may be about two hundred thousand couples whose wives are breeders; from which number I subtract thirty thousand couples, who are able to maintain their own children (although I apprehend there cannot be so many, under the present distresses of the kingdom); but this being granted, there will remain one hundred and seventy thousand breeders. I again subtract fifty thousand for those women who miscarry, or whose children die by accidents or disease within the year. There only remains an hundred and twenty thousand children of poor parents annually born. The question therefore is, how this number shall be reared and provided for? which, as I have already said, under the present situation of affairs, is utterly impossible by all the methods hitherto proposed. For we can neither employ them in handicraft or agriculture; we can neither build houses (I mean in the country) nor cultivate land; they can very seldom pick up a livelihood by stealing, till they arrive at six years old, except where they are of towardly parts; although I confess they learn the rudiments much earlier; during which time, they can however be properly looked upon only as probationers; as I have been informed by a principal gentleman in the county of Cavan, who protested to me that he never knew above one or two instances under the age of six, even in a part of the kingdom so renowned for the quickest proficiency in that art.

I am assured by our merchants that a boy or girl before twelve years old is no saleable commodity; and even when they come to this age they will not yield above three pounds or three pounds and half-a-crown at most on the exchange; which cannot turn to account either to the parents or the kingdom, the charge of nutriment and rags having been at least four times that value.

I shall now therefore humbly propose my own thoughts, which I hope will not be liable to the least objection.

I have been assured by a very knowing American of my acquaintance in London, that a young healthy child well nursed is at a year old a most delicious, nourishing, and wholesome food, whether stewed, roasted, baked, or boiled; and I make no doubt that it will equally serve in a fricassee or a ragout.

I do therefore humbly offer it to public consideration that of the hundred and twenty thousand children already computed, twenty thousand may be reserved for breed, whereof only one-fourth part to be males; which is more than we allow to sheep, black cattle or swine; and my reason is, that these children are seldom the fruits of marriage, a circumstance not much regarded by our savages; therefore one male will be sufficient to serve four females. That the remaining hundred thousand may, at a year old, be offered in sale to the persons of quality and fortune through the kingdom; always advising the mother to let them suck plentifully in the last month, so as to render them plump and fat for a good table. A child will make two dishes at an entertainment for friends; and when the family dines alone, the fore or hind quarter will make a reasonable dish, and seasoned with a little pepper or salt will be very good boiled on the fourth day, especially in winter.

I have reckoned upon a medium that a child just born will weigh twelve pounds, and in a solar year, if tolerably nursed, will increase to twenty-eight pounds.

I grant this food will be somewhat dear, and therefore very proper for landlords, who, as they have already devoured most of the parents, seem to have the best title to the children.

Infants' flesh will be in season throughout the year, but more plentifully in March, and a little before and after: for we are told by a grave author, an eminent French physician, that fish being a prolific diet, there are more children born in Roman Catholic countries about nine months after Lent than at any other season; therefore, reckoning a year after Lent, the markets will be more glutted than usual, because the number of popish infants is at least three to one in this kingdom: and therefore it will have one other collateral advantage, by lessening the number of papists among us.

I have already computed the charge of nursing a beggar's child (in which list I reckon all cottagers, laborers, and four-fifths of the farmers) to be about two shillings per annum, rags included; and I believe no gentleman would repine to give ten shillings for the carcass of a good fat child, which, as I have said, will make four dishes of excellent nutritive meat, when he has only some particular friend or his own family to dine with him. Thus the squire will learn to be a good landlord, and grow popular among his tenants; the mother will have eight shillings net profit, and be fit for work till she produces another child.

Those who are more thrifty (as I must confess the times require) may flay the carcass; the skin of which artificially dressed will make admirable gloves for ladies, and summer boots for fine gentlemen.

As to our city of Dublin, shambles may be appointed for this purpose in the most convenient parts of it, and butchers we may be assured will not be wanting; although I rather recommend buying the children alive, and dressing them hot from the knife as we do roasting pigs.

A very worthy person, a true lover of his country, and whose virtues I highly esteem, was lately pleased, in discoursing on this matter, to offer a refinement upon my scheme. He said that many gentlemen of this kingdom, having of late destroyed their deer, he conceived that the want of venison might be well supplied by the bodies of young lads and maidens, not exceeding fourteen years of age nor under twelve; so great a number of both sexes in every country being now ready to starve for want of work and service; and these to be disposed of by their parents, if alive, or otherwise by their nearest relations. But with due deference to so excellent a friend and so deserving a patriot, I cannot be altogether in his sentiments; for as to the males, my American acquaintance assured me from frequent experience that their flesh was generally tough and lean, like that of our school-boys, by continual exercise, and their taste disagreeable; and to fatten them would not answer the charge. Then as to the females, it would, I think, with humble submission, be a loss to the public, because they soon would become breeders themselves: and besides, it is not improbable that some scrupulous people might be apt to censure such a practice (although indeed very unjustly), as a little bordering upon cruelty; which, I confess, has always been with me the strongest objection against any project, however so well intended.

But in order to justify my friend, he confessed that this expedient was put into his head by the famous Psalmanazar, a native of the island Formosa, who came from thence to London above twenty years ago: and in conversation told my friend, that in his country when any young person happened to be put to death, the executioner sold the carcass to persons of quality as a prime dainty; and that in his time the body of a plump girl of fifteen, who was crucified for an attempt to poison the emperor, was sold to his imperial majesty's prime minister of state, and other great mandarins of the court, in joints from the gibbet, at four hundred crowns. Neither indeed can I deny, that if the same use were made of several plump young girls in this town, who, without one single groat to their fortunes, cannot stir abroad without a chair, and appear at the playhouse and assemblies in foreign fineries which they never will pay for, the kingdom would not be the worse.

Some persons of a desponding spirit are in great concern about that vast number of poor people, who are aged, diseased, or maimed, and I have been desired to employ my thoughts what course may be taken to ease the nation of so grievous an encumbrance. But I am not in the least pain upon that matter, because it is very well known that they are every day dying and rotting by cold and famine, and filth and vermin, as fast as can be reasonably expected. And as to the younger laborers, they are now in as hopeful a condition; they cannot get work, and consequently pine away for want of nourishment, to a degree that if at any time they are accidentally hired to common labor, they have not strength to perform it; and thus the country and themselves are happily delivered from the evils to come.

I have too long digressed, and therefore shall return to my subject. I think the advantages by the proposal which I have made are obvious, and many, as well as of the highest importance.

For first, as I have already observed, it would greatly lessen the number of papists, with whom we are yearly overrun, being the principal breeders of the nation as well as our most dangerous enemies; and who stay at home on purpose with a design to deliver the kingdom to the Pretender, hoping to take their advantage by the absence of so many good protestants, who have chosen rather to leave their country than stay at home and pay tithes against their conscience to an episcopal curate.

Secondly, The poorer tenants will have something valuable of their own, which by law may be made liable to distress, and help to pay their landlord's rent, their corn and cattle being already seized, and money a thing unknown.

Thirdly, Whereas the maintenance of an hundred thousand children, from two years old and upward, cannot be computed at less than ten shillings a-piece per annum, the nation's stock will be thereby increased fifty thousand pounds per annum, besides the profit of a new dish introduced to the tables of all gentlemen of fortune in the kingdom who have any refinement in taste. And the money will circulate among ourselves, the goods being entirely of our own growth and manufacture.

Fourthly, The constant breeders, beside the gain of eight shillings sterling per annum by the sale of their children, will be rid of the charge of maintaining them after the first year.

Fifthly, This food would likewise bring great custom to taverns; where the vintners will certainly be so prudent as to procure the best receipts for dressing it to perfection, and consequently have their houses frequented by all the fine gentlemen, who justly value themselves upon their knowledge in good eating; and a skilful cook, who understands how to oblige his guests, will contrive to make it as expensive as they please.

Sixthly, This would be a great inducement to marriage, which all wise nations have either encouraged by rewards or enforced by laws and penalties. It would increase the care and tenderness of mothers toward their children, when they were sure of a settlement for life to the poor babes, provided in some sort by the public, to their annual profit instead of expense. We should see an honest emulation among the married women, which of them could bring the fattest child to the market. Men would become as fond of their wives during the time of their pregnancy as they are now of their mares in foal, their cows in calf, or sows when they are ready to farrow; nor offer to beat or kick them (as is too frequent a practice) for fear of a miscarriage.

Many other advantages might be enumerated. For instance, the addition of some thousand carcasses in our exportation of barreled beef, the propagation of swine's flesh, and improvement in the art of making good bacon, so much wanted among us by the great destruction of pigs, too frequent at our tables; which are in no way comparable in taste or magnificence to a well-grown, fat, yearling child, which roasted whole will make a considerable figure at a lord mayor's feast, or any other public entertainment. But this and many others I omit, being studious of brevity.

Supposing that one thousand families in this city would be constant customers for infants' flesh, beside others who might have it at merry-meetings, particularly weddings and christenings, I compute that

Dublin would take off annually about twenty thousand carcasses; and the rest of the kingdom (where probably they will be sold somewhat cheaper) the remaining eighty thousand.

I can think of no one objection that will possibly be raised against this proposal, unless it should be urged that the number of people will be thereby much lessened in the kingdom. This I freely own, and it was indeed one principal design in offering it to the world. I desire the reader will observe, that I calculate my remedy for this one individual kingdom of Ireland, and for no other that ever was, is, or, I think, ever can be upon earth. Therefore let no man talk to me of other expedients: of taxing our absentees at five shillings a pound: of using neither clothes nor household furniture, except what is of our own growth and manufacture: of utterly rejecting the materials and instruments that promote foreign luxury: of curing the expensiveness of pride, vanity, idleness, and gambling in our women: of introducing a vein of parsimony, prudence, and temperance: of learning to love our country, in the want of which we differ even from Laplanders and the inhabitants of Topinamboo: of quitting our animosities and factions, nor acting any longer like the Jews, who were murdering one another at the very moment their city was taken: of being a little cautious not to sell our country and conscience for nothing: of teaching landlords to have at least one degree of mercy toward their tenants: lastly, of putting a spirit of honesty, industry, and skill into our shop-keepers; who, if a resolution could now be taken to buy only our native goods, would immediately unite to cheat and exact upon us in the price, the measure and the goodness, nor could ever yet be brought to make one fair proposal of just dealing, though often and earnestly invited to it.

Therefore, I repeat, let no man talk to me of these and the like expedients, till he has at least some glimpse of hope that there will be ever some hearty and sincere attempt to put them in practice.

But as to myself, having been wearied out for many years with offering vain, idle, visionary thoughts, and at length utterly despairing of success, I fortunately fell upon this proposal; which, as it is wholly new, so it has something solid and real, of no expense and little trouble, full in our own power, and whereby we can incur no danger in disobliging England. For this kind of commodity will not bear exportation, the flesh being of too tender a consistence to admit a long continuance in salt, although perhaps I could name a country which would be glad to eat up our whole nation without it.

After all, I am not so violently bent upon my own opinion as to reject any offer proposed by wise men, which shall be found equally innocent, cheap, easy, and effectual. But before something of that kind shall be advanced in contradiction to my scheme, and offering a better, I desire the author or authors will be pleased maturely to consider two points. First, as things now stand, how they will be able to find food and raiment for an hundred thousand useless mouths and backs. And secondly, there being a round million of creatures in human figure throughout this kingdom, whose whole subsistence put into a common stock would leave them in debt two millions of pounds sterling, adding those who are beggars by profession to the bulk of farmers, cottagers, and laborers, with their wives and children, who are beggars in effect; I desire those politicians, who dislike my overture, and may perhaps be so bold as to attempt an answer, that they will first ask the parents of these mortals, whether they would not at this day think it a great happiness to have been sold for food at a year old in the manner I prescribe, and thereby have avoided such a perpetual scene of misfortunes as they have since gone through by the oppression of landlords, the impossibility of paying rent without money or trade, the want of common sustenance, with neither house nor clothes to cover them from the inclemencies of the weather, and the most inevitable prospect of entailing the like or greater miseries upon their breed for ever.

I profess, in the sincerity of my heart, that I have not the least personal interest in endeavoring to promote this necessary work, having no other motive than the public good of my country, by advancing our trade, providing for infants, relieving the poor, and giving some pleasure to the rich. I have no children by which I can propose to get a single penny; the youngest being nine years old, and my wife past child-bearing.

DIRECTIONS TO SERVANTS

RULES THAT CONCERN ALL SERVANTS IN GENERAL [1]

WHEN your master or lady calls a servant by name, if that servant be not in the way, none of you are to answer, for then there will be no end of your drudgery:

---

[1] Excerpts from "Rules that govern all Servants in General," a sort of preface to *Directions to Servants*.

and masters themselves allow that if a servant comes when he is called it is sufficient.

When you have done a fault be always pert and insolent and behave yourself as if you were the injured person; this will immediately put your master or lady off their mettle.

Take all tradesmen's parts against your master, and when you are sent to buy anything, never offer to cheapen it but generously pay the full demand. This is highly to your master's honor, and may be some shillings in your pocket; and you are to consider, if your master hath paid too much, he can better afford the loss than a poor tradesman.

Never submit to stir a finger in any business but that for which you were particularly hired. For example, if the groom be drunk or absent and the butler be ordered to shut the stable door, the answer is ready: "An please your honor, I don't understand horses." If a corner of the hanging wants a single nail to fasten it, and the footman be directed to tack it up, he may say he doth not understand that sort of work, but his honor may send for the upholsterer.

Masters and ladies are usually quarrelling with the servants for not shutting the doors after them:[2] but neither masters nor ladies consider that those doors must be open before they can be shut and that the labor is double to open and shut the doors; therefore the best and shortest and easiest way is to do neither. But if you are so often teased to shut the door that you cannot easily forget it, then give the door such a clap as you go out as will shake the whole room and make every thing rattle in it, to put your master

---

[2] A matter of importance when rooms were heated individually by fireplaces and halls and stairways were cold.

and lady in mind that you observe their directions.

Write your own name and your sweetheart's with the smoke of a candle on the ceiling of the kitchen or the servants' hall, to show your learning.

I could never endure to see maid servants so ungenteel as to walk the streets with their petticoats pinned up; it is a foolish excuse to allege their petticoats will be dirty when they have so easy a remedy as to walk three or four times down a clean flight of stairs after they come home.

When your master or lady comes home and wants a servant who happens to be abroad, your answer must be that he had but just that minute stepped out, being sent for by a cousin who was dying.

When you are chidden for a fault, as you go out of the room and downstairs, mutter loud enough to be plainly heard; this will make him believe you are innocent.

Whoever comes to visit your master or lady when they are abroad,[3] never burden your memory with the person's name, for indeed you have too many other things to remember. Besides, it is a porter's business and your master's fault he does not keep one; and who can remember names? and you will certainly mistake them, and you can neither write nor read.

Where there are little masters and misses in a house they are usually great impediments to the diversions of the servants; the only remedy is to bribe them with *goody goodies,* that they may not tell tales to papa and mamma.

If your master or lady happen once in their lives to accuse you wrongfully, you are a happy servant, for you have nothing more to do, than for every fault

[3] out

you commit while you are in their service to put them in mind of that false accusation and protest yourself equally innocent in the present case.

The servants' candlesticks are generally broken, for nothing can last for ever. But you may find out many expedients: you may conveniently stick your candle in a bottle, or with a lump of butter against the wainscot, in a powder-horn, or in an old shoe, or in a cleft stick, or in the barrel of a pistol, or upon its own grease on a table, in a coffee-cup, or a drinking-glass, horn can, a tea-pot, a twisted napkin, a mustard-pot, an inkhorn, a marrowbone, a piece of dough, or you may cut a hole in the loaf and stick it there.

Lay all faults upon a lap-dog, or favorite cat, a monkey, a parrot, a child; or on the servant who was last turned off: by this rule you will excuse yourself, do no hurt to anybody else and save your master or lady from the trouble and vexation of chiding.

When you want proper instruments for any work you are about, use all expedients you can invent rather than leave your work undone. For instance, if the poker be out of the way or broken, stir the fire with the tongs; if the tongs be not at hand, use the muzzle of the bellows, the wrong end of the fire-shovel, the handle of the fire brush, the end of a mop, or your master's cane. If you want paper to singe a fowl, tear the first book you see about the house. Wipe your shoes, for want of a clout, with the bottom of a curtain, or a damask napkin.

There is nothing so pernicious in a family as a tell-tale, against whom it must be the principal business of you all to unite: whatever office he serves in, take all opportunities to spoil the business he is about and to cross him in everything. For instance, if the butler be a tell-tale, break his glasses whenever he leaves the pantry-door open; or lock the cat or the mastiff in it who will do as well: mislay a fork or a spoon so as he may never find it. If it be the cook, whenever she turns her back throw a lump of soot or a handful of salt into the pot, or smoking coals into the dripping pan, or daub the roast meat with the back of the chimney, or hide the key of the jack. If a footman be suspected, let the cook daub the back of his new livery; or when he is going up with a dish of soup, let her follow him softly with a ladle full and dribble it all the way upstairs to the dining room, and then let the house-maid make such a noise that her lady may hear it.

DIRECTIONS TO THE BUTLER [4]

IN waiting at the side-board, take all possible care to save your own trouble and your master's drinking glasses: therefore first, since those who dine at the same table are supposed to be friends, let them all drink out of the same glass without washing,[5] which will save you much pains as well as the hazard of breaking them. Give no person any liquor until he hath called for it thrice at least; by which means, some out of modesty and others out of forgetfulness will call the seldomer, and thus your master's liquor will be saved.

[4] Excerpts from "Directions to the Butler" in *Directions to Servants*.
[5] Every fresh glass of wine required a fresh glass. To fill up an empty or half-empty glass was a barbarous solecism.

DIRECTIONS TO SERVANTS

If any one desires a glass of bottled ale, first shake the bottle [6] to see whether any thing be in it; then taste it, to see what liquor it is, that you may not be mistaken; and lastly, wipe the mouth of the bottle with the palm of your hand to show your cleanliness.

Because butlers are apt to forget to bring up their ale and beer in time enough, be sure you remember to have up yours two hours before dinner; and place them in the sunny part of the room to let people see that you have not been negligent.

Clean your plate, wipe your knives, and rub the dirty tables with the napkins and table-cloths used that day; for it is but one washing, and besides it will save you wearing out the coarse rubbers; [7] and in reward of such good husbandry, my judgment is, that you may lawfully make use of the finest damask napkins for night caps for yourself.

When you cut bread for toast, do not stand idly watching it, but lay it on the coals and mind your other business, then come back, and if you find it toasted quite through, scrape off the burnt side and serve it up.

When any salt is spilled on the table, do not let it be lost, but when dinner is done fold up the table-cloth with the salt in it, then shake the salt out into the salt-cellar to serve next day: but the shortest and surest way is, when you remove the cloth, to wrap the knives, forks, spoons, salt-cellars, broken-bread and scraps of meat all together in the table-cloth, by which you will be sure to lose nothing, unless you

---

[6] Wine and ales, of course, are never to be shaken, and beer and ales should not be exposed to the light.

[7] cheap cloths for rubbing and polishing

think it better to shake them out of the window amongst the beggars, that they may with more convenience eat the scraps.

After supper, if it be dark, carry your plate and china together in the same basket to save candle-light, for you know your pantry well enough to put them up in the dark.

In bottling wine, fill your mouth full of corks — together with a large plug of tobacco which will give to the wine the true taste of the weed, so delightful to all good judges in drinking.

When you are to get water on for tea after dinner [8] (which in many families is part of your office) to save firing, and to make more haste, pour it into the tea-kettle from the pot where cabbage or fish have been boiling, which will make it much wholesomer by curing the acid and corroding quality of the tea.

Snuff the candles at supper as they stand on the table, which is much the securest way; because, if the burning snuff happens to get out of the snuffers you have a chance that it may fall into a dish of soup, sack-posset, rice-milk, or the like, where it will be immediately extinguished with very little stink.

That the salt may lie smooth in the salt-cellar, press it down with your moist palm.

You need not wipe your knife to cut bread for the table, because in cutting a slice or two it will wipe itself.

Always lock a cat in the closet where you keep your china plates, for fear the mice may steal in and break them.

A good butler always breaks off the point of his corkscrew in two days by trying which is hardest, the

[8] Tea used to be served, as we serve coffee, after dinner.

point of the screw or the neck of the bottle: in this case, to supply the want of a screw, after the stump hath torn the cork in pieces, make use of a silver fork, and when the scraps of the cork are almost drawn out, flirt the mouth of the bottle into the cistern three or four times until you quite clear it.

If a gentleman dines often with your master and gives you nothing when he goes away, you may use several methods to show him some mark of your displeasure and quicken his memory: if he calls for bread or drink, you may pretend not to hear, or send it to another who called after him: if he asks for wine, let him stay a while and then send him small-beer; give him always foul glasses; send him a spoon when he wants a knife; wink at the footman to leave him without a plate: by these and the like expedients, you may probably be a better man by half a crown before he leaves the house, provided you watch an opportunity of standing by when he is going.

If your master hath a large stock of glasses and you or your fellow-servants happen to break any of them without your master's knowledge, keep it a secret till there are not enough left to serve the table, then tell your master that the glasses are gone; this will be but one vexation to him, which is much better than fretting once or twice a week; and it is the office of a good servant to discompose his master and his lady as seldom as he can; and here the cat and dog will be of great use to take the blame from you.

Whet the backs of your knives until they are as sharp as the edge, which will have this advantage, that when gentlemen find them blunt on one side they may try the other; and to show you spare no pains in sharpening the knives, whet them so long, till you wear out a good part of the iron and even the bottom of the silver handle. This doth credit to your master, for it shows good house-keeping,[9] and the goldsmith may one day make you a present.

Do all in the dark to save your master's candles.

DIRECTIONS TO THE HOUSE-MAID [10]

IF your master and lady go into the country for a week or more, never wash the bed-chamber or dining-room until just the hour before you expect them to return: thus the rooms will be perfectly clean to receive them, and you will not be at the trouble to wash them so soon again.

Leave a pail of dirty water with the mop in it, a coal-box, a bottle, a broom, a chamber-pot, and such other unsightly things, either in a blind entry or upon the darkest part of the back stairs, that they may not be seen; and if people break their shins by trampling on them, it is their own fault.

Brush down the cobwebs with a broom that is wet and dirty, which will make them stick the faster to it and bring them down more effectually.

When you rid up the parlor hearth in a morning, throw the last night's ashes into a sieve; and what falls through, as you carry it down [11] will serve instead of sand for the room and the stairs.

---

[9] profuse entertaining, generous hospitality. The goldsmith would get the damaged knives to repair.

[10] Excerpts from "Directions to the House-maid" in *Directions to Servants*.

[11] Drawing-rooms and parlors were formerly on what we call the second floor of a house. The dining room was on the first floor and the kitchen in the basement.

When you have scoured the brasses and irons in the parlor chimney, lay the foul wet cloth upon the nearest chair, that your lady may see you have not neglected your work: observe the same rule when you clean the brass locks, only with this addition — to leave the marks of your fingers on the doors to show you have not forgot.

Bring up none but large coals to the dining-room and your lady's chamber; they make the best fires, and if you find them too big it is easy to break them on the marble hearth.

When you go to bed, be sure to take care of fire; and therefore blow the candle out with your breath, and then thrust it under your bed. Note, the smell of the snuff is very good against vapors.[12]

Lock up a cat or a dog in some room or closet, so as to make such a noise all over the house as may frighten away the thieves if any should attempt to break or steal in.

When you wash any of the rooms toward the street over night, throw the foul water out of the street-door; but be sure not to look before you for fear those on whom the water lights might think you uncivil and that you did it on purpose. If he who suffers breaks the windows in revenge and your lady chides you and gives positive orders that you should carry the pail down and empty it in the sink, you have an easy remedy: when you wash an upper room carry down the pail so as to let the water dribble on the stairs all the way down to the kitchen; by which not only your load will be lighter, but you will convince your lady that it is better to throw the water out of the windows or

---

[12] melancholy, the blues

down the street-door steps: besides, this latter practice will be very diverting to you and the family in a frosty night to see a hundred people falling on their noses or back-sides before your door, when the water is frozen.

NED SOFTLY[1]

JOSEPH ADDISON (1672–1719)

I YESTERDAY came hither[2] about two hours before the company generally make their appearance, with a design to read over all the newspapers, but upon my sitting down I was accosted by Ned Softly who saw me from a corner in the other end of the room, where, I found, he had been writing something. "Mr. Bickerstaff,"[3] says he, "I observe by a late paper of yours that you and I are just of a humor,[4] for you must know, of all impertinences there is nothing which I so much hate as news. I never read a *Gazette* in my life, and never trouble my head about our armies, whether they win or lose, or in what part of the world they lie encamped." Without giving me time to reply, he drew a paper of verses out of his pocket, telling me that he had something which would entertain me more agreeably, and that he would desire my judgment upon every line, for that we had time enough before us till the company came in.

Ned Softly is a very pretty poet and a great admirer of easy lines. Waller is his favorite, and as that admirable writer has the best and worst verses of any

[1] *Tatler*, No. 163
[2] Will's Coffee-house, from which this *Tatler* was written
[3] the pseudonym under which Addison and Steele wrote *The Tatler*
[4] of the same disposition

among our great English poets, Ned Softly has got all the bad ones without book, which he repeats, upon occasion, to show his reading and garnish his conversation. Ned is indeed a true English reader, incapable of relishing the great and masterly strokes of this art, but wonderfully pleased with the little Gothic [5] ornaments of epigrammatical conceits,[6] turns, points and quibbles which are so frequent in the most admired of our English poets, and practised by those who want genius and strength to represent, after the manner of the ancients, simplicity in its natural beauty and perfection.

Finding myself unavoidably engaged in such a conversation, I was resolved to turn my pain into a pleasure, and to divert myself as well as I could with so very odd a fellow. "You must understand," says Ned, "that the sonnet I am going to read to you was written upon a lady who showed me some verses of her own making and is, perhaps, the best poet of our age. But you shall hear it." Upon which he began to read as follows:

To Mira, on her incomparable Poems

I

When dressed in laurel wreaths you shine,
  And tune your soft melodious notes,
You seem a sister of the Nine,
  Or Phoebus' self in petticoats.

II

I fancy, when your song you sing,
  (Your song you sing with so much art)
Your pen was plucked from Cupid's wing;
  For, ah! it wounds me like his dart.

[5] barbarous
[6] strokes of wit

"Why," says I, "this is a little nosegay of conceits, a very lump of salt: every verse hath something in it that piques; and then the dart in the last line is certainly as pretty a sting in the tail of an epigram (for so I think you critics call it) as ever entered into the thought of a poet." "Dear Mr. Bickerstaff," says he, shaking me by the hand, "everybody knows you to be a judge of these things; and to tell you truly, I read over Roscommon's translation of Horace's *Art of Poetry* three several times before I sat down to write the sonnet which I have shown you. But you shall hear it again, and pray observe every line of it, for not one of them shall pass without your approbation.

When dressed in laurel wreaths you shine.

"That is," says he, "when you have your garland on; when you are writing verses." To which I replied, "I know your meaning: a metaphor!" "The same," said he, and went on:

And tune your soft melodious notes.

"Pray observe the gliding of that verse; there is scarce a consonant in it: I took care to make it run upon liquids. Give me your opinion of it." "Truly," said I, "I think it is as good as the former." "I am very glad to hear you say so," says he; "but mind the next:

You seem a sister of the Nine.

"That is," says he, "you seem a sister of the Muses; for, if you look into ancient authors, you will find it was their opinion that there were nine of them." "I remember it very well," said I; "but pray proceed."

Or Phoebus' self in petticoats.

"Phoebus," says he, "was the god of poetry. These little instances, Mr. Bickerstaff, show a gentleman's reading. Then, to take off from the air of learning, which Phoebus and the Muses have given to this first stanza, you may observe how it falls all of a sudden into the familiar 'in petticoats.'!

Or Phoebus' self in petticoats.

"Let us now," says I, "enter upon the second stanza; I find the first line is still a continuation of the metaphor:

I fancy, when your song you sing.

"It is very right," says he, "but pray observe the turn of words in those two lines. I was a whole hour in adjusting of them, and have still a doubt upon me, whether in the second line it should be 'Your song you sing,' or, 'You sing your song.' You shall hear them both:

I fancy, when your song you sing,
  (Your song you sing with so much art)

or

I fancy, when your song you sing,
  (You sing your song with so much art.)

"Truly," said I, "the turn is so natural either way, that you have made me almost giddy with it." "Dear sir," said he, grasping me by the hand, "you have a great deal of patience; but pray what do you think of the next verse?

Your pen was plucked from Cupid's wing.

"Think!" says I; "I think you have made Cupid look like a little goose." "That was my meaning," says he: "I think the ridicule is well enough hit off. But we come now to the last, which sums up the whole matter:

For, ah! it wounds me like his dart.

"Pray, how do you like that *ah!* Doth it not make a pretty figure in that place? *Ah!* — it looks as if I felt the dart, and cried out as being pricked with it!

For, ah! it wounds me like his dart.

"My friend, Dick Easy," continued he, "assured me, he would rather have written that *ah!* than to have been the author of the Aeneid. He indeed objected that I made Mira's pen like a quill in one of the lines, and like a dart in the other. But as to that —"

"Oh! as to that," says I, "it is but supposing Cupid to be like a porcupine, and his quills and darts will be the same thing." He was going to embrace me for the hint; but half a dozen critics coming into the room, whose faces he did not like, he conveyed the sonnet into his pocket and whispered me in the ear, "he would show it to me again as soon as his man had written it over fair."

SIGNOR NICOLINI AND THE LIONS [1]

THERE is nothing that of late years has afforded matter of greater amusement to the town than Signor Nicolini's combat with a lion in the Haymarket, which has been very often exhibited to the general satisfaction of most of the nobility and gentry in the kingdom of

[1] *Spectator*, No. 13. Nicolini was the operatic rage of the day. He is praised in the 405th *Spectator* and the 115th *Tatler*. The Haymarket is a theatre.

Great Britain. Upon the first rumor of this intended combat, it was confidently affirmed, and is still believed by many in both galleries, that there would be a tame lion sent from the tower every opera night in order to be killed by Hydaspes; this report, though altogether groundless, so universally prevailed in the upper regions of the playhouse that some of the most refined politicians in those parts of the audience gave it out in whisper that the lion was a cousin-german of the tiger who made his appearance in King William's days, and that the stage would be supplied with lions at the public expense during the whole session. Many likewise were the conjectures of the treatment which this lion was to meet with from the hands of Signor Nicolini; some supposed that he was to subdue him in recitativo, as Orpheus used to serve the wild beasts in his time, and afterwards to knock him on the head; some fancied that the lion would not pretend to lay his paws upon the hero, by reason of the received opinion that a lion will not hurt a virgin. Several, who pretended to have seen the opera in Italy, had informed their friends that the lion was to act a part in High Dutch and roar twice or thrice to a thorough bass before he fell at the feet of Hydaspes. To clear up a matter that was so variously reported, I have made it my business to examine whether this pretended lion is really the savage he appears to be, or only a counterfeit.

But before I communicate my discoveries, I must acquaint the reader that upon my walking behind the scenes last winter, as I was thinking on something else, I accidentally jostled against a monstrous animal that extremely startled me and, upon my nearer survey of it, appeared to be a lion rampant. The lion seeing me very much surprised told me, in a gentle voice, that

I might come by him if I pleased; "for," says he, "I do not intend to hurt anybody." I thanked him very kindly, and passed by him; and in a little time after saw him leap upon the stage and act his part with very great applause. It has been observed by several that the lion has changed his manner of acting twice or thrice since his first appearance, which will not seem strange when I acquaint my reader that the lion has been changed upon the audience three several times. The first lion was a candle-snuffer who, being a fellow of a testy, choleric temper, overdid his part and would not suffer himself to be killed so easily as he ought to have done: besides, it was observed of him that he grew more surly every time he came out of the lion; and having dropped some words in ordinary conversation, as if he had not fought his best, and that he suffered himself to be thrown upon his back in the scuffle, and that he would wrestle with Mr. Nicolini for what he pleased, out of his lion's skin, it was thought proper to discard him; and it is verily believed, to this day, that had he been brought upon the stage another time, he would certainly have done mischief. Besides, it was objected against the first lion that he reared himself so high upon his hinder paws and walked in so erect a posture that he looked more like an old man than a lion.

The second lion was a tailor by trade, who belonged to the playhouse and had the character of a mild and peaceable man in his profession. If the former was too furious, this was too sheepish for his part; insomuch, that after a short modest walk upon the stage, he would fall at the first touch of Hydaspes, without grappling with him and giving him an opportunity of showing his variety of Italian trips. It is said, indeed, that he once gave him a rip in his flesh-color doublet; but this was only to make work for himself in his private character of a tailor. I must not omit that it was this second lion who treated me with so much humanity behind the scenes.

The acting lion at present is, as I am informed, a country gentleman who does it for his diversion but desires his name may be concealed. He says, very handsomely, in his own excuse, that he does not act for gain, that he indulges an innocent pleasure in it, and that it is better to pass away an evening in this manner than in gaming and drinking; but at the same time says, with a very agreeable raillery upon himself, that if his name should be known, the ill-natured world might call him "the ass in the lion's skin." This gentleman's temper is made out of such a happy mixture of the mild and the choleric that he outdoes both his predecessors, and has drawn together greater audiences than have been known in the memory of man.

I must not conclude my narrative without taking notice of a groundless report that has been raised to a gentleman's disadvantage, of whom I must declare myself an admirer; namely, that Signor Nicolini and the lion have been seen sitting peaceably by one another and smoking a pipe together behind the scenes; by which their enemies would insinuate it is but a sham combat which they represent upon the stage; but upon inquiry I find that if any such correspondence has passed between them, it was not till the combat was over, when the lion was to be looked upon as dead, according to the received rules of the drama. Besides, this is what is practised every day in Westminster-hall, where nothing is more usual than to see a couple of lawyers, who have been tearing each other to

SIGNOR NICOLINI AND THE LIONS

pieces in the court, embracing one another as soon as they are out of it.

I would not be thought, in any part of this relation, to reflect upon Signor Nicolini, who, in acting this part, only complies with the wretched taste of his audience; he knows very well that the lion has many more admirers than himself; as they say of the famous equestrian statue on the Pont-Neuf, at Paris, that more people go to see the horse than the king who sits upon it. On the contrary, it gives me a just indignation to see a person whose action gives new majesty to kings, resolution to heroes and softness to lovers, thus sinking from the greatness of his behavior and degraded into the character of the London 'Prentice.[2] I have often wished that our tragedians would copy after this great master of action. Could they make the same use of their arms and legs, and inform their faces with as significant looks and passions, how glorious would an English tragedy appear with that action which is capable of giving dignity to the forced thoughts, cold conceits[3] and unnatural expressions of an Italian opera! In the mean time, I have related this combat of the lion to show what are at present the reigning entertainments of the politer part of Great Britain.

Audiences have often been reproached by writers for the coarseness of their taste; but our present grievance does not seem to be the want of a good taste, but of common sense.

[2] a character in an old roaring melodrama
[3] forced expressions

ON NEWS-WRITERS AND READERS [1]

THERE is no humor in my countrymen which I am more inclined to wonder at than their general thirst after news. There are about half a dozen ingenious men who live very plentifully upon this curiosity of their fellow-subjects. They all of them receive the same advices from abroad, and very often in the same words; but their way of cooking it is so different that there is no citizen who has an eye to the public good that can leave the coffee-house with peace of mind before he has given every one of them a reading. These several dishes of news are so very agreeable to the palate of my countrymen that they are not only pleased with them when they are served up hot, but when they are again set cold before them by those penetrating politicians who oblige the public with their reflections and observations upon every piece of intelligence that is sent us from abroad. The text is given us by one set of writers, and the comment by another.

But, notwithstanding we have the same tale told us in so many different papers and, if occasion requires, in so many articles of the same paper; notwithstanding, in a scarcity of foreign posts, we hear the same story repeated by different advices from Paris, Brussels, the Hague, and from every great town in Europe; notwithstanding the multitudes of annotations, explanations, reflections and various readings which it passes through, our time lies heavy on our hands till the arrival of a fresh mail: we long to receive further particulars, to hear what will be the next step, or what will be the

[1] *Spectator*, No. 452

consequences of that which has been already taken. A westerly wind [2] keeps the whole town in suspense and puts a stop to conversation.

This general curiosity has been raised and inflamed by our late wars, and, if rightly directed, might be of good use to a person who has such a thirst awakened in him. Why should not a man who takes delight in reading everything that is new apply himself to history, travels, and other writings of the same kind, where he will find perpetual fuel for his curiosity and meet with much more pleasure and improvement than in these papers of the week? An honest tradesman who languishes a whole summer in expectation of a battle — and perhaps is baulked at last — may here meet with half a dozen in a day. He may read the news of a whole campaign in less time than he now bestows upon the productions of a single post. Fights, conquests, and revolutions lie thick together. The reader's curiosity is raised and satisfied every moment, and his passions disappointed or gratified, without being detained in a state of uncertainty from day to day or lying at the mercy of the sea and wind; in short, the mind is not here kept in a perpetual gape after knowledge, nor punished with that eternal thirst which is the portion of all our modern newsmongers and coffee-house politicians.

All matters of fact which a man did not know before are news to him, and I do not see how any haberdasher in Cheapside is more concerned in the present quarrel of the Cantons than he was in that of the League. At least, I believe every one will allow me, it is of more importance to an Englishman to know the

---

[2] which would prevent ships coming from the continent to England

history of his ancestors than that of his contemporaries who live upon the banks of the Danube or the Boristhenes. As for those who are of another mind, I shall recommend to them the following letter from a projector who is willing to turn a penny by this remarkable curiosity of his countrymen: —

"Mr. Spectator,
"You must have observed that men who frequent coffee-houses and delight in news are pleased with everything that is matter of fact, so it be what they have not heard before. A victory or a defeat is equally agreeable to them. The shutting of a cardinal's mouth pleases them one post, and the opening of it another. They are glad to hear the French court is removed to Marli, and are afterwards as much delighted with its return to Versailles. They read the advertisements with the same curiosity as the articles of public news, and are as pleased to hear of a piebald horse, that is strayed out of a field near Islington, as of a whole troop that have been engaged in any foreign adventure. In short, they have a relish for everything that is news, let the matter of it be what it will; or, to speak more properly, they are men of a voracious appetite but no taste. Now, Sir, since the great fountain of news (I mean the war) is very near being dried up, and since these gentlemen have contracted such an inextinguishable thirst after it, I have taken their case and my own into consideration and have thought of a project which may turn to the advantage of us both. I have thoughts of publishing a daily paper which shall comprehend in it all the most remarkable occurrences in every little town, village and hamlet that lie within ten miles of London, or, in other words, within the

verge of the penny-post. I have pitched upon this scene of intelligence[3] for two reasons: first, because the carriage of letters will be very cheap; and secondly, because I may receive them every day. By this means my readers will have their news fresh, and many worthy citizens, who cannot sleep with any satisfaction at present, for want of being informed how the world goes, may go to bed contentedly, it being my design to put out my paper every night at nine o'clock precisely. I have already established correspondences in these several places and received very good intelligence.

"By my last advices from Knightsbridge I hear that a horse was clapped into the pound on the third instant, and that he was not released when the letters came away.

"We are informed from Pankridge[4] that a dozen weddings were lately celebrated in the mother church of that place, but are referred to their next letters for the names of the parties concerned.

"Letters from Brumpton advise that the widow Blight had received several visits from John Mildew, which affords great matter of speculation in those parts.

"By a fisherman who lately touched at Hammersmith there is advice from Putney that a certain person, well known in that place, is like to lose his election for churchwarden; but this being boat-news, we cannot give entire credit to it.

"Letters from Paddington bring little more than that William Squeak, the sow-gelder, passed through that place the fifth instant.

"They advise from Fulham that things remained

---
[3] news
[4] Pancras, then a fashionable place for weddings. All of the places mentioned are now parts of London.

there in the same state they were. They had intelligence, just as the letters came away, of a tub of excellent ale just set abroach at Parson's Green; but this wanted confirmation.

"I have here, Sir, given you a specimen of the news with which I intend to entertain the town; and which, when drawn up regularly in the form of a newspaper, will, I doubt not, be very acceptable to many of those public-spirited readers who take more delight in acquainting themselves with other people's business than their own. I hope a paper of this kind, which lets us know what is done near home, may be more useful to us than those which are filled with advices from Zug and Bender, and make some amends for that dearth of intelligence which we may justly apprehend from times of peace. If I find that you receive this project favorably, I will shortly trouble you with one or two more; and in the mean time am, most worthy Sir, with all due respect,

"Your most obedient,
"And most humble servant."

ON CONVERSATION [1]

SIR RICHARD STEELE (1672–1729)

It is no easy matter, when people are advancing in anything, to prevent their going too fast for want of patience. This happens in nothing more frequently than in the prosecution of studies. Hence it is that we meet crowds who attempt to be eloquent before they can speak. They affect the flowers of rhetoric before they understand the parts of speech. In the ordinary conversation of this town there are so many who can, as they call it, talk well, that there is not one in twenty that talks to be understood. This proceeds from an ambition to excel or, as the term is, to shine, in company. The matter is not to make themselves understood, but admired. They come together with a certain emulation rather than benevolence. When you fall among such companions, the safe way is to give yourself up and let the orators declaim for your esteem, and trouble yourself no further. It is said that a poet must be born so, but I think it may be much better said of an orator, especially when we talk of our town poets and orators; but the town poets are full of rules and laws, the town orators go through thick and thin and are, forsooth, persons of such eminent natural parts [2] and knowledge of the world that they despise all men as

[1] *Tatler,* No. 244
[2] abilities

inexperienced scholastics who wait for an occasion before they speak, or who speak no more than is necessary. They had half persuaded me to go to the tavern the other night, but that a gentleman whispered me, "Prithee, Isaac,[3] go with us; there is Tom Varnish will be there, and he is a fellow that talks as well as any man in England."

I must confess, when a man expresses himself well upon any occasion, and his falling into an account of any subject arises from a desire to oblige the company, or from fulness of the circumstance itself, so that his speaking of it at large is occasioned only by the openness of a companion — I say, in such a case as this, it is not only pardonable but agreeable when a man takes the discourse to himself, but when you see a fellow watch for opportunities for being copious, it is excessively troublesome. A man that stammers, if he has understanding, is to be attended with patience and good-nature, but he that speaks more than he need has no right to such an indulgence. The man who has a defect in his speech takes pains to come to you, while a man of a weak capacity with fluency of speech triumphs in outrunning you. The stammerer strives to be fit for your company; the loquacious man endeavours to show you, you are not fit for his.

With thoughts of this kind do I always enter into that man's company who is recommended as a person that talks well; but if I were to choose the people with whom I would spend my hours of conversation, they should be certainly such as labored no farther than to make themselves readily and clearly apprehended, and would have patience and curiosity to understand me. To have good sense and the ability to express it are

[3] Isaac Bickerstaff, Steele's pseudonym

ON CONVERSATION

the most essential and necessary qualities in companions. When thoughts rise in us fit to utter, among familiar friends there needs but very little care in clothing them.

Urbanus is, I take it, a man one might live with whole years, and enjoy all the freedom and improvement imaginable, and yet be insensible of a contradiction to you in all the mistakes you can be guilty of. His great good-will to his friends has produced in him such a general deference in his discourse that if he differs from you in his sense of anything, he introduces his own thoughts by some agreeable circumlocution, or he has often observed such and such a circumstance that made him of another opinion. Again, where another would be apt to say, "This I am confident of; I may pretend [4] to judge of this matter as well as anybody," Urbanus says, "I am verily persuaded; I believe one may conclude." In a word, there is no man more clear in his thoughts and expressions than he is, or speaks with greater diffidence. You shall hardly find one man of any consideration, but you shall observe one of less consequence form himself after him. This happens to Urbanus, but the man who steals from him almost every sentiment he utters in a whole week disguises the theft by carrying it with quite a different air. Umbratilis knows Urbanus's doubtful way of speaking proceeds from good-nature and good-breeding and not from uncertainty in his opinions. Umbratilis therefore has no more to do but repeat the thoughts of Urbanus in a positive manner, and appear to the undiscerning a wiser man than the person from whom he borrows; but those who know him can see the servant in his

[4] claim

master's habit, and the more he struts the less do his clothes appear his own.

In conversation the medium is neither to affect silence nor eloquence; not to value our approbation, and to endeavour to excel us who are of your company, are equal injuries. The great enemies therefore to good company, and those who transgress most against the laws of equality (which is the life of it), are the clown,[5] the wit and the pedant. A clown, when he has sense, is conscious of his want of education, and with an awkward bluntness hopes to keep himself in countenance by overthrowing the use of all polite behaviour. He takes advantage of the restraint good-breeding lays upon others not to offend him, to trespass against them, and is under the man's own shelter while he intrudes upon him. The fellows of this class are very frequent in the repetition of the words "rough" and "manly." When these people happen to be by their fortunes of the rank of gentlemen, they defend their other absurdities by an impertinent courage; and to help out the defect of their behaviour, add their being dangerous to their being disagreeable. This gentleman (though he displeases, professes to do so, and knowing that, dares still go on to do so) is not so painful a companion as he who will please you against your will, and resolves to be a wit.

This man, upon all occasions and whoever he falls in company with, talks in the same circle and in the same round of chat which he has learned at one of the tables of this[6] coffee-house. As poetry is in itself an elevation above ordinary and common sentiments, so there is no fop so near a madman in indifferent com-

[5] boor, yokel
[6] Will's, from which this *Tatler* was written

pany as a poetical one. He is not apprehensive that the generality of the world are intent upon the business of their own fortune and profession, and have as little capacity as curiosity to enter into matters of ornament or speculation. I remember at a full table in the City [7] one of these ubiquitary wits was entertaining the company with a soliloquy (for so I call it when a man talks to those who do not understand him) concerning wit and humor. An honest gentleman who sat next to me and was worth half a plum [8] stared at him, and observing there was some sense, as he thought, mixed with his impertinence,[9] whispered me, "Take my word for it, this fellow is more knave than fool." This was all my good friend's applause of the wittiest man of talk that I was ever present at, which wanted nothing to make it excellent but that there was no occasion for it.

The pedant is so obvious to ridicule that it would be to be one to offer to explain him. He is a gentleman so well known that there is none but those of his own class who do not laugh at and avoid him. Pedantry proceeds from much reading and little understanding. A pedant among men of learning and sense is like an ignorant servant giving an account of a polite conversation. You may find he has brought with him more than could have entered into his head without being there, but still that he is not a bit wiser than if he had not been there at all.

[7] "The City" means the mercantile part of the city.
[8] *i.e.,* was pretty well off
[9] nonsense

BIOGRAPHY [1]

SAMUEL JOHNSON (1709-1784)

ALL joy or sorrow for the happiness or calamities of others is produced by an act of the imagination that realizes the event, however fictitious, or approximates it, however remote, by placing us for a time in the condition of him whose fortune we contemplate; so that we feel, while the deception lasts, whatever motions would be excited by the same good or evil happening to ourselves.

Our passions are therefore more strongly moved in proportion as we can more readily adopt the pains or pleasure proposed to our minds by recognizing them as once our own or considering them as naturally incident to our state of life. It is not easy for the most artful writer to give us an interest in happiness or misery which we think ourselves never likely to feel and with which we have never yet been made acquainted. Histories of the downfall of kingdoms and revolutions of empires are read with great tranquillity; the imperial tragedy pleases common auditors only by its pomp of ornament and grandeur of ideas; and the man whose faculties have been engrossed by business, and whose heart never fluttered but at the rise or fall of the stocks, wonders how the attention can be seized or the affection agitated by a tale of love.

[1] The 60th *Rambler: The Dignity and Usefulness of Biography.*

Those parallel circumstances and kindred images to which we readily conform our minds are, above all other writings, to be found in narratives of the lives of particular persons; and therefore no species of writing seems more worthy of cultivation than biography, since none can be more delightful or more useful, none can more certainly enchain the heart by irresistible interest, or more widely diffuse instruction to every diversity of condition.

The general and rapid narratives of history, which involve a thousand fortunes in the business of a day and complicate innumerable incidents in one great transaction, afford few lessons applicable to private life, which derives its comforts and its wretchedness from the right or wrong management of things which nothing but their frequency makes considerable, *Parva si non fiunt quotidie,*[2] says Pliny, and which can have no place in those relations which never descend below the consultation of senates, the motions of armies and the schemes of conspirators.

I have often thought that there has rarely passed a life of which a judicious and faithful narrative would not be useful. For, not only every man has, in the mighty mass of the world, great numbers in the same condition with himself, to whom his mistakes and miscarriages, escapes and expedients, would be of immediate and apparent use, but there is such an uniformity in the state of man, considered apart from adventitious and separable decorations and disguises, that there is scarce any possibility of good or ill but is common to human kind. A great part of the time of those who are placed at the greatest distance by fortune,

---

[2] (Things) inconsiderable (in themselves) if they did not happen every day.

or by temper,[3] must unavoidably pass in the same manner, and though, when the claims of nature are satisfied, caprice and vanity and accident begin to produce discriminations and peculiarities, yet the eye is not very heedful or quick which cannot discover the same causes still terminating their influence in the same effects, though sometimes accelerated, sometimes retarded, or perplexed by multiplied combinations. We are all prompted by the same motives, all deceived by the same fallacies, all animated by hope, obstructed by danger, entangled by desire and seduced by pleasure.

It is frequently objected to relations of particular lives that they are not distinguished by any striking or wonderful vicissitudes. The scholar who passed his life among his books, the merchant who conducted only his own affairs, the priest whose sphere of action was not extended beyond that of his duty, are considered as no proper objects of public regard, however they might have excelled in their several stations, whatever might have been their learning, integrity, and piety. But this notion arises from false measures of excellence and dignity, and must be eradicated by considering that in the esteem of uncorrupted reason what is of most use is of most value.

It is, indeed, not improper to take honest advantages of prejudice and to gain attention by a celebrated name; but the business of the biographer is often to pass slightly over those performances and incidents which produce vulgar greatness, to lead the thoughts into domestic privacies and display the minute details of daily life where exterior appendages are cast aside and men excel each other only by prudence and by virtue. The account of Thuanus is, with great propriety,

[3] temperament

said by its author to have been written that it might lay open to posterity the private and familiar character of that man, *cuius ingenium et candorem ex ipsius scriptis sunt olim semper miraturi,* whose candor and genius will to the end of time be by his writings preserved in admiration.

There are many invisible circumstances which, whether we read as enquirers after natural or moral knowledge, whether we intend to enlarge our science[4] or increase our virtue, are more important than public occurrences. Thus Sallust, the great master of nature, has not forgot in his account of Catiline to remark that *his walk was now quick, and again slow,* as an indication of a mind revolving something with violent commotion. Thus the story of Melanchthon affords a striking lecture on the value of time by informing us that when he made an appointment he expected not only the hour but the minute to be fixed, that the day might not run out in the idleness of suspense; and all the plans and enterprises of De Witt are now of less important to the world than that part of his personal character which represents him as *careful of his health and negligent of his life.*

But biography has often been allotted to writers who seem very little acquainted with the nature of their task, or very negligent about the performance. They rarely afford any other account than might be collected from public papers but imagine themselves writing a life when they exhibit a chronological series of actions or preferments; and so little regard the manners or behavior of their heroes that more knowledge may be gained of a man's real character by a short conversation with one of his servants than from a formal and

[4] knowledge

studied narrative begun with his pedigree and ended with his funeral.

If now and then they condescend to inform the world of particular facts, they are not always so happy as to select the most important. I know not well what advantage posterity can receive from the only circumstance by which Tickell has distinguished Addison from the rest of mankind, *the irregularity of his pulse;* nor can I think myself overpaid for the time spent in reading the life of Malherb by being enabled to relate, after the learned biographer, that Malherb had two predominant opinions: one, that the looseness of a single woman might destroy all her boast of ancient descent; the other, that the French beggars made use very improperly and barbarously of the phrase *noble Gentleman,* because either word included the sense of both.

There are, indeed, some natural reasons why these narratives are often written by such as were not likely to give much instruction or delight, and why most accounts of particular persons are barren and useless. If a life be delayed till interest and envy are at an end, we may hope for impartiality, but must expect little intelligence,[5] for the incidents which give excellence to biography are of a volatile and evanescent kind, such as soon escape the memory and are rarely transmitted by tradition. We know how few can portray a living acquaintance, except by his most prominent and observable particularities and the grosser features of his mind, and it may be easily imagined how much of this little knowledge may be lost in imparting it and how soon a succession of copies will lose all resemblance of the original.

[5] information

If the biographer writes from personal knowledge and makes haste to gratify the public curiosity, there is danger lest his interest, his fear, his gratitude or his tenderness, overpower his fidelity and tempt him to conceal if not to invent. There are many who think it an act of piety to hide the faults or failings of their friends, even when they can no longer suffer by their detection; we therefore see whole ranks of characters adorned with uniform panegyric and not to be known from one another but by extrinsic and casual circumstances. "Let me remember," says Hale, "when I find myself inclined to pity a criminal, that there is likewise a pity due to the country." If we owe regard to the memory of the dead, there is yet more respect to be paid to knowledge, to virtue, and to truth.

FRIENDSHIP [1]

WHEN Socrates was building himself a house at Athens, being asked by one that observed the littleness of the design why a man so eminent would not have an abode more suitable to his dignity, he replied that he should think himself sufficiently accommodated if he could see that narrow habitation filled with real friends. Such was the opinion of this great master of human life concerning the infrequency of such an union of minds as might deserve the name of friendship, that among the multitudes whom vanity or curiosity, civility or veneration, crowded about him, he did not expect that very spacious apartments would be necessary to contain all that should regard him with sincere kindness or adhere to him with steady fidelity.

[1] The 64th *Rambler: The Requisites to True Friendship.*

So many qualities are indeed requisite to the possibility of friendship, and so many accidents must concur to its rise and its continuance, that the greatest part of mankind content themselves without it, and supply its place as they can with interest and dependence.

Multitudes are unqualified for a constant and warm reciprocation of benevolence, as they are incapacitated for any other elevated excellence, by perpetual attention to their interest and unresisting subjection to their passions. Long habits may superinduce inability to deny any desire or repress, by superior motives, the importunities of any immediate gratification, and an inveterate selfishness will imagine all advantages diminished in proportion as they are communicated.

But not only this hateful and confirmed corruption, but many varieties of disposition, not inconsistent with common degrees of virtue, may exclude friendship from the heart. Some ardent enough in their benevolence, and defective neither in officiousness [2] nor liberality, are mutable and uncertain, soon attracted by new objects, disgusted without offence and alienated without enmity. Others are soft and flexible, easily influenced by reports or whispers, ready to catch alarms from every dubious circumstance and to listen to every suspicion which envy and flattery shall suggest, to follow the opinion of every confident adviser and move by the impulse of the last breath. Some are impatient of contradiction, more willing to go wrong by their own judgment than to be indebted for a better or a safer way to the sagacity of another, inclined to consider counsel as insult, and enquiry as want of confidence, and to confer their regard on no other terms than unreserved submission and implicit compliance.

[2] kindness

Some are dark and involved, equally careful to conceal good and bad purposes; and pleased with producing effects by invisible means and showing their design only in its execution. Others are universally communicative, alike open to every eye and equally profuse of their own secrets and those of others, without the necessary vigilance of caution or the honest arts of prudent integrity, ready to accuse without malice and to betray without treachery. Any of these may be useful to the community and pass through the world with the reputation of good purposes and uncorrupted morals, but they are unfit for close and tender intimacies. He cannot properly be chosen for a friend whose kindness is exhaled by its own warmth or frozen by the first blast of slander; he cannot be a useful counselor who will hear no opinion but his own; he will not much invite confidence whose principal maxim is to suspect; nor can the candor and frankness of that man be much esteemed who spreads his arms to humankind and makes every man, without distinction, a denizen of his bosom.

That friendship may be at once fond and lasting there must not only be equal virtue on each part, but virtue of the same kind; not only the same end must be proposed, but the same means must be approved by both. We are often, by superficial accomplishments and accidental endearments, induced to love those whom we cannot esteem; we are sometimes, by great abilities and incontestible evidences of virtue, compelled to esteem those whom we cannot love. But friendship, compounded of esteem and love, derives from one its tenderness and its permanence from the other; and therefore requires not only that its candidates should gain the judgment, but that they should attract the affections; that they should not only be firm in the day of distress but gay in the hour of jollity; not only useful in exigencies, but pleasing in familiar life; their presence should give cheerfulness as well as courage, and dispel alike the gloom of fear and of melancholy.

To this mutual complacency is generally requisite an uniformity of opinions, at least of those active and conspicuous principles which discriminate parties in government and sects in religion and which every day operate more or less on the common business of life. For though great tenderness has, perhaps, been sometimes known to continue between men eminent in contrary factions, yet such friends are to be shown rather as prodigies than examples; and it is no more proper to regulate our conduct by such instances than to leap a precipice because some have fallen from it and escaped with life.

It cannot but be extremely difficult to preserve private kindness in the midst of public opposition, in which will necessarily be involved a thousand incidents, extending their influence to conversation and privacy. Men engaged, by moral or religious motives, in contrary parties will generally look with different eyes upon every man and decide almost every question upon different principles. When such occasions of dispute happen, to comply is to betray our cause and to maintain friendship by ceasing to deserve it; to be silent is to lose the happiness and dignity of independence, to live in perpetual constraint and to desert, if not to betray; and who shall determine which of two friends shall yield where neither believes himself mistaken and both confess the importance of the question? What then remains but contradiction and debate? And from those what can be expected but acrimony and vehemence, the insolence of triumph, the vexation of defeat and, in time, a weariness of contest and an extinction of benevolence? Exchange of endearments and intercourse of civility may continue indeed, as boughs may for a while be verdant when the root is wounded, but the poison of discord is infused, and though the countenance may preserve its smile the heart is hardening and contracting.

That man will not long be agreeable whom we see only in times of seriousness and severity, and therefore to maintain the softness and serenity of benevolence it is necessary that friends partake each other's pleasures as well as cares and be led to the same diversions by similitude of taste. This is, however, not to be considered as equally indispensable with conformity of principles, because any man may honestly, according to the precepts of Horace, resign the gratifications of taste to the humor of another, and friendship may well deserve the sacrifice of pleasure though not of conscience.

It was once confessed to me by a painter that no professor of his art ever loved another. This declaration is so far justified by the knowledge of life as to damp the hopes of warm and constant friendship between men whom their studies have made competitors and whom every favorer and every censurer are hourly inciting against each other. The utmost expectation that experience can warrant is that they should forbear open hostilities and secret machinations and when the whole fraternity is attacked be able to unite against a common foe. Some however, though few, may perhaps be found in whom emulation has not been able to overpower generosity, who are distinguished from lower beings by nobler motives than the love of fame, and can preserve the sacred flame of friendship from the gusts of pride and the rubbish of interest.[3]

Friendship is seldom lasting but between equals or where the superiority on one side is reduced by some equivalent advantage on the other. Benefits which cannot be repaid and obligations which cannot be discharged are not commonly found to increase affection; they excite gratitude indeed, and heighten veneration, but commonly take away that easy freedom and familiarity of intercourse without which, though there may be fidelity and zeal and admiration, there cannot be friendship. Thus imperfect are all earthly blessings; the great effect of friendship is beneficence, yet by the first act of uncommon kindness it is endangered, like plants that bear their fruit and die. Yet this consideration ought not to restrain bounty or repress compassion; for duty is to be preferred before convenience, and he that loses part of the pleasures of friendship by his generosity, gains in its place the gratulation of his conscience.

POPULARITY [1]

NONE of the desires dictated by vanity is more general or less blameable than that of being distinguished for the arts of conversation.[2] Other accomplishments may be possessed without opportunity of exerting them, or wanted without danger that the defect can often be remarked, but as no man can live, otherwise than in an

---
[3] self-interest, selfishness
[1] The 188th *Rambler: Popularity Not Always due to Merit.*
[2] social intercourse in general

hermitage, without hourly pleasure or vexation from the fondness or neglect of those about him, the faculty of giving pleasure is of continual use. Few are more frequently envied than those who have the power of forcing attention wherever they come, whose entrance is considered as a promise of felicity and whose departure is lamented, like the recess of the sun from northern climates, as a privation of all that enlivens fancy or inspirits gaiety.

It is apparent that to excellence in this valuable art some peculiar qualifications are necessary, for everyone's experience will inform him that the pleasure which men are able to give in conversation holds no stated proportion to their knowledge or their virtue. Many find their way to the tables and the parties of those who never consider them as of the least importance in any other place; we have all, at one time or other, been content to love those whom we could not esteem, and been persuaded to try the dangerous experiment of admitting him for a companion whom we knew to be too ignorant for a counsellor and too treacherous for a friend.

I question whether some abatement of character is not necessary to general acceptance. Few spend their time with much satisfaction under the eye of uncontestable superiority; and, therefore, among those whose presence is courted at assemblies of jollity there are seldom found men eminently distinguished for powers or acquisitions. The wit whose vivacity condemns slower tongues to silence, the scholar whose knowledge allows no man to fancy that he instructs him,[3] the critic who suffers no fallacy to pass undetected, and the reasoner who condemns the idle to thought and

[3] The antecedent of "him," is, of course, "the scholar."

the negligent to attention are generally praised and feared, reverenced and avoided.

He that would please must rarely aim at such excellence as depresses his hearers in their own opinion or debars them from the hope of contributing reciprocally to the entertainment of the company. Merriment extorted by sallies of imagination, sprightliness of remark or quickness of reply, is too often what the Latins call the *Sardinian Laughter,* a distortion of the face without gladness of heart.

For this reason no style of conversation is more extensively acceptable than the narrative. He who has stored his memory with slight anecdotes, private incidents and personal peculiarities, seldom fails to find his audience favorable. Almost every man listens with eagerness to contemporary history, for almost every man has some real or imaginary connection with a celebrated character, some desire to advance or oppose a rising name. Vanity often co-operates with curiosity. He that is a hearer in one place qualifies himself to become a speaker in another; for though he cannot comprehend a series of argument or transport the volatile spirit of wit without evaporation, he yet thinks himself able to treasure up the various incidents of a story, and pleases his hopes with the information which he shall give to some inferior society.

Narratives are for the most part heard without envy, because they are not supposed to imply any intellectual qualities above the common rate. To be acquainted with facts not yet echoed by plebeian mouths may happen to one man as well as to another, and to relate them when they are known has in appearance so little difficulty that everyone concludes himself equal to the task.

But it is not easy, and in some situations of life not possible, to accumulate such a stock of materials as may support the expense of continual narration; and it frequently happens that they who attempt this method of ingratiating themselves please only at the first interview and, for want of new supplies of intelligence [4] wear out their stories by continual repetition.

There would be, therefore, little hope of obtaining the praise of being a good companion were it not to be gained by more compendious methods; but such is the kindness of mankind to all, except those who aspire to real merit and rational dignity, that every understanding may find some way to excite benevolence, and whoever is not envied may learn the art of procuring love. We are willing to be pleased, but are not willing to admire; we favor the mirth or officiousness that solicits our regard, but oppose the worth or spirit that enforces it.

The first place among those that please because they desire only to please is due to the *merry fellow,* whose laugh is loud and whose voice is strong, who is ready to echo every jest with obstreperous approbation and countenance every frolic with vociferations of applause. It is not necessary to a merry fellow to have in himself any fund of jocularity or force of conception; it is sufficient that he always appears in the highest exaltation of gladness, for the greater part of mankind are gay or serious by infection and follow without resistance the attraction of example.

Next to the merry fellow is the *good-natured man,* a being generally without benevolence or any other virtue than such as indolence and insensibility confer. The characteristic of a good-natured man is to bear

[4] information

a joke; to sit unmoved and unaffected amidst noise and turbulence, profaneness and obscenity; to hear every tale without contradiction; to endure insult without reply, and to follow the stream of folly whatever course it shall happen to take. The good-natured man is commonly the darling of the petty wits with whom they exercise themselves in the rudiments of raillery, for he never takes advantage of failings nor disconcerts a puny satirist with unexpected sarcasms, but while the glass continues to circulate contentedly bears the expense of uninterrupted laughter and retires rejoicing at his own importance.

The *modest man* is a companion of a yet lower rank, whose only power of giving pleasure is not to interrupt it. The modest man satisfies himself with peaceful silence, which all his companions are candid [5] enough to consider as proceeding not from an inability to speak but willingness to hear.

Many, without being able to attain any general character of excellence, have some single art of entertainment which serves them as a passport through the world. One I have known for fifteen years the darling of a weekly club, because every night, precisely at eleven, he begins his favorite song and during the vocal performance, by corresponding motions of his hand, chalks out a giant upon the wall. Another has endeared himself to a long succession of acquaintances by sitting among them with his wig reversed; another by contriving to smut the nose of any stranger who was to be initiated in the club; another by purring like a cat, and then pretending to be frightened; and another by yelping like a hound and calling to the drawers to drive out the dog.

[5] ingenuous

Such are the arts by which cheerfulness is promoted and sometimes friendship established; arts which those who despise them should not rigorously blame, except when they are practiced at the expense of innocence, for it is always necessary to be loved, but not always necessary to be reverenced.

WILL MARVEL'S JOURNEY [1]

I SUPPED three nights ago with my friend Will Marvel. His affairs obliged him lately to take a journey into Devonshire from which he has just returned. He knows me to be a very patient hearer and was glad of my company, as it gave him an opportunity of disburdening himself by a minute relation of the casualties of his expedition.

Will is not one of those who go out and return with nothing to tell. He has a story of his travels which will strike a home-bred citizen with horror, and has in ten days suffered so often the extremes of terror and joy that he is in doubt whether he shall ever again expose either his body or mind to such danger and fatigue.

When he left London the morning was bright and a fair day was promised. But Will is born to struggle with difficulties. That happened to him which has sometimes, perhaps, happened to others. Before he had gone more than ten miles it began to rain. What course was to be taken? His soul disdained to turn back. He did what the King of Prussia [2] might have done; he flapped his hat,[3] buttoned up his cape and

[1] The 49th *Idler*
[2] Frederick the Great
[3] fastened the flaps under his chin

went forwards, fortifying his mind by the stoical consolation that whatever is violent will be short.

His constancy was not long tried; at the distance of about half a mile he saw an inn which he entered, wet and weary, and found civil treatment and proper refreshment. After a respite of about two hours he looked abroad, and seeing the sky clear called for his horse and passed the first stage without any other memorable accident.

Will considered that labor must be relieved by pleasure and that the strength which great undertakings required must be maintained by copious nutriment; he therefore ordered himself an elegant supper, drank two bottles of claret, and passed the beginning of the night in sound sleep, but, waking before light, was forewarned of the troubles of the next day by a shower beating against his windows with such violence as to threaten the dissolution of nature. When he arose he found what he expected, that the country was under water. He joined himself, however, to a company that was travelling the same way and came safely to the place of dinner, though every step of his horse dashed the mud into the air.

In the afternoon, having parted from his company, he set forward alone and passed many collections of water, of which it was impossible to guess the depth and which he now cannot review without some censure of his own rashness; but what a man undertakes he must perform, and Marvel hates a coward at his heart.

Few that lie warm in their beds think what others undergo who have, perhaps, been as tenderly educated and have as acute sensations as themselves. My friend was now to lodge the second night almost fifty miles from home, in a house which he never had seen before, among people to whom he was totally a stranger, not knowing whether the next man he should meet would prove good or bad; but seeing an inn of a good appearance, he rode resolutely into the yard, and knowing that respect is often paid in proportion as it is claimed, delivered his injunction to the hostler with spirit and entering the house called vigorously about him.

On the third day up rose the sun and Mr. Marvel. His troubles and his dangers were now such as he wishes no other man ever to encounter. The ways were less frequented and the country more thinly inhabited. He rode many a lonely hour through mire and water, and met not a single soul for two miles together with whom he could exchange a word. He cannot deny that, looking round upon the dreary region and seeing nothing but bleak fields and naked trees, hills obscured by fogs and flats covered with inundations, he did for some time suffer melancholy to prevail upon him, and wished himself again safe at home. One comfort he had, which was to consider that none of his friends were in the same distress, for whom, if they had been with him, he should have suffered more than for himself; he could not forbear sometimes to consider how happily the Idler is settled in an easier condition, who, surrounded like him with terrors, could have done nothing but lie down and die.

Amidst these reflections he came to a town and found a dinner which disposed him to more cheerful sentiments. But the joys of life are short and its miseries are long; he mounted and travelled fifteen miles more through dirt and desolation.

At last the sun set, and all the horrors of darkness came upon him. He then repented the weak indulgence in which he had gratified himself at noon with too long an interval of rest. Yet he went forward along a path which he could no longer see, sometimes rushing suddenly into water and sometimes incumbered with stiff clay, ignorant whither he was going and uncertain whether his next step might not be the last.

In this dismal gloom of nocturnal peregrination his horse unexpectedly stood still. Marvel had heard many relations of the instinct of horses, and was in doubt what danger might be at hand. Sometimes he fancied that he was on the bank of a river, still and deep, and sometimes that a dead body lay across the track. He sat still awhile to recollect his thoughts, and as he was about to alight and explore the darkness, out stepped a man with a lantern and opened the turnpike. He hired a guide to the town, arrived in safety and slept in quiet.

The rest of his journey was nothing but danger. He climbed and descended precipices on which vulgar [4] mortals tremble to look; he passed marshes like the *Serbonian bog, where armies whole have sunk;* [5] he forded rivers where the current roared like the Egre [6] or the Severn; [7] or ventured himself on bridges that trembled under him, from which he looked down on foaming whirlpools or dreadful abysses; he wandered over houseless heaths, amidst all the rage of the elements, with the snow driving in his face and the tempest howling in his ears.

Such are the colors in which Marvel paints his adventures. He has accustomed himself to sounding

[4] common
[5] *Paradise Lost,* ii. 594. It is significant that Marvel speaks in epic phraseology.
[6] a mountainous torrent in Abyssinia
[7] a shallow, placid river in western England

words and hyperbolical images till he has lost the power of true description. In a road through which the heaviest carriages pass without difficulty and the post-boy every day and night goes and returns, he meets with hardships like those which are endured in Siberian deserts, and misses nothing of romantic danger but a giant and a dragon. When his dreadful story is told in proper terms, it is only that the way was dirty in winter and that he experienced the common vicissitudes of rain and sunshine.

MARVEL PARALLELED [1]

THE character of Mr. Marvel has raised the merriment of some and the contempt of others who do not sufficiently consider how often they hear and practice the same arts of exaggerated narration.

There is not, perhaps, among the multitudes of all conditions that swarm upon the earth a single man who does not believe that he has something extraordinary to relate of himself, and who does not, at one time or another, summon the attention of his friends to the casualties of his adventures and the vicissitudes of his fortune; casualties and vicissitudes that happen alike in lives uniform and diversified, to the commander of armies and the writer at a desk, to the sailor who resigns himself to the wind and water and the farmer whose longest journey is to the market.

In the present state of the world man may pass through Shakespeare's seven stages of life and meet nothing singular or wonderful. But such is every man's attention to himself that what is common and

[1] The 50th *Idler*

unheeded when it is only seen, becomes remarkable and peculiar when we happen to feel it.

It is well enough known to be according to the usual process of nature that men should sicken and recover, that some designs should succeed and others miscarry, that friends should be separated and meet again, that some should be made angry by endeavors to please them, and some be pleased when no care has been used to gain their approbation; that men and women should at first come together by chance, like each other so well as to commence acquaintance, improve acquaintance into fondness, increase or extinguish fondness by marriage, and have children of different degrees of intellects and virtue, some of whom die before their parents and others survive them.

Yet let any man tell his own story, and nothing of all this has ever befallen him according to the common order of things; something has always discriminated his case; some unusual concurrence of events has appeared which made him more happy or more miserable than other mortals; for in pleasures or calamities, however common, every one has comforts and afflictions of his own.

It is certain that without some artificial augmentations many of the pleasures of life, and almost all its embellishments, would fall to the ground. If no man was to express more delight than he felt, those who felt most would raise little envy. If travellers were to describe the most labored performances of art with the same coldness as they survey them, all expectations of happiness from change of place would cease. The pictures of Raphael would hang without spectators, and the gardens of Versailles might be inhabited by hermits. All the pleasure that is received ends in an opportunity of splendid falsehood, in the power of gaining notice by the display of beauties which the eye was weary of beholding, and a history of happy moments, of which, in reality, the most happy was the last.

The ambition of superior sensibility [2] and superior eloquence disposes the lovers of arts to receive rapture at one time and communicate it at another, and each labors first to impose upon himself and then to propagate the imposture.

Pain is less subject than pleasure to caprices of expression. The torments of disease and the grief for irremediable misfortunes sometimes are such as no words can declare, and can only be signified by groans or sobs or inarticulate ejaculations. Man has from nature a mode of utterance peculiar to pain, but he has none peculiar to pleasure, because he never has pleasure but in such degrees as the ordinary use of language may equal or surpass.

It is nevertheless certain that many pains as well as pleasures are heightened by rhetorical affectation and that the picture is, for the most part, bigger than the life.

When we describe our sensations of another's sorrows, either in friendly or ceremonious condolence, the customs of the world scarcely admit of rigid veracity. Perhaps the fondest friendship would enrage oftener than comfort, were the tongue on such occasions faithfully to represent the sentiments of the heart; and I think the strictest moralists allow forms of address to be used without much regard to their literal acceptation when either respect or tenderness requires

[2] sensitiveness, powers of perception or appreciation

them, because they are universally known to denote not the degree but the species of our sentiments.

But the same indulgence cannot be allowed to him who aggravates dangers incurred or sorrow endured by himself, because he darkens the prospect of futurity and multiplies the pains of our condition by useless terror. Those who magnify their delights are less criminal deceivers, yet they raise hopes which are sure to be disappointed. It would be undoubtedly best if we could see and hear everything as it is, that nothing might be too anxiously dreaded or too ardently pursued.

SHAKESPEARE[1]

THE poet, of whose works I have undertaken the revision, may now begin to assume the dignity of an ancient and claim the privilege of established fame and prescriptive veneration. He has long outlived his century, the term commonly fixed as the test of literary merit. Whatever advantages he might once derive from personal allusions, local customs or temporary opinions, have for many years been lost; and every topic of merriment or motive of sorrow which the modes of artificial life afforded him now only obscure the scenes which they once illuminated. The effects of favour and competition are at an end; the tradition of his friendships and his enmities has perished; his works support no opinion with arguments nor supply any faction with invectives; they can neither indulge vanity nor gratify malignity; but are read without any other reason than the desire of pleasure, and are therefore praised only as pleasure is obtained; yet, thus unas-

[1] From *The Preface to Shakespeare,* 1765.

sisted by interest or passion, they have passed through variations of taste and changes of manners, and, as they devolved from one generation to another, have received new honours at every transmission.

But because human judgment, though it be gradually gaining upon certainty, never becomes infallible; and approbation, though long continued, may yet be only the approbation of prejudice or fashion; it is proper to inquire by what peculiarities of excellence Shakespeare has gained and kept the favour of his countrymen.

Nothing can please many, and please long, but just representations of general nature. Particular manners can be known to few, and therefore few only can judge how nearly they are copied. The irregular combinations of fanciful invention may delight awhile by that novelty of which the common satiety of life sends us all in quest, but the pleasures of sudden wonder are soon exhausted and the mind can only repose on the stability of truth.

Shakespeare is, above all writers, at least above all modern writers, the poet of nature, the poet that holds up to his readers a faithful mirror of manners and of life. His characters are not modified by the customs of particular places, unpractised by the rest of the world, by the peculiarities of studies or professions, which can operate but upon small numbers, or by the accidents of transient fashions or temporary opinions; they are the genuine progeny of common humanity, such as the world will always supply and observation will always find. His persons act and speak by the influence of those general passions and principles by which all minds are agitated and the whole system of life is continued in motion. In the writings of other poets a character is too often an individual; in those of Shakespeare it is commonly a species.

It is from this wide extension of design that so much instruction is derived. It is this which fills the plays of Shakespeare with practical axioms and domestic wisdom. It was said of Euripides that every verse was a precept; and it may be said of Shakespeare that from his works may be collected a system of civil and economical prudence.[2] Yet his real power is not shown in the splendor of particular passages, but by the progress of his fable and the tenor of his dialogue, and he that tries to recommend him by select quotations will succeed like the pedant in Hierocles who, when he offered his house to sale, carried a brick in his pocket as a specimen.

It will not easily be imagined how much Shakespeare excels in accommodating his sentiments to real life but by comparing him with other authors. It was observed of the ancient schools of declamation that the more diligently they were frequented the more was the student disqualified for the world, because he found nothing there which he should ever meet in any other place. The same remark may be applied to every stage but that of Shakespeare. The theatre, when it is under any other direction, is peopled by such characters as were never seen, conversing in a language which was never heard upon topics which will never arise in the commerce of mankind. But the dialogue of this author is often so evidently determined by the incident which produces it, and is pursued with so much ease and simplicity that it seems scarcely to claim the merit of fiction but to have been gleaned by diligent selection out of common conversation and common occurrences.

[2] a system of social and domestic conduct

Upon every other stage the universal agent is love, by whose power all good and evil is distributed and every action quickened or retarded. To bring a lover, a lady and a rival into the fable; to entangle them in contradictory obligations, to perplex them with oppositions of interest, and harass them with violence of desires inconsistent with each other; to make them meet in rapture and part in agony; to fill their mouths with hyperbolical joy and outrageous sorrow; to distress them as nothing human ever was distressed; to deliver them as nothing human ever was delivered; is the business of a modern dramatist. For this, probability is violated, life is misrepresented, and language is depraved. But love is only one of many passions, and as it has no great influence upon the sum of life, it has little operation in the dramas of a poet who caught his ideas from the living world and exhibited only what he saw before him. He knew that any other passion, as it was regular or exorbitant, was a cause of happiness or calamity.

Characters thus ample and general were not easily discriminated and preserved, yet perhaps no poet ever kept his personages more distinct from each other. I will not say with Pope that every speech may be assigned to the proper speaker, because many speeches there are which have nothing characteristical; but, perhaps, though some may be equally adapted to every person, it will be difficult to find that any can be properly transferred from the present possessor to another claimant. The choice is right when there is reason for choice.

Other dramatists can only gain attention by hyperbolical or aggravated characters, by fabulous and unexampled excellence or depravity, as the writers of barbarous romances invigorated the reader by a giant and a dwarf, and he that should form his expectations of human affairs from the play, or from the tale, would be equally deceived. Shakespeare has no heroes; his scenes are occupied only by men, who act and speak as the reader thinks that he should himself have spoken or acted on the same occasion: even where the agency is supernatural, the dialogue is level with life. Other writers disguise the most natural passions and most frequent incidents, so that he who contemplates them in the book will not know them in the world: Shakespeare approximates [3] the remote and familiarizes the wonderful; the event which he represents will not happen, but, if it were possible, its effects would probably be such as he has assigned; and it may be said that he has not only shown human nature as it acts in real exigences, but as it would be found in trials to which it cannot be exposed.

This therefore is the praise of Shakespeare, that his drama is the mirror of life, that he who has mazed his imagination in following the phantoms which other writers raise up before him may here be cured of his delirious ecstasies by reading human sentiments in human language, by scenes from which a hermit may estimate the transactions of the world and a confessor predict the progress of the passions.

His adherence to general nature has exposed him to the censure of critics who form their judgments upon narrower principles. Dennis and Rymer think his Romans not sufficiently Roman, and Voltaire censures his kings as not completely royal. Dennis is offended that Menenius, a senator of Rome, should play the buffoon, and Voltaire perhaps thinks decency violated

[3] brings near

when the Danish usurper is represented as a drunkard. But Shakespeare always makes nature predominate over accident; and, if he preserves the essential character, is not very careful of distinctions superinduced and adventitious. His story requires Romans or kings, but he thinks only on men. He knew that Rome, like every other city, had men of all dispositions, and, wanting a buffoon, he went into the senate-house for that which the senate-house would certainly have afforded him. He was inclined to show an usurper and a murderer not only odious, but despicable; he therefore added drunkenness to his other qualities, knowing that kings love wine like other men and that wine exerts its natural power upon kings. These are the petty cavils of petty minds; a poet overlooks the casual distinction of country and condition, as a painter, satisfied with the figure, neglects the drapery.

The censure which he has incurred by mixing comic and tragic scenes, as it extends to all his works, deserves more consideration. Let the fact be first stated and then examined.

Shakespeare's plays are not in the rigorous and critical sense either tragedies or comedies, but compositions of a distinct kind, exhibiting the real state of sublunary nature, which partakes of good and evil, joy and sorrow, mingled with endless variety of proportion and innumerable modes of combination; and expressing the course of the world, in which the loss of one is the gain of another; in which, at the same time, the reveller is hasting to his wine, and the mourner burying his friend; in which the malignity of one is sometimes defeated by the frolic of another; and many mischiefs and many benefits are done and hindered without design.

Out of this chaos of mingled purposes and casualties the ancient poets, according to the laws which custom had prescribed, selected some the crimes of men and some their absurdities, some the momentous vicissitudes of life and some the lighter occurrences, some the terrors of distress and some the gaieties of prosperity. Thus rose the two modes of imitation known by the names of tragedy and comedy, compositions intended to promote different ends by contrary means, and considered as so little allied that I do not recollect among the Greeks or Romans a single writer who attempted both.

Shakespeare has united the powers of exciting laughter and sorrow not only in one mind but in one composition. Almost all his plays are divided between serious and ludicrous characters, and, in the successive evolutions of the design, sometimes produce seriousness and sorrow and sometimes levity and laughter.

That this is a practice contrary to the rules of criticism will be readily allowed, but there is always an appeal open from criticism to nature. The end of writing is to instruct; the end of poetry is to instruct by pleasing. That the mingled drama may convey all the instruction of tragedy or comedy cannot be denied, because it includes both in its alternations of exhibition, and approaches nearer than either to the appearance of life, by showing how great machinations and slender designs may promote or obviate one another, and the high and the low co-operate in the general system by unavoidable concatenation.

It is objected that by this change of scenes the passions are interrupted in their progression and that the principal event, being not advanced by a due gradation of preparatory incidents, wants at last the power to move which constitutes the perfection of dramatic poetry. This reasoning is so specious that it is received as true even by those who in daily experience feel it to be false. The interchanges of mingled scenes seldom fail to produce the intended vicissitudes of passion. Fiction cannot move so much but that the attention may be easily transferred; and though it must be allowed that pleasing melancholy be sometimes interrupted by unwelcome levity, yet let it be considered likewise that melancholy is often not pleasing and that the disturbance of one man may be the relief of another, that different auditors have different habitudes and that, upon the whole, all pleasure consists in variety.

The players [4] who in their edition divided our author's works into comedies, histories and tragedies, seem not to have distinguished the three kinds by any very exact or definite ideas.

An action which ended happily to the principal persons, however serious or distressful through its intermediate incidents, in their opinion constituted a comedy. This idea of a comedy continued long amongst us, and plays were written which, by changing the catastrophe, were tragedies today and comedies tomorrow.

Tragedy was not in those times a poem of more general dignity or elevation than comedy; it required only a calamitous conclusion, with which the common criticism of that age was satisfied, whatever lighter pleasure it afforded in its progress.

History was a series of actions with no other than chronological succession, independent on each other and without any tendency to introduce or regulate the

[4] John Heming and Henry Condell, actors, who issued the first complete edition of Shakespeare's plays in a folio volume in 1623.

conclusion. It is not always very nicely distinguished from tragedy. There is not much nearer approach to unity of action in the tragedy of *Antony and Cleopatra* than in the history of *Richard the Second*. But a history might be continued through many plays; as it had no plan, it had no limits.

Through all these denominations of the drama Shakespeare's mode of composition is the same: an interchange of seriousness and merriment, by which the mind is softened at one time and exhilarated at another. But whatever be his purpose, whether to gladden or depress, or to conduct the story without vehemence or emotion through tracts of easy and familiar dialogue, he never fails to attain his purpose; as he commands us, we laugh or mourn or sit silent with quiet expectation, in tranquillity without indifference.

When Shakespeare's plan is understood, most of the criticisms of Rymer and Voltaire vanish away. The play of *Hamlet* is opened, without impropriety, by two sentinels; Iago bellows at Brabantio's window without injury to the scheme of the play, though in terms which a modern audience would not easily endure; the character of Polonius is seasonable and useful, and the grave-diggers themselves may be heard with applause.

Shakespeare engaged in dramatic poetry with the world open before him; the rules of the ancients were yet known to few, the public judgment was unformed, he had no example of such fame as might force him upon imitation, nor critics of such authority as might restrain his extravagance; he therefore indulged his natural disposition, and his disposition, as Rymer has remarked, led him to comedy. In tragedy he often writes, with great appearance of toil and study, what is written at last with little felicity, but in his comic scenes he seems to produce without labor what no labor can improve. In tragedy he is always struggling after some occasion to be comic, but in comedy he seems to repose, or to luxuriate, as in a mode of thinking congenial to his nature. In his tragic scenes there is always something wanting, but his comedy often surpasses expectation or desire. His comedy pleases by the thoughts and the language, and his tragedy for the greater part by incident and action. His tragedy seems to be skill, his comedy to be instinct.

The force of his comic scenes has suffered little diminution from the changes made by a century and a half, in manners or in words. As his personages act upon principles arising from genuine passion, very little modified by particular forms, their pleasures and vexations are communicable to all times and to all places; they are natural, and therefore durable: the adventitious peculiarities of personal habits are only superficial dyes, bright and pleasing for a little while, yet soon fading to a dim tinct, without any remains of former lustre; but the discriminations of true passion are the colours of nature: they pervade the whole mass, and can only perish with the body that exhibits them. The accidental compositions of heterogeneous modes are dissolved by the chance which combined them, but the uniform simplicity of primitive qualities neither admits increase nor suffers decay. The sand heaped by one flood is scattered by another, but the rock always continues in its place. The stream of time, which is continually washing the dissoluble fabrics of other poets, passes without injury by the adamant of Shakespeare.

If there be, what I believe there is, in every nation a style which never becomes obsolete, a certain mode of phraseology so consonant and congenial to the analogy and principles of its respective language as to remain unsettled and altered, this style is probably to be sought in the common intercourse of life, among those who speak only to be understood, without ambition of elegance. The polite are always catching modish innovations, and the learned depart from established forms of speech in the hope of finding or making better; those who wish for distinction forsake the vulgar, when the vulgar is right; but there is a conversation above grossness and below refinement, where propriety resides, and where this poet seems to have gathered his comic dialogue. He is therefore more agreeable to the ears of the present age than any other author equally remote, and among his other excellencies deserves to be studied as one of the original masters of our language.

These observations are to be considered not as unexceptionably constant, but as containing general and predominant truth. Shakespeare's familiar dialogue is affirmed to be smooth and clear, yet not wholly without ruggedness or difficulty, as a country may be eminently fruitful, though it has spots unfit for cultivation; his characters are praised as natural, though their sentiments are sometimes forced and their actions improbable, as the earth upon the whole is spherical, though its surface is varied with protuberances and cavities.

Shakespeare with his excellencies has likewise faults, and faults sufficient to obscure and overwhelm any other merit.[5] I shall show them in the proportion in which they appear to me, without envious malignity or superstitious veneration. No question can be more innocently discussed than a dead poet's pretensions to

[5] *i.e.,* the merit of any other (writer)

renown, and little regard is due to that bigotry which sets candor [6] higher than truth.

His first defect is that to which may be imputed most of the evil in books or in men. He sacrifices virtue to convenience, and is so much more careful to please than to instruct that he seems to write without any moral purpose. From his writings indeed a system of social duty may be selected, for he that thinks reasonably must think morally; but his precepts and axioms drop casually from him; he makes no just distribution of good or evil, nor is always careful to show in the virtuous a disapprobation of the wicked; he carries his persons indifferently through right and wrong, and at the close dismisses them without further care and leaves their examples to operate by chance. This fault the barbarity of his age cannot extenuate, for it is always a writer's duty to make the world better, and justice is a virtue independent on time or place.

The plots are often so loosely formed that a very slight consideration may improve them, and so carelessly pursued that he seems not always fully to comprehend his own design. He omits opportunities of instructing or delighting which the train of his story seems to force upon him, and apparently rejects those exhibitions which would be more affecting for the sake of those which are more easy.

It may be observed that in many of his plays the latter part is evidently neglected. When he found himself near the end of his work and in view of his reward, he shortened the labor to snatch the profit. He therefore remits his efforts where he should most vigorously exert them, and his catastrophe is improbably produced or imperfectly represented.

[6] The word is used here in the unusual sense of *kindness*.

He had no regard to distinction of time or place, but gives to one age or nation, without scruple, the customs, institutions and opinions of another, at the expense not only of likelihood but of possibility. These faults Pope had endeavoured, with more zeal than judgment, to transfer to his imagined interpolators. We need not wonder to find Hector quoting Aristotle when we see the loves of Theseus and Hippolyta combined with the gothic mythology of fairies. Shakespeare, indeed, was not the only violator of chronology, for in the same age Sidney, who wanted not the advantages of learning, has, in his *Arcadia,* confounded the pastoral with the feudal times, the days of innocence, quiet and security with those of turbulence, violence and adventure.

In his comic scenes he is seldom very successful when he engages his characters in reciprocations of smartness and contests of sarcasm; their jests are commonly gross and their pleasantry licentious; neither his gentlemen nor his ladies have much delicacy, nor are sufficiently distinguished from his clowns [7] by any appearance of refined manners. Whether he represented the real conversation of his time is not easy to determine; the reign of Elizabeth is commonly supposed to have been a time of stateliness, formality and reserve, yet perhaps the relaxations of that severity were not very elegant. There must, however, have been always some modes of gaiety preferable to others, and a writer ought to choose the best.

In tragedy his performance seems constantly to be worse as his labor is more. The effusions of passion which exigence forces out are, for the most part, striking and energetic; but whenever he solicits his inven-

[7] boors

tion or strains his faculties, the offspring of his throes is tumour,[8] meanness,[9] tediousness and obscurity.

In narration he affects a disproportionate pomp of diction and a wearisome train of circumlocution, and tells the incident imperfectly in many words which might have been more plainly delivered in few. Narration in dramatic poetry is naturally tedious, as it is unanimated and inactive and obstructs the progress of the action; it should therefore always be rapid and enlivened by frequent interruption. Shakespeare found it an encumbrance, and instead of lightening it by brevity endeavoured to recommend it by dignity and splendor.

His declamations or set speeches are commonly cold and weak, for his power was the power of nature; when he endeavoured, like other tragic writers, to catch opportunities of amplification and, instead of inquiring what the occasion demanded, to show how much his stores of knowledge could supply, he seldom escapes without the pity or resentment of his reader.

It is incident to him to be now and then entangled with an unwieldy sentiment which he cannot well express and will not reject; he struggles with it a while and, if it continues stubborn, compromises it in words such as occur, and leaves it to be disentangled and evolved by those who have more leisure to bestow upon it.

Not that always where the language is intricate the thought is subtle, or the image always great where the line is bulky; the equality of words to things is very often neglected, and trivial sentiments and vulgar ideas disappoint the attention, to which they are recommended by sonorous epithets and swelling figures.

[8] bombast
[9] triviality

But the admirers of this great poet have most reason to complain when he approaches nearest to his highest excellence and seems fully resolved to sink them in dejection and mollify them with tender emotions by the fall of greatness, the danger of innocence or the crosses of love. What he does best, he soon ceases to do. He is not soft and pathetic without some idle conceit [10] or contemptible equivocation.[11] He no sooner begins to move, than he counteracts himself, and terror and pity, as they are rising in the mind, are checked and blasted by sudden frigidity.

A quibble [11] is to Shakespeare what luminous vapors are to the traveller: he follows it at all adventures; it is sure to lead him out of his way, and sure to engulf him in the mire. It has some malignant power over his mind, and its fascinations are irresistible. Whatever be the dignity or profundity of his disquisition, whether he be enlarging knowledge or exalting affection, whether he be amusing attention with incidents or enchaining it in suspense, let but a quibble spring up before him, and he leaves his work unfinished. A quibble is the golden apple for which he will always turn aside from his career [12] or stoop from his elevation. A quibble, poor and barren as it is, gave him such delight that he was content to purchase it by the sacrifice of reason, propriety and truth. A quibble was to him the fatal Cleopatra for which he lost the world and was content to lose it. . . .[13]

[10] far-fetched figure of speech
[11] pun
[12] course
[13] The remainder of the essay is a defense of Shakespeare's neglect of the classical unities, a consideration of the extent of his general knowledge, and a discussion of the previous editions of his plays.

POOR RELATIONS

CHARLES LAMB (1775–1834)

A Poor Relation is the most irrelevant thing in nature, — a piece of impertinent correspondency, — an odious approximation, — a haunting conscience, — a preposterous shadow, lengthening in the noontide of our prosperity, — an unwelcome remembrancer, — a perpetually recurring mortification, — a drain on your purse, — a more intolerable dun upon your pride, — a drawback upon success, — a rebuke to your rising, — a stain in your blood, — a blot on your 'scutcheon, — a rent in your garment, — a death's head at your banquet, — Agathocles' pot,[1] — a Mordecai[2] in your gate, — a Lazarus[3] at your door, — a lion in your path, — a frog in your chamber, — a fly in your ointment, — a mote in your eye, — a triumph to your enemy, an apology to your friends, — the one thing not needful, — the hail in harvest, — the ounce of sour in a pound of sweet.

He is known by his knock. Your heart telleth you "That is Mr. ——." A rap, between familiarity and respect; that demands, and, at the same time, seems to despair of, entertainment. He entereth smiling and — embarrassed. He holdeth out his hand to you to

[1] Agathocles, tyrant of Syracuse, was the son of a humble potter.
[2] Esther iii. 2
[3] Luke xvi. 20. The other figures are from the Bible, also.

shake, and — draweth it back again. He casually looketh in about dinner time — when the table is full. He offereth to go away, seeing you have company — but is induced to stay. He filleth a chair, and your visitor's two children are accommodated at a side table. He never cometh upon open days, when your wife says with some complacency, "My dear, perhaps Mr. ⸺ will drop in to-day." He remembereth birthdays — and professeth he is fortunate to have stumbled upon one. He declareth against fish, the turbot being small — yet suffereth himself to be importuned into a slice against his first resolution. He sticketh by the port — yet will be prevailed upon to empty the remainder glass of claret, if a stranger press it upon him. He is a puzzle to the servants, who are fearful of being too obsequious, or not civil enough, to him. The guests think "they have seen him before." Everyone speculateth upon his condition; and the most part take him to be — a tide waiter.[4] He calleth you by your Christian name, to imply that his other is the same with your own. He is too familiar, by half, yet you wish he had less diffidence. With half the familiarity he might pass for a casual dependent; with more boldness he would be in no danger of being taken for what he is. He is too humble for a friend, yet taketh on him more state than befits a client. He is a worse guest than a country tenant, inasmuch as he bringeth up no rent — yet 't is odds, from his garb and demeanour, that your guests take him for one. He is asked to make one at the whist table; refuseth on the score of poverty, and — resents being left out. When the company break up he proffereth to go for a coach — and

[4] either a customs inspector or (in the figurative sense) one who lives on vague expectations

lets the servant go. He recollects your grandfather; and will thrust in some mean and quite unimportant anecdote of — the family. He knew it when it was not quite so flourishing as "he is blest in seeing it now." He reviveth past situations to institute what he calleth — favourable comparisons. With a reflecting sort of congratulation, he will inquire the price of your furniture; and insults you with a special commendation of your window-curtains. He is of opinion that the urn is the more elegant shape, but, after all, there was something more comfortable about the old tea-kettle — which you must remember. He dare say you must find a great convenience in having a carriage of your own, and appealeth to your lady if it is not so. Inquireth if you have had your arms done on vellum yet; and did not know, till lately, that such-and-such had been the crest of the family. His memory is unseasonable; his compliments perverse; his talk a trouble; his stay pertinacious; and when he goeth away, you dismiss his chair into a corner, as precipitately as possible, and feel fairly rid of two nuisances.

There is a worse evil under the sun, and that is — a female Poor Relation. You may do something with the other; you may pass him off tolerably well; but your indigent she-relative is hopeless. "He is an old humorist,"[5] you may say, "and affects to go threadbare. His circumstances are better than folks would take them to be. You are fond of having a character at your table, and truly he is one." But in the indications of female poverty there can be no disguise. No woman dresses below herself from caprice. The truth must out without shuffling. "She is plainly related to the L——s; or what does she at their house?"

[5] eccentric

She is, in all probability, your wife's cousin. Nine times out of ten, at least, this is the case. Her garb is something between a gentlewoman and a beggar, yet the former evidently predominates. She is most provokingly humble, and ostentatiously sensible [6] to her inferiority. He may require to be repressed sometimes — *aliquando sufflaminandus erat* [7] — but there is no raising her. You send her soup at dinner, and she begs to be helped — after the gentlemen. Mr. —— requests the honour of taking wine with her; she hesitates between Port and Madeira, and chooses the former [8] — because he does. She calls the servant *Sir;* and insists on not troubling him to hold her plate. The housekeeper patronizes her. The children's governess takes upon her to correct her, when she has mistaken the piano for a harpsichord.

Richard Amlet, Esq., in the play,[9] is a notable instance of the disadvantages to which this chimerical notion of *affinity constituting a claim to acquaintance* may subject the spirit of a gentleman. A little foolish blood is all that is betwixt him and a lady of great estate. His stars are perpetually crossed by the malignant maternity of an old woman, who persists in calling him "her son Dick." But she has wherewithal in the end to recompense his indignities, and float him again upon the brilliant surface, under which it had been her seeming business and pleasure all along to sink him. All men, besides, are not of Dick's temperament. I knew an Amlet in real life, who, wanting Dick's buoyancy, sank indeed. Poor W—— was of my own standing at Christ's, a fine classic, and a

[6] sensitive
[7] the Latin equivalent of the preceding phrase
[8] Port was particularly a man's drink.
[9] *The Confederacy,* a comedy by Sir John Vanbrugh

youth of promise. If he had a blemish, it was too much pride; but its quality was inoffensive; it was not of that sort which hardens the heart, and serves to keep inferiors at a distance; it only sought to ward off derogation from itself. It was the principle of self-respect carried as far as it could go, without infringing upon that respect which he would have every one else equally maintain for himself. He would have you to think alike with him on this topic. Many a quarrel have I had with him, when we were rather older boys, and our tallness made us more obnoxious to observation in the blue clothes, because I would not thread the alleys and blind ways of the town with him to elude notice, when we have been out together on a holiday in the streets of this sneering and prying metropolis. W—— went, sore with these notions, to Oxford, where the dignity and sweetness of a scholar's life, meeting with the alloy of a humble introduction, wrought in him a passionate devotion to the place, with a profound aversion from the society. The servitor's gown (worse than his school array) clung to him with Nessian [10] venom. He thought himself ridiculous in a garb under which Latimer must have walked erect; and in which Hooker, in his young days, possibly flaunted in a vein of no discommendable vanity. In the depths of college shades, or in his lonely chamber, the poor student shrunk from observation. He found shelter among books, which insult not; and studies that ask no questions of a youth's finances. He was lord of his library, and seldom cared for looking out beyond his domains. The healing influence

---

[10] Hercules was killed by wearing a shirt that had been poisoned with the blood of the centaur, Nessus. The servitor's gown, like the blue coat of Christ's Hospital School, designated that the wearer was a charity student.

of studious pursuits was upon him, to soothe and to abstract. He was almost a healthy man; when the waywardness of his fate broke out against him with a second and worse malignity. The father of W—— had hitherto exercised the humble profession of house-painter at N——, near Oxford. A supposed interest with some of the heads of colleges had now induced him to take up his abode in that city, with the hope of being employed upon some public works which were talked of. From that moment I read in the countenance of the young man the determination which at length tore him from academical pursuits for ever. To a person unacquainted with our Universities, the distance between the gownsmen and the townsmen, as they are called — the trading part of the latter especially — is carried to an excess that would appear harsh and incredible. The temperament of W——'s father was diametrically the reverse of his own. Old W—— was a little, busy, cringing tradesman, who, with his son upon his arm, would stand bowing and scraping, cap in hand, to anything that wore the semblance of a gown — insensible to the winks and opener remonstrances of the young man, to whose chamber-fellow, or equal in standing, perhaps, he was thus obsequiously and gratuitously ducking. Such a state of things could not last. W—— must change the air of Oxford or be suffocated. He chose the former; and let the sturdy moralist, who strains the point of the filial duties as high as they can bear, censure the dereliction; he cannot estimate the struggle. I stood with W——, the last afternoon I ever saw him, under the eaves of his paternal dwelling. It was in the fine lane leading from the High Street to the back of —— college, where W——

kept his rooms. He seemed thoughtful, and more reconciled. I ventured to rally him — finding him in a better mood — upon a representation of the Artist Evangelist, which the old man, whose affairs were beginning to flourish, had caused to be set up in a splendid sort of frame over his really handsome shop, either as a token of prosperity, or badge of gratitude to his saint. W—— looked up at the Luke, and, like Satan, "knew his mounted sign — and fled."[11] A letter on his father's table the next morning announced that he had accepted a commission in a regiment about to embark for Portugal. He was among the first who perished before the walls of St. Sebastian.

I do not know how, upon a subject which I began with treating half seriously, I should have fallen upon a recital so eminently painful; but this theme of poor relationship is replete with so much matter for tragic as well as comic associations, that it is difficult to keep the account distinct without blending. The earliest impressions which I received on this matter are certainly not attended with anything painful, or very humiliating, in the recalling. At my father's table (no very splendid one) was to be found, every Saturday, the mysterious figure of an aged gentleman, clothed in neat black, of a sad yet comely appearance. His deportment was of the essence of gravity; his words few or none; and I was not to make a noise in his presence. I had little inclination to have done so — for my cue was to admire in silence. A particular elbow chair was appropriated to him, which was in no case to be violated. A peculiar sort of sweet pudding, which appeared on no other occasion, distin-

[11] See *Paradise Lost,* iv, 1013–1015.

guished the days of his coming. I used to think him a prodigiously rich man. All I could make out of him was that he and my father had been schoolfellows a world ago at Lincoln, and that he came from the Mint.[12] The Mint I knew to be a place where all the money was coined — and I thought he was the owner of all that money. Awful ideas of the Tower twined themselves about his presence. He seemed above human infirmities and passions. A sort of melancholy grandeur invested him. From some inexplicable doom I fancied him obliged to go about in an eternal suit of mourning; a captive — a stately being, let out of the Tower on Saturdays. Often have I wondered at the temerity of my father, who, in spite of an habitual general respect which we all in common manifested towards him, would venture now and then to stand up against him in some argument, touching their youthful days. The houses of the ancient city of Lincoln are divided (as most of my readers know) between the dwellers on the hill, and in the valley. This marked distinction formed an obvious division between the boys who lived above (however brought together in a common school) and the boys whose paternal residence was on the plain; a sufficient cause of hostility in the code of these young Grotiuses.[13] My father had been a leading mountaineer; and would still maintain the general superiority, in skill and hardihood, of the *Above Boys* (his own faction) over the *Below Boys* (so were they called), of which party his contemporary had been a chieftain. Many and hot were the skirmishes on this topic — the only one upon

[12] a slum in London in which debtors were free from arrest
[13] Hugo Grotius (1583-1645), a famous jurist who wrote on the causes of war

which the old gentleman was ever brought out — and bad blood bred; even sometimes almost to the recommencement (so I expected) of actual hostilities. But my father, who scorned to insist upon advantages, generally contrived to turn the conversation upon some adroit by-commendation of the old Minster; in the general preference of which, before all other cathedrals in the island, the dweller on the hill, and the plain-born, could meet on a conciliating level, and lay down their less important differences. Once only I saw the old gentleman really ruffled, and I remembered with anguish the thought that came over me: "Perhaps he will never come here again." He had been pressed to take another plate of the viand, which I have already mentioned as the indispensable concomitant of his visits. He had refused with a resistance amounting to rigour — when my aunt, an old Lincolnian, but who had something of this in common with my cousin Bridget, that she would sometimes press civility out of season — uttered the following memorable application — "Do take another slice, Mr. Billet, for you do not get pudding every day." The old gentleman said nothing at the time — but he took occasion in the course of the evening, when some argument had intervened between them, to utter with an emphasis which chilled the company, and which chills me now as I write it — "Woman, you are superannuated." John Billet did not survive long, after the digesting of this affront; but he survived long enough to assure me that peace was actually restored! and, if I remember aright, another pudding was discreetly substituted in the place of that which had occasioned the offence. He died at the Mint (anno 1781) where he had long held, what he accounted, a comfortable independence; and with five pounds, fourteen shillings and a penny, which were found in his escrutoire after his decease, left the world, blessing God that he had enough to bury him, and that he had never been obliged to any man for a sixpence. This was — a Poor Relation.

VULGARITY AND AFFECTATION

WILLIAM HAZLITT (1778–1830)

FEW subjects are more nearly allied than these two — vulgarity and affectation. It may be said of them truly that "thin partitions do their bounds divide." There cannot be a surer proof of a low origin or of an innate meanness[1] of disposition than to be always talking and thinking of being genteel.[2] One must feel a strong tendency to that which one is always trying to avoid: whenever we pretend, on all occasions, a mighty contempt for anything, it is a pretty clear sign that we feel ourselves very nearly on a level with it. Of the two classes of people, I hardly know which is to be regarded with most distaste, the vulgar aping the genteel, or the genteel constantly sneering at and endeavoring to distinguish themselves from the vulgar. These two sets of persons are always thinking of one another; the lower of the higher with envy, the more fortunate of their less happy neighbors with contempt. They are habitually placed in opposition to each other; jostle in their pretensions at every turn; and the same objects and train of thought (only reversed by the relative situation of either party) occupy their whole time and attention. The one are straining every nerve, and outraging common sense, to be thought genteel;

[1] pettiness
[2] well-bred, fashionable

the others have no other object or idea in their heads than not to be thought vulgar. This is but poor spite; a very pitiful style of ambition. To be merely not that which one heartily despises is a very humble claim to superiority; to despise what one really is, is still worse. Most of the characters in Miss Burney's novels — the Branghtons, the Smiths, the Dubsters, the Cecilias, the Delvilles, etc. — are well met in this respect, and much of a piece: the one half are trying not to be taken for themselves, and the other half not to be taken for the first. They neither of them have any pretensions of their own, or real standard of worth. "A feather will turn the scale of their avoirdupois"; though the fair authoress was not aware of the metaphysical identity of her principal and subordinate characters. Affectation is the master-key to both.

Gentility is only a more select and artificial kind of vulgarity. It cannot exist but by a sort of borrowed distinction. It plumes itself up and revels in the homely pretensions of the mass of mankind. It judges of the worth of everything by name, fashion and opinion; and hence, from the conscious absence of real qualities or sincere satisfaction in itself, it builds its supercilious and fantastic conceit on the wretchedness and wants of others. Violent antipathies are always suspicious, and betray a secret affinity. The difference between the "Great Vulgar and the Small" is mostly in outward circumstances. The coxcomb criticises the dress of the clown,[3] as the pedant cavils at the bad grammar of the illiterate, or the prude is shocked at the backslidings of her frail acquaintance. Those who have the fewest resources in themselves naturally seek the food of their self-love elsewhere. The most ignorant people

[3] country fellow

VULGARITY AND AFFECTATION

find most to laugh at in strangers: scandal and satire prevail most in country-places; and a propensity to ridicule the slightest or most palpable deviation from what we happen to approve, ceases with the progress of common sense and decency. True worth does not exult in the faults and deficiencies of others; as true refinement turns away from grossness and deformity instead of being tempted to indulge in an unmanly triumph over it. Raphael would not faint away at the daubing of a signpost,[4] nor Homer hold his head the higher for being in the company of a Grub Street bard. Real power, real excellence, does not seek for a foil in inferiority; nor fear contamination from coming in contact with that which is coarse and homely. It reposes on itself, and is equally free from spleen and affectation. But the spirit of gentility is the mere essence of spleen and affectation; of affected delight in its own *would-be* qualifications, and of ineffable disdain poured out upon the involuntary blunders or accidental disadvantages of those whom it chooses to treat as its inferiors. Thus a fashionable Miss titters till she is ready to burst her sides at the uncouth shape of a bonnet or the abrupt drop of a curtsey (such as Jeanie Deans[5] would make) in a country-girl who comes to be hired by her Mamma as a servant; yet to show how little foundation there is for this hysterical expression of her extreme good opinion of herself and contempt for the untutored rustic, she would herself the next day be delighted with the very same shaped bonnet if brought her by a French milliner and told it was all the fashion, and in a week's time

---

[4] inn signs, usually vilely decorated
[5] the rustic, but noble-hearted, heroine of Scott's *Heart of Midlothian*

will become quite familiar with the maid, and chatter with her (upon equal terms) about caps and ribbons and lace by the hour together. There is no difference between them but that of situation in the kitchen or in the parlor: let circumstances bring them together, and they fit like hand and glove. It is like mistress, like maid. Their talk, their thoughts, their dreams, their likings and dislikes are the same. The mistress's head runs continually on dress and finery, so does the maid's: the young lady longs to ride in a coach and six, so does the maid, if she could; Miss forms a beau idéal of a lover with black eyes and rosy cheeks, which does not differ from that of her attendant; both like a smart man, the one the footman and the other his master, for the same reason; both like handsome furniture and fine houses; both apply the terms *shocking* and *disagreeable* to the same things and persons; both have a great notion of balls, plays, treats, song-books, and love-tales; both like a wedding or a christening, and both would give their little fingers to see a coronation — with this difference, that the one has a chance of getting a seat at it, and the other is dying with envy that she has not. Indeed, this last is a ceremony that delights equally the greatest monarch and the meanest of his subjects — the vilest of the rabble. Yet this which is the height of gentility and consummation of external distinction and splendor, is, I should say, a vulgar ceremony. For what degree of refinement, of capacity, of virtue is required in the individual who is so distinguished, or is necessary to his enjoying this idle and imposing parade of his person? Is he delighted with the stagecoach and gilded panels? So is the poorest wretch that gazes at it. Is he struck with the spirit, the beauty, and symmetry of the eight

VULGARITY AND AFFECTATION

cream-colored horses? There is not one of the immense multitude who flock to see the sight from town or country, St. Giles's or Whitechapel, young or old, rich or poor, gentle or simple, who does not agree to admire the same object. Is he delighted with the yeomen of the guard, the military escort, the groups of ladies, the badges of sovereign power, the kingly crown, the marshal's truncheon and the judge's robe, the array that precedes and follows him, the crowded streets, the windows hung with eager looks? so are the mob, for they "have eyes and see them"! There is no one faculty of mind or body, natural or acquired, essential to the principal figure in this procession more than is common to the meanest and most despised attendant on it. A waxwork figure would answer the same purpose: a Lord Mayor of London has as much tinsel to be proud of. I would rather have a king do something that no one else has the power or magnanimity to do, or say something that no one else has the wisdom to say, or look more handsome, more thoughtful, or benign than any one else in his dominions. But I see nothing to raise one's idea of him in his being made a show of: if the pageant would do as well without the man, the man would do as well without the pageant! Kings have been declared to be "lovers of low company"; and this maxim, besides the reason sometimes assigned for it, viz. that they meet with less opposition to their wills from such persons, will I suspect be found to turn at last on the consideration I am here stating, that they also meet with more sympathy in their tastes. The most ignorant and thoughtless have the greatest admiration of the baubles, the outward symbols of pomp and power, the sound and show, which are the habitual delight and mighty prerogative of kings. The stupidest slave worships the gaudiest tyrant. The same gross motives appeal to the same gross capacities, flatter the pride of the superior and excite the servility of the dependant; whereas a higher reach of moral and intellectual refinement might seek in vain for higher proofs of internal worth and inherent majesty in the object of its idolatry, and not finding the divinity lodged within, the unreasonable expectation raised would probably end in mortification on both sides! — There is little to distinguish a king from his subjects but the rabble's shout — if he loses that and is reduced to the forlorn hope of gaining the suffrages of the wise and good, he is of all men the most miserable. — But enough of this.

"I like it," says Miss Branghton in *Evelina*[6] (meaning the opera), "because it is not vulgar." That is, she likes it, not because there is anything to like in it, but because other people are prevented from liking or knowing anything about it. Janus Weathercock, Esq., laugheth to scorn and spitefully entreateth and hugely condemneth my dramatic criticisms in the *London,* for a like exquisite reason. I must therefore make an example of him *in terrorem* to all such hypercritics. He finds fault with me and calls my taste vulgar because I go to Sadler's Wells[7] ("a place he has heard of" — O Lord, sir!) — because I notice the Miss Dennetts, "great favorites with the Whitechapel orders" — praise Miss Valancy, "a bouncing Columbine at Ashley's and them there places, as his barber informs him" (has he no way of establishing himself in his own good opinion but by triumphing

---

[6] Fanny Burney's novel, referred to earlier
[7] a popular, but unfashionable, theatre in an unaristocratic part of London

VULGARITY AND AFFECTATION

over his barber's bad English?) — and finally, because I recognised the existence of the Coburg and Surrey theatres, at the names of which he cries "Faugh" with great significance, as if he had some personal disgust at them, and yet he would be supposed never to have entered them. It is not his cue as a well-bred critic. *C'est beau ça.* Now this appears to me a very rude, unmeaning, indiscriminate, wholesale, and vulgar way of thinking. It is prejudicing things in the lump, by names and places and classes, instead of judging them by what they are in themselves, by their real qualities and shades of distinction. There is no selection, truth or delicacy in such a mode of proceeding. It is affecting ignorance, and making it a title to wisdom. It is a vapid assumption of superiority. It is exceeding impertinence. It is rank coxcombry. It is nothing in the world else. To condemn because the multitude admire is as essentially vulgar as to admire because they admire. There is no exercise of taste or judgment in either case: both are equally repugnant to good sense, and of the two I should prefer the good-natured side. I would as soon agree with my barber as differ from him; and why should I make a point of reversing the sentence of the Whitechapel orders? Or how can it affect my opinion of the merits of an actor at the Coburg or the Surrey theatres, that these theatres are in or out of the Bills of Mortality?[8] This is an easy, shorthand way of judging, as gross as it is mechanical. It is not a difficult matter to settle questions of taste by consulting the map of London, or to prove your liberality by geographical distinctions. Janus jumbles things together strangely. If he had seen Mr. Kean[9]

[8] *i.e.*, the city limits
[9] the most famous actor of the day

in a provincial theatre, at Exeter or Taunton, he would have thought it vulgar to admire him; but when he had been stamped in London, Janus would no doubt show his discernment and the subtlety of his tact [10] for the display of character and passion by not being behind the fashion. The Miss Dennetts are "little unformed girls," for no other reason than because they danced at one of the minor theatres: let them but come out on the opera boards, and let the beauty and fashion of the season greet them with a fairy shower of delighted applause, and they would outshine Milanie "with the foot of fire." His gorge rises at the mention of a certain quarter of the town: whatever passes current in another he "swallows total grist unsifted, husks and all." This is not taste, but folly. At this rate, the hackney-coachman who drives him, or his horse Contributor whom he has introduced as a select personage to the vulgar reader, knows as much of the matter as he does. — In a word, the answer to all this in the first instance is to say what vulgarity is. Now its essence, I imagine, consists in taking manners, actions, words, opinions on trust from others, without examining one's own feelings or weighing the merits of the case. It is coarseness or shallowness of taste arising from want of individual refinement, together with the confidence and presumption inspired by example and numbers. It may be defined to be a prostitution of the mind or body to ape the more or less obvious defects of others, because by so doing we shall secure the suffrages of those we associate with. To affect a gesture, an opinion, a phrase, because it is the rage with a large number of persons, or to hold it in abhorrence because another set of persons very

[10] feeling

little, if at all, better informed, cry it down to distinguish themselves from the former, is in either case equal vulgarity and absurdity. — A thing is not vulgar merely because it is common. 'T is common to breathe, to see, to feel, to live. Nothing is vulgar that is natural, spontaneous, unavoidable. Grossness is not vulgarity, ignorance is not vulgarity, awkwardness is not vulgarity; but all these become vulgar when they are affected and shown off on the authority of others, or to fall in with the *fashion* or the company we keep. Caliban [11] is coarse enough, but surely he is not vulgar. We might as well spurn the clod under our feet and call it vulgar. Cobbett [12] is coarse enough, but he is not vulgar. He does not belong to the herd. Nothing real, nothing original, can be vulgar; but I should think an imitator of Cobbett a vulgar man. Emery's Yorkshireman is vulgar, because he is a Yorkshireman. It is the cant and gibberish, the cunning and low life of a particular district; it has "a stamp exclusive and provincial." He might "gabble most brutishly," and yet not fall under the letter of the definition; but "his speech bewrayeth him," his dialect (like the jargon of a Bond Street lounger) is the damning circumstance. If he were a mere blockhead, it would not signify; but he thinks himself a *knowing hand,* according to the notions and practices of those with whom he was brought up, and which he thinks *the go* everywhere. In a word, this character is not the offspring of untutored nature but of bad habits; it is made up of ignorance and conceit. It has a mixture of *slang* in it. All slang phrases are for the same reason vulgar; but there is nothing vulgar in the common English

---

[11] a semi-human monster in Shakespeare's *The Tempest*
[12] William Cobbett (1762–1835), a vigorous radical journalist

idiom. Simplicity is not vulgarity; but the looking to affectation of any sort for distinction is. A cockney is a vulgar character, whose imagination cannot wander beyond the suburbs of the metropolis; so is a fellow who is always thinking of the High Street, Edinburgh. We want a name for this last character. An opinion is vulgar that is stewed in the rank breath of the rabble: nor is it a bit purer or more refined for having passed through the well-cleansed teeth of a whole court. The inherent vulgarity is in having no other feeling on any subject than the crude, blind, headlong, gregarious notion acquired by sympathy with the mixed multitude or with a fastidious minority, who are just as insensible to the real truth, and as indifferent to everything but their own frivolous and vexatious pretensions. The upper are not wiser than the lower orders, because they resolve to differ from them. The fashionable have the advantage of the unfashionable in nothing but the fashion. The true vulgar are the *servum pecus imitatorum* — the herd of pretenders to what they do not feel and to what is not natural to them, whether in high or low life. To belong to any class, to move in any rank or sphere of life, is not a very exclusive distinction or test of refinement. Refinement will in all classes be the exception, not the rule; and the exception may fall out in one class as well as another. A king is but an hereditary title. A nobleman is only one of the House of Peers. To be a knight or alderman is confessedly a vulgar thing. The king the other day made Sir Walter Scott a baronet, but not all the power of the Three Estates could make another author of *Waverley*. Princes, heroes, are often commonplace people: Hamlet was not a vulgar character, neither was Don

Quixote. To be an author, to be a painter, is nothing. It is a trick, it is a trade.

> An author! 't is a venerable name:
> How few deserve it, yet what numbers claim!

Nay, to be a Member of the Royal Academy or a Fellow of the Royal Society is but a vulgar distinction; but to be a Virgil, a Milton, a Raphael, a Claude, is what fell to the lot of humanity but once! I do not think *they* were vulgar people; though, for anything I know to the contrary, the first Lord of the Bedchamber may be a very vulgar man; for anything I know to the contrary he may not be so. — Such are pretty much my notions of gentility and vulgarity.

There is a well-dressed and an ill-dressed mob, both which I hate. *Odi profanum vulgus, et arceo.*[13] The vapid affectation of the one to me is even more intolerable than the gross insolence and brutality of the other. If a set of low-lived fellows are noisy, rude, and boisterous to show their disregard of the company, a set of fashionable coxcombs are, to a nauseous degree, finical and effeminate to show their thorough breeding. The one are governed by their feelings, however coarse and misguided, which is something; the others consult only appearances, which are nothing, either as a test of happiness or virtue. Hogarth[14] in his prints has trimmed the balance of pretension between the downright blackguard and the *soi-disant*[15] fine gentleman unanswerably. It does not appear in his moral demonstrations (whatever it may do in the genteel letter writing of Lord Chesterfield or the chiv-

[13] I hate the common crowd, and keep at a distance.
[14] a popular, satirical painter and engraver of the eighteenth century
[15] self-styled

alrous rhapsodies of Burke) that vice by losing all its grossness loses half its evil. It becomes more contemptible, not less disgusting. What is there in common, for instance, between his beaux and belles, his rakes and his coquettes, and the men and women, the true heroic and ideal characters in Raphael? But his people of fashion and quality are just upon a par with the low, the selfish, the *unideal* characters in the contrasted view of human life, and are often the very same characters, only changing places. If the lower ranks are actuated by envy and uncharitableness towards the upper, the latter have scarcely any feelings but of pride, contempt, and aversion to the lower. If the poor would pull down the rich to get at their good things, the rich would tread down the poor as in a vine-press, and squeeze the last shilling out of their pockets and the last drop of blood out of their veins. If the headstrong self-will and unruly turbulence of a common alehouse are shocking, what shall we say to the studied insincerity, the insipid want of common sense, the callous insensibility of the drawing-room and boudoir? I would rather see the feelings of our common nature (for they are the same at bottom) expressed in the most naked and unqualified way, than see every feeling of our nature suppressed, stifled, hermetically sealed under the smooth, cold, glittering varnish of pretended refinement and conventional politeness. The one may be corrected by being better informed; the other is incorrigible, wilful, heartless depravity. I cannot describe the contempt and disgust I have felt at the tone of what would be thought good company, when I have witnessed the sleek, smiling, glossy, gratuitous assumption of superiority to every feeling of humanity, honesty, or principle, as a part of the etiquette, the mental

VULGARITY AND AFFECTATION

and moral *costume* of the table, and every profession of toleration or favor for the lower orders, that is, for the great mass of our fellow-creatures, treated as an indecorum and breach of the harmony of well-regulated society. In short, I prefer a bear-garden to the adder's den; or, to put this case in its extremest point of view, I have more patience with men in a rude state of nature outraging the human form than I have with apes "making mops and mows" at the extravagances they have first provoked. I can endure the brutality (as it is termed) of mobs better than the inhumanity of courts. The violence of the one rages like a fire; the insidious policy of the other strikes like a pestilence, and is more fatal and inevitable. The slow poison of despotism is worse than the convulsive struggles of anarchy. "Of all evils," says Hume, "anarchy is the shortest lived." The one may "break out like a wild overthrow"; but the other from its secret, sacred stand, operates unseen, and undermines the happiness of kingdoms for ages, lurks in the hollow cheek, and stares you in the face in the ghastly eye of want and agony and woe. It is dreadful to hear the noise and uproar of an infuriated multitude stung by the sense of wrong and maddened by sympathy;[16] it is more appalling to think of the smile answered by other gracious smiles, of the whisper echoed by other assenting whispers, which doom them first to despair and then to destruction. Popular fury finds its counterpart in courtly servility. If every outrage is to be apprehended from the one, every iniquity is deliberately sanctioned by the other, without regard to justice or decency. The word of a king, "Go thou and do likewise," makes the stoutest heart dumb: truth and honesty shrink before it. If there are watchwords

[16] fellow feeling

for the rabble, have not the polite and fashionable their hackneyed phrases, their fulsome, unmeaning jargon as well? Both are to me anathema! . . .[17]

ON THE FEELING OF IMMORTALITY IN YOUTH

Life is a pure flame, and we live by an invisible sun within us. — SIR THOMAS BROWNE

No young man believes he shall ever die. It was a saying of my brother's, and a fine one. There is a feeling of Eternity in youth, which makes us amends for everything. To be young is to be as one of the Immortal Gods. One half of time indeed is flown — the other half remains in store for us with all its countless treasures; for there is no line drawn, and we see no limit to our hopes and wishes. We make the coming age our own. —

The vast, the unbounded prospect lies before us.

Death, old age, are words without a meaning, that pass by us like the idle air which we regard not. Others may have undergone, or may still be liable to them — we "bear a charmed life," which laughs to scorn all such sickly fancies. As in setting out on a delightful journey, we strain our eager gaze forward —

Bidding the lovely scenes at distance hail, —

---

[17] The remainder of the essay is a long description of a character in an old play, *Eastward Hoe*. It is really a footnote or appendix to the essay as a whole, from which its omission detracts nothing.

IMMORTALITY IN YOUTH

and see no end to the landscape, new objects presenting themselves as we advance; so, in the commencement of life, we set no bounds to our inclinations, nor to the unrestricted opportunities of gratifying them. We have as yet found no obstacle, no disposition to flag; and it seems that we can go on so for ever. We look round in a new world, full of life, and motion and ceaseless progress; and feel in ourselves all the vigour and spirit to keep pace with it, and do not foresee from any present symptoms how we shall be left behind in the natural course of things, decline into old age, and drop into the grave. It is the simplicity, and as it were *abstractedness* of our feelings in youth, that (so to speak) identifies us with nature, and (our experience being slight and our passions strong) deludes us into a belief of being immortal like it. Our short-lived connection with existence, we fondly flatter ourselves, is an indissoluble and lasting union — a honey-moon that knows neither coldness, jar, nor separation. As infants smile and sleep, we are rocked in the cradle of our wayward fancies, and lulled into security by the roar of the universe around us — we quaff the cup of life with eager haste without draining it, instead of which it only overflows the more — objects press around us, filling the mind with their magnitude and with the throng of desires that wait upon them, so that we have no room for the thoughts of death. From that plenitude of our being, we cannot change all at once to dust and ashes, we cannot imagine "this sensible,[1] warm motion, to become a kneaded clod" — we are too much dazzled by the brightness of the waking dream around us to look into the darkness of the tomb. We no more see our end than our beginning: the one is lost in oblivion and

[1] sensitive

vacancy, as the other is hid from us by the crowd and hurry of approaching events. Or the grim shadow is seen lingering in the horizon, which we are doomed never to overtake, or whose last, faint, glimmering outline touches upon Heaven and translates us to the skies! Nor would the hold that life has taken of us permit us to detach our thoughts from present objects and pursuits, even if we would. What is there more opposed to health, than sickness; to strength and beauty, than decay and dissolution; to the active search of knowledge than mere oblivion? Or is there none of the usual advantage to bar the approach of Death, and mock his idle threats; Hope supplies their place, and draws a veil over the abrupt termination of all our cherished schemes. While the spirit of youth remains unimpaired, ere the "wine of life is drank up" we are like people intoxicated or in a fever, who are hurried away by the violence of their own sensations: it is only as present objects begin to pall upon the sense, as we have been disappointed in our favourite pursuits, cut off from our closest ties, that passion loosens its hold upon the breast, that we by degrees become weaned from the world, and allow ourselves to contemplate, "as in a glass, darkly," the possibility of parting with it for good. The example of others, the voice of experience, has no effect upon us whatever. Casualties we must avoid: the slow and deliberate advances of age we can play at *hide-and-seek* with. We think ourselves too lusty and too nimble for that blear-eyed decrepit old gentleman to catch us. Like the foolish fat scullion, in Sterne,[2] when she hears that Master Bobby is dead, our only reflection is — "So am not I!" The idea of death, instead of staggering our confidence, rather seems

[2] See *Tristram Shandy,* Bk. V, Chap. vii.

to strengthen and enhance our possession and our enjoyment of life. Others may fall around us like leaves, or be mowed down like flowers by the scythe of Time: these are but tropes and figures to the unreflecting ears and overweening presumption of youth. It is not till we see the flowers of Love, Hope, and Joy, withering around us, and our own pleasures cut up by the roots, that we bring the moral home to ourselves, that we abate something of the wanton extravagance of our pretensions, or that the emptiness and dreariness of the prospect before us reconciles us to the stillness of the grave!

> Life! thou strange thing, that hast a power to feel
> Thou art, and to perceive that others are.[3]

Well might the poet begin his indignant invective against an art, whose professed object is its destruction, with this animated apostrophe to life. Life is indeed a strange gift, and its privileges are most miraculous. Nor is it singular that when the splendid boon is first granted us, our gratitude, our admiration, and our delight should prevent us from reflecting on our own nothingness, or from thinking it will ever be recalled. Our first and strongest impressions are taken from the mighty scene that is opened to us, and we very innocently transfer its durability as well as magnificence to ourselves. So newly found, we cannot make up our minds to parting with it yet and at least put off that consideration to an indefinite term. Like a clown[4] at a fair, we are full of amazement and rapture, and have no thoughts of going home, or that it will soon be night. We know our existence only from external objects, and we measure it by them. We can never be satisfied

[3] Fawcett's *Art of War*, 1794
[4] country fellow, yokel

with gazing; and nature will still want us to look on and applaud. Otherwise, the sumptuous entertainment, "the feast of reason and the flow of soul," to which they were invited seems little better than a mockery and a cruel insult. We do not go from a play till the scene is ended, and the lights are ready to be extinguished. But the fair face of things still shines on; shall we be called away before the curtain falls, or ere we have scarce had a glimpse of what is going on? Like children, our step-mother Nature holds us up to see the raree-show of the universe; and then, as if life were a burthen to support, lets us instantly down again. Yet in that short interval, what "brave sublunary things" does not the spectacle unfold; like a bubble, at one minute reflecting the universe, and the next, shook to air! — To see the golden sun and azure sky, the outstretched ocean, to walk upon the green earth, and to be lord of a thousand creatures, to look down giddy precipices or over distant flowery vales, to see the world spread out under one's finger in a map, to bring the stars near, to view the smallest insects in a microscope, to read history, and witness the revolutions of empires and the succession of generations, to hear of the glory of Sidon and Tyre, or Babylon and Susa, as of a faded pageant, and to say all these were, and are now nothing, to think that we exist in such a point of time, and in such a corner of space, to be at once spectators and a part of the moving scene, to watch the return of the seasons, of spring and autumn, to hear

> — The stockdove plain amid the forest deep,
> That drowsy rustles to the sighing gale —

to traverse desert wildernesses, to listen to the midnight choir, to visit lighted halls, or plunge into the dungeon's gloom, or sit in crowded theatres and see life itself mocked, to feel heat and cold, pleasure and pain, right and wrong, truth and falsehood, to study the works of art and refine the sense of beauty to agony, to worship fame and to dream of immortality, to have read Shakespeare and belong to the same species as Sir Isaac Newton; to be and to do all this, and then in a moment to be nothing, to have it all snatched from one like a juggler's ball or a phantasmagoria; there is something revolting and incredible to sense in the transition, and no wonder that, aided by youth and warm blood, and the flush of enthusiasm, the mind contrives for a long time to reject it with disdain and loathing as a monstrous and improbable fiction, like a monkey on a house-top, that is loath, amidst its fine discoveries and specious antics, to be tumbled head-long into the street, and crushed to atoms, the sport and laughter of the multitude!

The change, from the commencement to the close of life, appears like a fable, after it has taken place; how should we treat it otherwise than as a chimera before it has come to pass? There are some things that happened so long ago, places or persons we have formerly seen, of which such dim traces remain, we hardly know whether it was sleeping or waking they occurred; they are like dreams within the dream of life, a mist, a film before the eye of memory, which, as we try to recall them more distinctly, elude our notice altogether. It is but natural that the lone interval that we thus look back upon, should have appeared long and endless in prospect. There are others so distinct and fresh, they seem but of yesterday — their very vividness might be deemed a pledge of their permanence. Then, however far back our impressions may go, we find others still older (for our years are multiplied in youth) ; descriptions of scenes that we had read, and people before our time, Priam and the Trojan war; and even then, Nestor was old and dwelt delighted on his youth, and spoke of the race of heroes that were no more; — what wonder that, seeing this long line of being pictured in our minds, and reviving as it were in us, we should give ourselves involuntary credit for an indeterminate period of existence? In the Cathedral at Peterborough there is a monument to Mary, Queen of Scots, at which I used to gaze when a boy, while the events of the period, all that had happened since, passed in review before me. If all this mass of feeling and imagination could be crowded into a moment's compass, what might not the whole of life be supposed to contain? We are heirs of the past; we count upon the future as our natural reversion. Besides, there are some of our early impressions so exquisitely tempered, it appears that they must always last — nothing can add to or take away from their sweetness and purity — the first breath of spring, the hyacinth dipped in the dew, the mild lustre of the evening-star, the rainbow after a storm — while we have the full enjoyment of these, we must be young; and what can ever alter us in this respect? Truth, friendship, love, books, are also proof against the canker of time; and while we live but for them, we can never grow old. We take out a new lease of existence from the objects on which we set our affections, and become abstracted, impassive, immortal in them. We cannot conceive how certain sentiments should ever decay or grow cold in our breasts; and, consequently, to maintain them in their first youthful glow and vigour, the flame of life must continue to burn as bright as ever, or rather, they are the fuel that feed the sacred lamp, that kindle "the purple light of love," and spread a golden cloud around our heads! Again, we not only flourish and survive in our affections (in which we will not listen to the possibility of a change, any more than we foresee the wrinkles on the brow of a mistress), but we have a farther guarantee against the thoughts of death in our favourite studies and pursuits, and in their continual advance. Art we know is long; life, we feel, should be so too. We see no end of the difficulties we have to encounter; perfection is slow of attainment, and we must have time to accomplish it in. Rubens complained that when he had just learnt his art, he was snatched away from it: we trust we shall be more fortunate! A wrinkle in an old head takes whole days to finish it properly: but to catch "the Raphael grace, the Guido air," no limit should be put to our endeavours. What a prospect for the future! What a task we have entered upon! and shall we be arrested in the middle of it? We do not reckon our time thus employed lost, or our pains thrown away, or our progress slow — we do not droop or grow tired, but "gain new vigour at our endless task"; — and shall Time grudge us the opportunity to finish what we have auspiciously begun, and have formed a sort of compact with nature to achieve? The fame of the great names we look up to is also imperishable; and shall not we, who contemplate it with such intense yearnings, imbibe a portion of ethereal fire, the *divinae particula aurae*,[5] which nothing can extinguish? I remember to have looked at a print of Rembrandt for hours together, without being conscious of the flight of time, trying to resolve it into its component parts, to connect its strong and sharp gradations, to learn the secret of its reflected lights, and found

[5] particles of divine ether

neither satiety nor pause in the prosecution of my studies. The print over which I was poring would last long enough; why should the idea in my mind, which was finer, more impalpable, perish before it? At this, I redoubled the ardour of my pursuit, and by the very subtlety and refinement of my inquiries, seemed to bespeak for them an exemption from corruption and the rude grasp of Death.[6]

Objects, on our first acquaintance with them, have that singleness and integrity of impression that it seems as if nothing could destroy or obliterate them, so firmly are they stamped and rivetted on the brain. We repose on them with a sort of voluptuous indolence, in full faith and boundless confidence. We are absorbed in the present moment, or return to the same point — idling away a great deal of time in youth, thinking we have enough and to spare. There is often a local feeling in the air, which is as fixed as if it were of marble; we loiter in dim cloisters, losing ourselves in thought and in their glimmering arches; a winding road before us seems as long as the journey of life, and as full of events. Time and experience dissipate this illusion; and by reducing them to detail, circumscribe the limits of our expectations. It is only as the pageant of life passes by and the masques turn their backs upon us, that we see through the deception, or believe that the train will have an end. In many cases, the slow progress and monotonous texture of our lives, before we mingle with the world and are embroiled in its affairs, has a tendency to aid the same feeling. We have a difficulty, when left to ourselves, and without the resource of books or some more lively pursuit, to

[6] Is it not this that frequently keeps artists alive so long, *viz.* the constant occupation of their minds with vivid images, with little of the *wear-and-tear* of the body? — HAZLITT

"beguile the slow and creeping hours of time," and argue that if it moves on always at this tedious snail's-pace, it can never come to an end. We are willing to skip over certain portions of it that separate us from favourite objects, that irritate ourselves at the unnecessary delay. The young are prodigal of life from a superabundance of it; the old are tenacious on the same score, because they have little left, and cannot enjoy even what remains of it.

For my part, I set out in life with the French Revolution, and that event had considerable influence on my early feelings, as on those of others. Youth was then doubly such. It was the dawn of a new era, a new impulse had been given to men's minds, and the sun of Liberty rose upon the sun of Life in the same day, and both were proud to run their race together. Little did I dream, while my first hopes and wishes went hand in hand with those of the human race, that long before my eyes should close, that dawn would be overcast, and set once more in the night of despotism — "total eclipse!" Happy that I did not. I felt for years, and during the best part of my existence, *heart-whole* in that cause, and triumphed in the triumphs over the enemies of man! At that time, while the fairest aspirations of the human mind seemed about to be realized, ere the image of man was defaced and his breast mangled in scorn, philosophy took a higher, poetry could afford a deeper range. At that time, to read the *Robbers*,[7] was indeed delicious, and to hear

> From the dungeon of the tower time-rent,
> That fearful voice, a famish'd father's cry,

---

[7] *The Robbers* (1781) and *Don Carlos* (1787) were tragedies by Schiller which expressed ideas of political and intellectual freedom dear to the young romanticists.

could be borne only amidst the fulness of hope, the crash of the fall of the strongholds of power, and the exulting sounds of the march of human freedom. What feelings the death-scene in *Don Carlos* sent into the soul! In that headlong career of lofty enthusiasm and the joyous opening of the prospects of the world and our own, the thought of death crossing it smote doubly cold upon the mind; there was a stifling sense of oppression and confinement, an impatience of our present knowledge, a desire to grasp the whole of our existence in one strong embrace, to sound the mystery of life and death, and in order to put an end to the agony of doubt and dread, to burst through our prison-house, and confront the King of Terrors in his grisly palace! . . . As I was writing out this passage, my miniature-picture when a child lay on the mantle-piece, and I took it out of the case to look at it. I could perceive few traces of myself in it; but there was the same placid brow, the dimpled mouth, the same timid, inquisitive glance as ever. But its careless smile did not seem to reproach me with having become a recreant to the sentiments that were then sown in my mind, or with having written a sentence that could call up a blush in this image of ingenuous youth!

"That time is past with all its giddy raptures." Since the future was barred to my progress, I have turned for consolation to the past, gathering up the fragments of my early recollections, and putting them into a form that might live. It is thus, that when we find our personal and substantial identity vanishing from us, we strive to gain a reflected and substituted one in our thoughts: we do not like to perish wholly, and wish to bequeath our names at least to posterity. As long as we can keep alive our cherished thoughts and nearest interests in the minds of others, we do not appear to have retired altogether from the stage, we still occupy a place in the estimation of mankind, exercise a powerful influence over them, and it is only our bodies that are trampled into dust or dispersed to air. Our darling speculations still find favour and encouragement, and we make as good a figure in the eyes of our descendants, nay, perhaps, a better than we did in our life-time. This is one point gained; the demands of our self-love are so far satisfied. Besides, if by the proofs of intellectual superiority we survive ourselves in this world, by exemplary virtue or unblemished faith we are taught to ensure an interest in another and a higher state of being, and to anticipate at the same time the applauses of men and angels.

> Even from the tomb the voice of nature cries;
> Even in our ashes live their wonted fires.

As we advance in life, we acquire a keener sense of the value of time. Nothing else, indeed, seems of any consequence; and we become misers in this respect. We try to arrest its few last tottering steps, and to make it linger on the brink of the grave. We can never leave off wondering how that which has ever been should cease to be, and would still live on, that we may wonder at our own shadow, and when "all the life of life is flown," dwell on the retrospect of the past. This is accompanied by a mechanical tenaciousness of whatever we possess, by a distrust and a sense of fallacious hollowness in all we see. Instead of the full, pulpy feeling of youth, everything is flat and insipid. The world is a painted witch that puts us off with false shows and tempting appearances. The ease, the jocund gaiety, the unsuspecting security of youth are fled: nor can we, without flying in the face of common sense,

> From the last dregs of life, hope to receive
> What its first sprightly runnings could not give.

If we can slip out of the world without notice or mischance, can tamper with bodily infirmity, and frame our minds to the becoming composure of *still-life,* before we sink into total insensibility, it is as much as we ought to expect. We do not in the regular course of nature die all at once: we have mouldered away gradually long before; faculty after faculty, attachment after attachment, we are torn from ourselves piecemeal while living; year after year takes something from us; and death only consigns the last remnant of what we were to the grave. The revulsion is not so great, and a quiet *euthanasia* is a winding-up of the plot that is not out of reason or nature.

That we should thus in a manner outlive ourselves, and dwindle imperceptibly into nothing, is not surprising, even when in our prime the strongest impressions leave so little traces of themselves behind, and the last object is driven out by the succeeding one. How little effect is produced on us at any time by the books we have read, the scenes we have witnessed, the sufferings we have gone through! Think only of the variety of feelings we experience in reading an interesting romance or being present at a fine play — what beauty, what sublimity, what soothing, what heart-rending emotions! You would suppose these would last for ever, or at least subdue the mind to a correspondent tone and harmony — while we turn over the page, while the scene is passing before us, it seems as if nothing could ever after shake our resolution, that "treason domestic, foreign levy, nothing could touch us farther!" The first splash of mud we get on entering the street, the first pettifogging shop-keeper that cheats us out of twopence, and the whole vanishes clean out of our remembrance, and we become the idle prey of the most petty and annoying circumstances. The mind soars by an effort to the grand and lofty: it is at home in the grovelling, the disagreeable, and the little. This happens in the height and heyday of our existence, when novelty gives a stronger impulse to the blood and takes a faster hold of the brain, (I have known the impression on coming out of a gallery of pictures then last half a day) — as we grow old, we become more feeble and querulous, every object "reverbs its own hollowness," and both worlds are not enough to satisfy the peevish importunity and extravagant presumption of our desires! There are a few superior, happy beings, who are born with a temper exempt from every trifling annoyance. This spirit sits serene and smiling as in its native skies, and a divine harmony (whether heard or not) plays around them. This is to be at peace. Without this, it is vain to fly into deserts, or to build a hermitage on the top of rocks, if regret and ill-humour follow us there: and with this, it is needless to make the experiment. The only true retirement is that of the heart; the only true leisure is the repose of the passions. To such persons it makes little difference whether they are young or old; and they die as they have lived, with graceful resignation.

DEMOCRACY[1]

THOMAS CARLYLE (1795–1881)

IF the Serene Highnesses and Majesties do not take note of that,[2] then, as I perceive, *that* will take note of itself! The time for levity, insincerity, and idle babble and play-acting, in all kinds, is gone by; it is a serious, grave time. Old long-vexed questions, not yet solved in logical words or parliamentary laws, are fast solving themselves in facts, somewhat unblessed to behold! This largest of questions, this question of Work and Wages, which ought, had we heeded Heaven's voice, to have begun two generations ago or more, cannot be delayed longer without hearing Earth's voice. "Labor" will verily need to be somewhat "organized," as they say, — God knows with what difficulty. Man will actually need to have his debts and earnings a little better paid by man; which, let Parliaments speak of them or be silent of them, are eternally his due from man, and cannot, without penalty and at length not without death-penalty, be withheld. How much ought to cease among us straightway; how much ought to begin straightway, while the hours yet are!

Truly they are strange results to which this of leaving all to "Cash"; of quietly shutting-up the God's Temple,

[1] from *Past and Present,* 1843
[2] the problem of labor and wages, with a statement of which Carlyle had concluded the preceding chapter

and gradually opening wide-open the Mammon's Temple, with "Laissez-faire, and Every man for himself," — have led us in these days! We have Upper, speaking Classes, who indeed do "speak" as never man spake before; the withered flimsiness, the godless baseness and barrenness of whose Speech might of itself indicate what kind of Doing and practical Governing went on under it! For speech is the gaseous element out of which most kinds of Practice and Performance, especially all kinds of moral Performance, condense themselves, and take shape; as the one is, so will the other be. Descending, accordingly, into the Dumb Class in its Stockport Cellars and Poor-Law Bastilles, have we not to announce that they also are hitherto unexampled in the History of Adam's Posterity?

Life was never a May-game for men: in all times the lot of the dumb millions born to toil was defaced with manifold sufferings, injustices, heavy burdens, avoidable and unavoidable; not play at all, but hard work that made the sinews sore and the heart sore. As bond-slaves, *villani, bordarii, sochemanni,* nay indeed as dukes, earls and kings, men were oftentimes made weary of their life; and had to say, in the sweat of their brow and of their soul, Behold, it is not sport, it is grim earnest, and our back can bear no more! Who knows not what massacrings and harryings there have been; grinding, long-continuing, unbearable injustices, — till the heart had to rise in madness, and some *"Eu Sachsen, nimith euer sachses,* You Saxons, out with your gully-knives, then!" You Saxons, some "arrestment," partial "arrestment of the Knaves and Dastards" has become indispensable! The page of Dryasdust is heavy with such details.

And yet I will venture to believe that in no time, since the beginnings of Society, was the lot of those same dumb millions of toilers so entirely unbearable as it is even in the days now passing over us. It is not to die, or even to die of hunger, that makes a man wretched; many men have died; all men must die, — the last exit of us all is in a Fire-Chariot of Pain. But it is to live miserable we know not why; to work sore and yet gain nothing; to be heart-worn, weary, yet isolated, unrelated, girt-in with a cold universal Laissez-faire: it is to die slowly all our life long, imprisoned in a deaf, dead, Infinite Injustice, as in the accursed iron belly of a Phalaris' Bull! This is and remains forever intolerable to all men whom God has made. Do we wonder at French Revolutions, Chartisms, Revolts of Three Days?[3] The times, if we will consider them, are really unexampled.

Never before did I hear of an Irish Widow reduced to "prove her sisterhood by dying of typhus-fever and infecting seventeen persons," — saying in such undeniable way, "You *see* I was your sister!" Sisterhood, brotherhood, was often forgotten; but not till the rise of these ultimate Mammon and Shotbelt Gospels did I ever see it so expressly denied. If no pious Lord or *Law-ward* would remember it, always some pious Lady (*"Hlaf-dig,"* Benefactress, *"Loaf-giveress,"* they say she is, — blessings on her beautiful heart!) was there, with mild mother-voice and hand, to remember it; some pious thoughtful *Elder,* what we now call "Prester," *Presbyter* or "Priest," was there to put all men in mind of it, in the name of the God who had made all.

[3] the revolution of July 1830, which drove Charles X from the throne of France.

Not even in Black Dahomey was it ever, I think, forgotten to the typhus-fever length. Mungo Park, resourceless, had sunk down to die under the Negro Village-Tree, a horrible White object in the eyes of all. But in the poor Black Woman, and her daughter who stood aghast at him, whose earthly wealth and funded capital consisted of one small calabash of rice, there lived a heart richer than *Laissez-faire:* they, with a royal munificence, boiled their rice for him; they sang all night to him, spinning assiduous on their cotton distaffs, as he lay to sleep: "Let us pity the poor white man; no mother has he to fetch him milk, no sister to grind him corn!" Thou poor black Noble One, — thou *Lady,* too: did not a God make thee too; was there not in thee too something of a God! —

Gurth,[4] born thrall of Cedric the Saxon, has been greatly pitied by Dryasdust and others. Gurth, with the brass collar round his neck, tending Cedric's pigs in the glades of the wood, is not what I call an exemplar of human felicity: but Gurth, with the sky above him, with the free air and tinted boscage and umbrage round him, and in him at least the certainty of supper and social lodging when he came home; Gurth to me seems happy, in comparison with many a Lancashire and Buckinghamshire man of these days, not born thrall of anybody! Gurth's brass collar did not gall him: Cedric *deserved* to be his master. The pigs were Cedric's, but Gurth too would get his parings of them. Gurth had the inexpressible satisfaction of feeling himself related indissolubly, though in a rude brass-collar way, to his fellow-mortals in this Earth. He had superiors, inferiors, equals. — Gurth is now "emancipated" long since; has what we call "Liberty." Liberty, I am told,

[4] the swineherd in Scott's *Ivanhoe*

is a divine thing. Liberty when it becomes the "Liberty to die by starvation" is not so divine!

Liberty? The true liberty of a man, you would say, consisted in his finding out, or being forced to find out the right path, and to walk thereon. To learn, or to be taught, what work he actually was able for; and then by permission, persuasion, and even compulsion, to set about doing of the same! That is his true blessedness, honor, "liberty" and maximum of wellbeing: if liberty be not that, I for one have small care about liberty. You do not allow a palpable madman to leap over precipices; you violate his liberty, you that are wise; and keep him, were it in strait-waistcoats, away from the precipices! Every stupid, every cowardly and foolish man is but a less palpable madman: his true liberty were that a wiser man, that any and every wiser man, could, by brass collars, or in whatever milder or sharper way, lay hold of him when he was going wrong, and order and compel him to go a little righter. O, if thou really art my *Senior,* Seigneur, my *Elder,* Presbyter or Priest, — if thou art in very deed my *Wiser,* may a beneficent instinct lead and impel thee to "conquer" me, to command me! If thou do know better than I what is good and right, I conjure thee in the name of God, force me to do it; were it by never such brass collars, whips and handcuffs, leave me not to walk over precipices! That I have been called, by all the Newspapers, a "free man" will avail me little, if my pilgrimage have ended in death and wreck. O that the Newspapers had called me slave, coward, fool, or what it pleased their sweet voices to name me, and I had attained not death, but life! — Liberty requires new definitions.

A conscious abhorrence and intolerance of Folly, of

Baseness, Stupidity, Poltroonery and all that brood of things, dwells deep in some men: still deeper in others an *un*conscious abhorrence and intolerance, clothed moreover by the beneficent Supreme Powers in what stout appetites, energies, egoisms so-called, are suitable to it; — These latter are your Conquerors, Romans, Normans, Russians, Indo-English; Founders of what we call Aristocracies. Which indeed have they not the most "divine right" to found; — being themselves truly Αριστοι, BRAVEST, BEST; and conquering generally a confused rabble of WORST, or at lowest, clearly enough, of WORSE. I think their divine right, tried, with affirmatory verdict, in the greatest Law-Court known to me, was good! A class of men who are dreadfully exclaimed against by Dryasdust; of whom nevertheless beneficent Nature has oftentimes had need; and may, alas, again have need.

When, across the hundredfold poor scepticisms, trivialisms and constitutional cobwebberies of Dryasdust, you catch any glimpse of a William the Conqueror, a Tancred of Hauteville or suchlike, — do you not discern veritably some rude outline of a true God-made King; whom not the Champion of England cased in tin, but all Nature and the Universe were calling to the throne? It is absolutely necessary that he get thither. Nature does not mean her poor Saxon children to perish, of obesity, stupor or other malady, as yet: a stern Ruler and Line of Rulers therefore is called in, — a stern but most beneficent *perpetual House-Surgeon* is by Nature herself called in, and even the appropriate *fees* are provided for him! Dryasdust talks lamentably about Hereward and the Fen Counties; fate of Earl Waltheof; Yorkshire and the North reduced to ashes: all which is undoubtedly lamentable. But even

Dryasdust apprises me of one fact: "A child, in this William's reign, might have carried a purse of gold from end to end of England." My erudite friend, it is a fact which out-weighs a thousand! Sweep away thy constitutional, sentimental and other cobwebberies; look eye to eye, if thou still have any eye, in the face of this big burly William Bastard: thou wilt see a fellow of most flashing discernment, of most strong lion-heart; — in whom, as it were, within a frame of oak and iron, the gods have planted the soul of "a man of genius"! Dost thou call that nothing? I call it an immense thing! — Rage enough was in this Willelmus Conquaestor, rage enough for his occasions; — and yet the essential element of him, as of all such men, is not scorching *fire,* but shining illuminative *light.* Fire and light are strangely interchangeable; nay, at bottom, I have found them different forms of the same most godlike "elementary substance" in our world: a thing worth stating in these days. The essential element of this Conquaestor is, first of all, the most sun-eyed perception of what *is* really what on this God's-Earth; — which, thou wilt find, does mean at bottom "Justice," and "Virtues" not a few: *Conformity* to what the Maker has seen good to make; that, I suppose, will mean Justice and a Virtue or two? —

Dost thou think Willelmus Conquaestor would have tolerated ten years' jargon, one hour's jargon, on the propriety of killing Cotton-manufacturers by partridge Corn-Laws? I fancy, this was not the man to knock out of his night's-rest with nothing but a noisy bedlamism in your mouth! "Assist us still better to bush the partridges; strangle Plugson who spins the shirts?" — *"Par la Splendeur de Dieu!"* — Dost thou think Willelmus Conquaestor, in this new time, with Steam-engine Captains of Industry on one hand of him, and Joe-Manton [5] Captains of Idleness on the other, would have doubted which *was* really the BEST; which did deserve strangling, and which not?

I have a certain indestructible regard for Willelmus Conquaestor. A resident House-Surgeon, provided by Nature for her beloved English People, and even furnished with the requisite fees, as I said; for he by no means felt himself doing Nature's work, this Willelmus, but his own work exclusively! And his work withal it was; informed *"par la Splendeur de Dieu."* — I say, it is necessary to get the work out of such a man, however harsh that be! When a world, not yet doomed for death, is rushing down to ever-deeper Baseness and Confusion, it is a dire necessity of Nature's to bring in her ARISTOCRACIES, her BEST, even by forcible methods. When their descendants or representatives cease entirely to *be* the Best, Nature's poor world will very soon rush down again to Baseness; and it becomes a dire necessity of Nature's to cast them out. Hence French Revolutions, Five-point Charters, Democracies, and a mournful list of *Etceteras,* in these our afflicted times.

To what extent Democracy has now reached, how it advances irresistible with ominous, ever-increasing speed, he that will open his eyes on any province of human affairs may discern. Democracy is everywhere the inexorable demand of these ages, swiftly fulfilling itself. From the thunder of Napoleon battles, to the jabbering of Open-vestry in St. Mary Axe, all things announce Democracy. A distinguished man, whom

---

[5] A famous gun maker from whom the aristocracy bought their sporting guns. Carlyle was always contemptuous of the partridge-shooting aristocracy.

some of my readers will hear again with pleasure, thus writes to me what in these days he notes from the Wahngasse of Weissnichtwo, where our London fashions seem to be in full vogue. Let us hear the Herr Teufelsdröckh[6] again, were it but the smallest word!

"Democracy, which means despair of finding any Heroes to govern you, and contented putting-up with the want of them, — alas, thou too, *mein Lieber,* seest well how close it is of kin to *Atheism,* and other sad *Isms:* he who discovers no God whatever, how shall he discover Heroes, the visible Temples of God? — Strange enough meanwhile it is, to observe with what thoughtlessness here in our rigidly Conservative Country, men rush into Democracy with full cry. Beyond doubt, his Excellenz the Titular-Herr Ritter Kauderwälsch von Pferdefuss-Quacksalber, he our distinguished Conservative Premier himself, and all but the thicker-headed of his Party, discern Democracy to be inevitable as death, and are even desperate of delaying it much!

"You cannot walk the streets without beholding Democracy announce itself: the very Tailor has become, if not properly Sansculottic, which to him would be ruinous, yet a Tailor unconsciously symbolizing, and prophesying with his scissors, the reign of Equality. What now is our fashionable coat? A thing of superfinest texture, of deeply meditated cut; with Malines-lace cuffs; quilted with gold; so that a man can carry, without difficulty, an estate of land on his back? *Keineswegs,* By no manner of means! The Sumptuary

---

[6] The philosopher hero of Carlyle's *Sartor Resartus,* a book in which religious and political ideas are discussed under the guise of a philosophy of clothes. Democracy here is the rising of the masses. Sans-culottism, a term taken from the French Revolution, means "the people without breeches," or clothes in general.

Laws have fallen into such a state of desuetude as was never before seen. Our fashionable coat is an amphibium between barnsack and drayman's doublet. The cloth of it is studiously coarse; the color a speckled soot-black or rust-brown gray; the nearest approach to a Peasant's. And for shape, — thou shouldst see it! The last consummation of the year now passing over us is definable as Three Bags; a big bag for the body, two small bags for the arms, and by way of collar a hem! The first Antique Cheruscan [7] who, of felt-cloth or bear's-hide, with bone or metal needle, set about making himself a coat, before Tailors had yet awakened out of Nothing, — did not he make it even so? A loose wide poke for body, with two holes to let out the arms; this was his original coat: to which holes it was soon visible that two small loose pokes, or sleeves, easily appended, would be an improvement.

"Thus has the Tailor-art, so to speak, overset itself, like most other things; changed its centre-of-gravity; whirled suddenly over from zenith to nadir. Your Stulz, with huge somerset, vaults from his high shop-board down to the depths of primal savagery, — carrying much along with him! For I will invite thee to reflect that the Tailor, as topmost ultimate froth of Human Society, is indeed swift-passing, evanescent, slippery to decipher; yet significant of much, nay of all. Topmost evanescent froth, he is churned-up from the very lees, and from all intermediate regions of the liquor. The general outcome he, visible to the eye, of what men aimed to do, and were obliged and enabled to do, in this one public department of symbolizing themselves to each other by covering of their skins. A smack of all Human Life lies in the Tailor: its wild struggles

[7] a primitive Germanic tribe

toward beauty, dignity, freedom, victory; and how, hemmed-in by Sedan and Huddersfield, by Nescience, Dulness, Prurience, and other sad necessities and laws of Nature, it has attained just to this: Gray savagery of Three Sacks with a hem.

"When the very Tailor verges toward Sansculottism, is it not ominous? The last Divinity of poor mankind dethroning himself; sinking *his* taper too, flame downmost, like the Genius of Sleep or of Death; admonitory that Tailor time shall be no more! — For, little as one could advise Sumptuary Laws at the present epoch, yet nothing is clearer than that where ranks do actually exist, strict division of costumes will also be enforced; that if we ever have a new Hierarchy and Aristocracy acknowledged veritably as such, for which I daily pray Heaven, the Tailor will reawaken; and be, by volunteering and appointment, consciously and unconsciously, a safeguard of that same." — Certain farther observations, from the same invaluable pen, on our never-ending changes of mode, our "perpetual nomadic and even ape-like appetite for change and mere change" in all the equipments of our existence, and the "fatal revolutionary character" thereby manifested, we suppress for the present. It may be admitted that Democracy, in all meanings of the word, is in full career; irresistible by any Ritter Kauderwälsch or other Son of Adam, as times go. "Liberty" is a thing men are determined to have.

But truly, as I had to remark in the mean while, "the liberty of not being oppressed by your fellow man" is an indispensable, yet one of the most insignificant fractional parts of Human Liberty. No man oppresses thee, can bid thee fetch or carry, come or go, without reason shown. True; from all men thou art emancipated: but from Thyself and from the Devil — ? No man, wiser, unwiser, can make thee come or go: but thy own futilities, bewilderments, thy false appetites for Money, Windsor Georges [8] and suchlike? No man oppresses thee, O free and independent Franchiser: but does not this stupid Porter-pot oppress thee? No Son of Adam can bid thee come or go; but this absurd Pot of Heavy-wet, this can and does! Thou art the thrall not of Cedric the Saxon, but of thy own brutal appetites and this scoured dish of liquor. And thou pratest of thy "liberty"? Thou entire blockhead!

Heavy-wet and gin: alas, these are not the only kinds of thraldom. Thou who walkest in a vain show, looking out with ornamental dilettante sniff and serene supremacy at all Life and all Death; and amblest jauntily; perking up thy poor talk into crotchets, thy poor conduct into fatuous somnambulisms; — and *art* as an "enchanted Ape" under God's sky, where thou mightest have been a man, had proper Schoolmasters and Conquerors, and Constables with cat-o'-nine tails, been vouchsafed thee; dost thou call that "liberty"? Or your unreposing Mammon-worshipper again, driven, as if by Galvanisms, by Devils and Fixed-Ideas, who rises early and sits late, chasing the impossible; straining every faculty to "fill himself with the east wind," — how merciful were it, could you, by mild persuasion, or by the severest tyranny so-called, check him in his mad path, and turn him into a wiser one! All painful tyranny, in that case again, were but mild "surgery";

---

[8] Saint George, patron of the Order of the Garter; his figure appeared on the badge of the order. It is used here as a symbol for all worldly honors.

the pain of it cheap, as health and life, instead of galvanism and fixed-idea, are cheap at any price.

Sure enough, of all paths a man could strike into, there *is,* at any given moment, a *best path* for every man; a thing which, here and now, it were of all things *wisest* for him to do; — which could he be but led or driven to do, he were then doing "like a man," as we phrase it; all men and gods agreeing with him, the whole Universe virtually exclaiming Well-done to him! His success, in such case, were complete; his felicity a maximum. This path, to find this path and walk in it, is the one thing needful for him. Whatsoever forwards him in that, let it come to him even in the shape of blows and spurnings, is liberty: whatsoever hinders him, were it ward-motes, open-vestries, poll-booths, tremendous cheers, rivers of heavy-wet, is slavery.

The notion that a man's liberty consists in giving his vote at election-hustings, and saying, "Behold, now I too have my twenty-thousandth part of a Talker in our National Palaver; will not all the gods be good to me?" — is one of the pleasantest! Nature nevertheless is kind at present; and puts it into the heads of many, almost of all. The liberty especially which has to purchase itself by social isolation, and each man standing separate from the other, having "no business with him" but a cash-account: this is such a liberty as the Earth seldom saw; — as the Earth will not long put up with, recommend it how you may. This liberty turns out, before it have long continued in action, with all men flinging up their caps round it, to be, for the Working Millions a liberty to die by want of food; for the Idle Thousands and Units, alas, a still more fatal liberty to live in want of work; to have no earnest duty to do in this God's-World any more. What becomes of a man in such predicament? Earth's laws are silent; and Heaven's speak in a voice which is not heard. No work, and the ineradicable need of work, give rise to new very wondrous life-philosophies, new very wondrous life-practices! Dilettantism, Pococurantism,[9] Beau-Brummelism,[10] with perhaps an occasional, half-mad, protesting burst of Byronism, establish themselves: at the end of a certain period, — if you go back to "the Dead Sea," there is, say our Moslem friends, a very strange "Sabbath-day" transacting itself there! — Brethren, we know but imperfectly yet, after ages of Constitutional Government, what Liberty and Slavery are.

Democracy, the chase of Liberty in that direction, shall go its full course; unrestrainable by him of Pferdefuss-Quacksalber, or any of *his* household. The Toiling Millions of Mankind, in most vital need and passionate instinctive desire of Guidance, shall cast away False-Guidance; and hope, for an hour, that No-Guidance will suffice them: but it can be for an hour only. The smallest item of human Slavery is the oppression of man by his Mock-Superiors; the palpablest, but I say at bottom the smallest. Let him shake-off such oppression, trample it indignantly under his feet; I blame him not, I pity and commend him. But oppression by your Mock-Superiors well shaken off, the grand problem yet remains to solve: That of finding government by your Real-Superiors! Alas, how shall we ever learn the solution of that, benighted, bewildered, sniffing, sneering, godforgetting unfortu-

---

[9] Pococurante, a character in Voltaire's *Candide,* though accomplished and wealthy, was eternally bored.
[10] Beau Brummel (1778–1840), the leading dandy in the reign of George IV

nates as we are? It is a work for centuries; to be taught us by tribulations, confusions, insurrections, obstructions; who knows if not by conflagration and despair! It is a lesson inclusive of all other lessons; the hardest of all lessons to learn.

One thing I do know: Those Apes, chattering on the branches by the Dead Sea, never got it learned; but chatter there to this day. To them no Moses need come a second time; a thousand Moses would be but so many painted Phantasms, interesting Fellow-Apes of new strange aspect, — whom they would "invite to dinner," be glad to meet with in lion-soirées. To them the voice of Prophecy, of heavenly monition, is quite ended. They chatter there, all Heaven shut to them, to the end of the world. The unfortunates! Oh, what is dying of hunger, with honest tools in your hand, with a manful purpose in your heart, and much real labor lying round you done, in comparison? You honestly quit your tools; quit a most muddy confused coil of sore work, short rations, of sorrows, dispiritments and contradictions, having now honestly done with it all; — and await, not entirely in a distracted manner, what the Supreme Powers, and the Silences and the Eternities may have to say to you.

A second thing I know: This lesson will have to be learned, — under penalties! England will either learn it, or England also will cease to exist among Nations. England will either learn to reverence its Heroes, and discriminate them from its Sham-Heroes and Valets and gaslighted Histrios; and to prize them as the audible God's-voice, amid all inane jargons and temporary market-cries, and say to them with heart-loyalty, "Be ye King and Priest, and Gospel and Guidance for us": or else England will continue to worship new and ever-new forms of Quackhood, — and so, with what resiliences and reboundings matters little, go down to the Father of Quacks! Can I dread such things of England? Wretched, thick-eyed, gross-hearted mortals, why will ye worship lies, and "Stuffed Clothes-suits created by the ninth-parts of men!" It is not your purses that suffer; your farm-rents, your commerces, your mill-revenues, loud as ye lament over these; no, it is not these alone, but a far deeper than these: it is your souls that lie dead, crushed down under despicable Nightmares, Atheisms, Brain-fumes; and are not souls at all, but mere succedanea for *salt* to keep your bodies and their appetites from putrefying! Your cotton-spinning and thrice-miraculous mechanism, what is this too, by itself, but a larger kind of Animalism? Spiders can spin, Beavers can build and show contrivance; the Ant lays-up accumulation of capital, and has, for aught I know, a Bank of Antland. If there is no soul in man higher than all that, did it reach to sailing on the cloud-rack, and spinning sea-sand; then I say, man is but an animal, a more cunning kind of brute: he has no soul, but only a succedaneum for salt. Whereupon, seeing himself to be truly of the beasts that perish, he ought to admit it, I think; — and also straightway universally to kill himself; and so, in a manlike manner at least *end,* and wave these brute-worlds *his* dignified farewell! —

LIFE WITHOUT PRINCIPLE [1]

HENRY DAVID THOREAU (1817–1862)

AT a lyceum, not long since, I felt that the lecturer had chosen a theme too foreign to himself, and so failed to interest me as much as he might have done. He described things not in or near to his heart, but toward his extremities and superficies. There was, in this sense, no truly central or centralizing thought in the lecture. I would have had him deal with his privatest experience, as the poet does. The greatest compliment that was ever paid me was when one asked me what *I thought,* and attended to my answer. I am surprised, as well as delighted, when this happens; it is such a rare use he would make of me, as if he were acquainted with the tool. Commonly, if men want anything of me, it is only to know how many acres I make of their land, — since I am a surveyor, — or, at most, what trivial news I have burdened myself with. They never will go to law for my meat; they prefer the shell. A man once came a considerable distance to ask me to lecture on Slavery; but on conversing with him, I found that he and his clique expected seven-eighths of the lecture to be theirs, and only one-eighth mine; so I declined. I take it for granted, when I am invited to

[1] From the *Atlantic Monthly,* October 1863.

lecture anywhere, — for I have had a little experience in that business, — that there is a desire to hear what *I think* on some subject, though I may be the greatest fool in the country, — and not that I should say pleasant things merely, or such as the audience will assent to; and I resolve, accordingly, that I will give them a strong dose of myself. They have sent for me, and engaged to pay for me, and I am determined that they shall have me, though I bore them beyond all precedent.

So now I would say something similar to you, my readers. Since *you* are my readers, and I have not been much of a traveller, I will not talk about people a thousand miles off, but come as near home as I can. As the time is short, I will leave out all the flattery, and retain all the criticism.

Let us consider the way in which we spend our lives.

This world is a place of business. What an infinite bustle! I am awaked almost every night by the panting of the locomotive. It interrupts my dreams. There is no sabbath. It would be glorious to see mankind at leisure for once. It is nothing but work, work, work. I cannot easily buy a blank-book to write thoughts in; they are commonly ruled for dollars and cents. An Irishman, seeing me making a minute in the fields, took it for granted that I was calculating my wages. If a man was tossed out of a window when an infant, and so made a cripple for life, or scared out of his wits by the Indians, it is regretted chiefly because he was thus incapacitated for — business! I think that there is nothing, not even crime, more opposed to poetry, to philosophy, ay, to life itself, than this incessant business.

There is a coarse and boisterous money-making fellow in the outskirts of our town who is going to build a bank-wall under the hill along the edge of his meadow. The powers have put this into his head to keep him out of mischief, and he wishes me to spend three weeks digging there with him. The result will be that he will perhaps get some more money to hoard, and leave for his heirs to spend foolishly. If I do this, most will commend me as an industrious and hard-working man; but if I choose to devote myself to certain labors which yield more real profit, though but little money, they may be inclined to look on me as an idler. Nevertheless, as I do not need the police of meaningless labor to regulate me, and do not see anything absolutely praiseworthy in this fellow's undertaking, any more than in many an enterprise of our own or foreign governments, however amusing it may be to him or them, I prefer to finish my education at a different school.

If a man walk in the woods for love of them half of each day, he is in danger of being regarded as a loafer; but if he spends his whole day as a speculator, shearing off those woods and making earth bald before her time, he is esteemed an industrious and enterprising citizen. As if a town had no interest in its forests but to cut them down!

Most men would feel insulted if it were proposed to employ them in throwing stones over a wall, and then in throwing them back, merely that they might earn their wages. But many are no more worthily employed now. For instance: just after sunrise one summer morning I noticed one of my neighbors walking beside his team, which was slowly drawing a heavy hewn stone swung under the axle, surrounded by an atmosphere of industry — his day's work begun, his brow commenced to sweat, a reproach to all sluggards and idlers — pausing abreast the shoulders of his oxen, and half turning round with a flourish of his merciful whip, while they gained their length on him. And I thought, Such is the labor which the American Congress exists to protect, — honest, manly toil, — honest as the day is long, — that makes his bread taste sweet, and keeps society sweet, — which all men respect and have consecrated: one of the sacred band, doing the needful, but irksome drudgery. Indeed, I felt a slight reproach, because I observed this from the window, and was not abroad and stirring about a similar business. The day went by, and at evening I passed the yard of another neighbor, who keeps many servants, and spends much money foolishly, while he adds nothing to the common stock, and there I saw the stone of the morning lying beside a whimsical structure intended to adorn this Lord Timothy Dexter's premises, and the dignity forthwith departed from the teamster's labor, in my eyes. In my opinion, the sun was made to light worthier toil than this. I may add that his employer has since run off, in debt to a good part of the town, and, after passing through Chancery, has settled somewhere else, there to become once more a patron of the arts.

The ways by which you may get money almost without exception lead downward. To have done anything by which you earned money *merely* is to have been truly idle or worse. If the laborer gets no more than the wages which his employer pays him, he is cheated, he cheats himself. If you would get money as a writer or a lecturer, you must be popular, which is to go down perpendicularly. Those services which the community will most readily pay for it is most disagreeable to render. You are paid for being something less than a man. The State does not commonly reward a genius any more wisely. Even the poet-laureate would rather not have to celebrate the accidents of royalty. He must be bribed with a pipe of wine; and perhaps another poet is called away from his muse to gauge that very pipe. As for my own business, even that kind of surveying which I could do with most satisfaction my employers do not want. They would prefer that I should do my work coarsely and not too well, ay, not well enough. When I observe that there are different ways of surveying, my employer commonly asks which will give him the most land, not which is most correct. I once invented a rule for measuring cord-wood, and tried to introduce it in Boston; but the measurer there told me that the sellers did not wish to have their wood measured correctly, — that he was already too accurate for them, and therefore they commonly got their wood measured in Charleston before crossing the bridge.

The aim of the laborer should be, not to get his living, to get "a good job," but to perform well a certain work; and, even in a pecuniary sense, it would be economy for a town to pay its laborers so well that they would not feel that they were working for low ends, as for a livelihood merely, but for scientific, or even moral ends. Do not hire a man who does your work for money, but him who does it for love of it.

It is remarkable that there are few men so well employed, so much to their minds, but that a little money or fame would commonly buy them off from their present pursuit. I see advertisements for *active* young men, as if activity were the whole of a young man's capital. Yet I have been surprised when one has with confidence proposed to me, a grown man, to embark in some enterprise of his, as if I had absolutely nothing to do, my life having been a complete failure hitherto.

LIFE WITHOUT PRINCIPLE   219

What a doubtful compliment this is to pay me! As if he had met me half-way across the ocean beating up against the wind, but bound nowhere, and proposed to me to go along with him! If I did, what do you think the underwriters would say? No, no! I am not without employment at this stage of the voyage. To tell the truth, I saw an advertisement for able-bodied seamen, when I was a boy, sauntering in my native port, and as soon as I came of age I embarked.

The community has no bribe that will tempt a wise man. You may raise money enough to tunnel a mountain, but you cannot raise money enough to hire a man who is minding *his own* business. An efficient and valuable man does what he can, whether the community pay him for it or not. The inefficient offer their inefficiency to the highest bidder, and are forever expecting to be put into office. One would suppose that they were rarely disappointed.

Perhaps I am more than usually jealous with respect to my freedom. I feel that my connection with and obligation to society are still very slight and transient. Those slight labors which afford me a livelihood, and by which it is allowed that I am to some extent serviceable to my contemporaries, are as yet commonly a pleasure to me, and I am not often reminded that they are a necessity. So far I am successful. But I foresee, that, if my wants should be much increased, the labor required to supply them would become a drudgery. If I should sell both my forenoons and afternoons to society, as most appear to do, I am sure that, for me, there would be nothing left worth living for. I trust that I shall never thus sell my birthright for a mess of pottage. I wish to suggest that a man may be very industrious, and yet not spend his time well. There is no more fatal blunderer than he who consumes the greater part of his life getting his living. All great enterprises are self-supporting. The poet, for instance, must sustain his body by his poetry, as a steam planing-mill feeds its boilers with the shavings it makes. You must get your living by loving. But as it is said of the merchants that ninety-seven in a hundred fail, so the life of men generally, tried by this standard, is a failure, and bankruptcy may be surely prophesied.

Merely to come into the world the heir of a fortune is not to be born, but to be still-born, rather. To be supported by the charity of friends, or a government pension, — provided you continue to breathe, — by whatever fine synonyms you describe these relations, is to go into the almshouse. On Sundays the poor debtor goes to church to take an account of stock, and finds, of course, that his outgoes have been greater than his income. In the Catholic Church, especially, they go into Chancery, make a clean confession, give up all, and think to start again. Thus men will lie on their backs, talking about the fall of man, and never make an effort to get up.

As for the comparative demand which men make on life, it is an important difference between two, that the one is satisfied with a level success, that his marks can all be hit by point-blank shots, but the other, however low and unsuccessful his life may be, constantly elevates his aim, though at a very slight angle to the horizon. I should much rather be the last man, — though, as the Orientals say, "Greatness doth not approach him who is forever looking down; and all those who are looking high are growing poor."

It is remarkable that there is little or nothing to be

remembered written on the subject of getting a living: how to make getting a living not merely honest and honorable, but altogether inviting and glorious; for if *getting* a living is not so, then living is not. One would think, from looking at literature, that this question had never disturbed a solitary individual's musings. Is it that men are too much disgusted with their experience to speak of it? The lesson of value which money teaches, which the Author of the Universe has taken so much pains to teach us, we are inclined to skip altogether. As for the means of living, it is wonderful how indifferent men of all classes are about it, even reformers, so called, — whether they inherit, or earn, or steal it. I think that society has done nothing for us in this respect, or at least has undone what she has done. Cold and hunger seem more friendly to my nature than those methods which men have adopted and advise to ward them off.

The title *wise* is, for the most part, falsely applied. How can one be a wise man, if he does not know any better how to live than other men? — if he is only more cunning and intellectually subtle? Does Wisdom work in a tread-mill? or does she teach how to succeed *by her example?* Is there any such thing as wisdom not applied to life? Is she merely the miller who grinds the finest logic? It is pertinent to ask if Plato got his *living* in a better way or more successfully than his contemporaries, — or did he succumb to the difficulties of life like other men? Did he seem to prevail over some of them merely by indifference, or by assuming grand airs? or find it easier to live, because his aunt remembered him in her will? The ways in which most men get their living, that is, live, are mere makeshifts, and a shirking of the real business of life, — chiefly because they do not know, but partly because they do not mean, any better.

The rush to California, for instance, and the attitude, not merely of merchants, but of philosophers and prophets, so called, in relation to it, reflect the greatest disgrace on mankind. That so many are ready to live by luck, and so get the means of commanding the labor of others less lucky, without contributing any value to society! And that is called enterprise! I know of no more startling development of the immorality of trade, and all the common modes of getting a living. The philosophy and poetry and religion of such a mankind are not worth the dust of a puff-ball. The hog that gets his living by rooting, stirring up the soil so, would be ashamed of such company. . . .

But why go to California for a text? She is the child of New England, bred at her own school and church. . . .[2]

I hardly know an *intellectual* man, even, who is so broad and truly liberal that you can think aloud in his society. Most with whom you endeavor to talk soon come to a stand against some institution in which they appear to hold stock, — that is, some particular, not universal, way of viewing things. They will continually thrust their own low roof, with its narrow skylight, between you and the sky, when it is the unobstructed heavens you would view. Get out of the way with your cobwebs, wash your windows, I say! In some lyceums they tell me that they have voted to exclude the subject of religion. But how do I know

[2] The omissions are illustrations from Thoreau's own times of some of his points. Leaving them out in no way affects the flow of his ideas. That the next paragraph does not seem related is not due to the omissions, but to a sudden shift in Thoreau's thought.

what their religion is, and when I am near to or far from it? I have walked into such an arena and done my best to make a clean breast of what religion I have experienced, and the audience never suspected what I was about. The lecture was as harmless as moonshine to them. Whereas, if I had read to them the biography of the greatest scamps in history, they might have thought that I had written the lives of the deacons of their church. Ordinarily, the inquiry is, Where did you come from? or, Where are you going? That was a more pertinent question which I overheard one of my auditors put to another once, — "What does he lecture for?" It made me quake in my shoes.

To speak impartially, the best men that I know are not serene, a world in themselves. For the most part, they dwell in forms, and flatter and study effect only more finely than the rest. We select granite for the underpinning of our houses and barns; we build fences of stone; but we do not ourselves rest on an underpinning of granitic truth, the lowest primitive rock. Our sills are rotten. What stuff is the man made of who is not coexistent in our thought with the purest and subtilest truth? I often accuse my finest acquaintances of an immense frivolity; for, while there are manners and compliments we do not meet, we do not teach one another the lessons of honesty and sincerity that the brutes do, or of steadiness and solidity that the rocks do. The fault is commonly mutual, however; for we do not habitually demand any more of each other.

That excitement about Kossuth,[3] consider how char-

[3] Lajos Kossuth (1802-1894), the great Hungarian patriot and orator, exiled after an unsuccessful attempt to free his country from Austrian tyranny. He visited America in 1851, where he was a nine days' wonder.

acteristic, but superficial, it was! — only another kind of politics or dancing. Men were making speeches to him all over the country, but each expressed only the thought, or the want of thought, of the multitude. No man stood on truth. They were merely banded together, as usual, one leaning on another, and altogether on nothing; as the Hindoos made the world rest on an elephant, the elephant on a tortoise, and the tortoise on a serpent, and had nothing to put under the serpent. For all fruit of that stir we have the Kossuth hat.

Just so hollow and ineffectual, for the most part, is our ordinary conversation. Surface meets surface. When our life ceases to be inward and private, conversation degenerates into mere gossip. We rarely meet a man who can tell us any news which he has not read in a newspaper, or been told by his neighbor; and, for the most part, the only difference between us and our fellow is that he has seen the newspaper, or been out to tea, and we have not. In proportion as our inward life fails, we go more constantly and desperately to the post-office. You may depend on it, that the poor fellow who walks away with the greatest number of letters, proud of his extensive correspondence, has not heard from himself this long while.

I do not know but it is too much to read one newspaper a week. I have tried it recently, and for so long it seems to me that I have not dwelt in my native region. The sun, the clouds, the snow, the trees say not so much to me. You cannot serve two masters. It requires more than a day's devotion to know and to possess the wealth of a day.

We may be well ashamed to tell what things we have read or heard in our day. I do not know why my news should be so trivial, — considering what one's dreams and expectations are, why the developments should be so paltry. The news we hear, for the most part, is not news to our genius. It is the stalest repetition. You are often tempted to ask why such stress is laid on a particular experience which you have had, — that, after twenty-five years, you should meet Hobbins, Registrar of Deeds, again on the sidewalk. Have you not budged an inch, then? Such is the daily news. Its facts appear to float in the atmosphere, insignificant as the sporules of fungi, and impinge on some neglected *thallus,* or surface of our minds, which affords a basis for them, and hence a parasitic growth. We should wash ourselves clean of such news. Of what consequence, though our planet explode, if there is no character involved in the explosion? In health we have not the least curiosity about such events. We do not live for idle amusement. I would not run round a corner to see the world blow up.

All summer, and far into the autumn, perchance, you unconsciously went by the newspapers and the news, and now you find it was because the morning and the evening were full of news to you. Your walks were full of incidents. You attended, not to the affairs of Europe, but to your own affairs in Massachusetts fields. If you chance to live and move and have your being in that thin stratum in which the events that make the news transpire, — thinner than the paper on which it is printed, — then these things will fill the world for you; but if you soar above or dive below that plane, you cannot remember nor be reminded of them. Really to see the sun rise or go down every day, so to relate ourselves to a universal fact, would preserve us sane forever. Nations! What are nations? Tartars, and Huns, and Chinamen! Like insects, they swarm. The historian strives in vain to make them memorable. It is for want of a man that there are so many men. It is individuals that populate the world. Any man thinking may say with the Spirit of Lodin, —

> I look down from my height on nations,
> And they become ashes before me; —
> Calm is my dwelling in the clouds;
> Pleasant are the great fields of my rest.

Pray, let us live without being drawn by dogs, Esquimaux-fashion, tearing over hill and dale, and biting each other's ears.

Not without a slight shudder at the danger, I often perceive how near I had come to admitting into my mind the details of some trivial affair, — the news of the street; and I am astonished to observe how willing men are to lumber their minds with such rubbish, — to permit idle rumors and incidents of the most insignificant kind to intrude on ground which should be sacred to thought. Shall the mind be a public arena, where the affairs of the street and the gossip of the tea-table chiefly are discussed? Or shall it be a quarter of heaven itself, — an hypaethral temple, consecrated to the service of the gods? I find it so difficult to dispose of the few facts which to me are significant, that I hesitate to burden my attention with those which are insignificant, which only a divine mind could illustrate. Such is, for the most part, the news in newspapers and conversation. It is important to preserve the mind's chastity in this respect. Think of admitting the details of a single case of the criminal court into our thoughts, to stalk profanely through their very *sanctum sanctorum* for an hour, ay, for many hours! to make a very bar-room of the mind's inmost apartment, as if for so long the dust of the street had occupied us, — the very street itself, with all its travel, its bustle, and filth had passed through our thoughts' shrine! Would it not be an intellectual and moral suicide? When I have been compelled to sit spectator and auditor in a court-room for some hours, and have seen my neighbors, who were not compelled, stealing in from time to time, and tiptoeing about with washed hands and faces, it has appeared to my mind's eye, that, when they took off their hats, their ears suddenly expanded into vast hoppers for sound, between which even their narrow heads were crowded. Like the vanes of windmills, they caught the broad, but shallow stream of sound, which, after a few titillating gyrations in their coggy brains, passed out the other side. I wondered if, when they got home, they were as careful to wash their ears as before their hands and faces. It has seemed to me, at such a time, that the auditors and the witnesses, the jury and the counsel, the judge and the criminal at the bar, — if I may presume him guilty before he is convicted, — were all equally criminal, and a thunderbolt might be expected to descend and consume them all together.

By all kinds of traps and sign-boards, threatening the extreme penalty of the divine law, exclude such trespassers from the only ground which can be sacred to you. It is so hard to forget what it is worse than useless to remember! If I am to be a thoroughfare, I prefer that it be of the mountain-brooks, the Parnassian streams, and not the town-sewers. There is inspiration, that gossip which comes to the ear of the attentive mind from the courts of heaven. There is the profane and stale revelation of the bar-room and the police court. The same ear is fitted to receive both communications. Only the character of the hearer determines to which it shall be open, and to which closed. I believe that the mind can be permanently profaned by the habit of attending to trivial things, so that all our thoughts shall be tinged with triviality. Our very intellect shall be macadamized, as it were, — its foundation broken into fragments for the wheels of travel to roll over; and if you would know what will make the most durable pavement, surpassing rolled stones, spruce blocks, and asphaltum, you have only to look into some of our minds which have been subjected to this treatment so long.

If we have thus desecrated ourselves, — as who has not? — the remedy will be by wariness and devotion to reconsecrate ourselves, and make once more a fane of the mind. We should treat our minds, that is, ourselves, as innocent and ingenuous children, whose guardians we are, and be careful what objects and what subjects we thrust on their attention. Read not the Times. Read the Eternities. Conventionalities are at length as bad as impurities. Even the facts of science may dust the mind by their dryness, unless they are in a sense effaced each morning, or rather rendered fertile by the dews of fresh and living truth. Knowledge does not come to us by details, but in flashes of light from heaven. Yes, every thought that passes through the mind helps to wear and tear it, and to deepen the ruts, which, as in the streets of Pompeii, evince how much it has been used. How many things there are concerning which we might well deliberate whether we had better know them, — had better let their peddling-carts be driven, even at the slowest trot or walk, over that bridge of glorious span by which we trust to pass at last from the farthest brink of time to the nearest shore of eternity! Have we no culture, no refinement, — but skill only to live coarsely and serve the Devil? — to acquire a little worldly wealth, or fame, or liberty, and make a false show with it, as if we were all husk and shell, with no tender and living kernel to us? Shall our institutions be like those chestnut-burs which contain abortive nuts, perfect only to prick the fingers. . . .[4]

In short, as a snow-drift is formed where there is a lull in the wind, so, one would say, where there is a lull of truth, an institution springs up. But the truth blows right on over it, nevertheless, and at length blows it down.

What is called politics is comparatively something so superficial and inhuman that, practically, I have never fairly recognized that it concerns me at all. The newspapers, I perceive, devote some of their columns specially to politics or government without charge; and this, one would say, is all that saves it; but, as I love literature, and, to some extent, the truth also, I never read those columns at any rate. I do not wish to blunt my sense of right so much. I have not got to answer for having read a single President's Message. A strange age of the world this when empires, kingdoms, and republics come a-begging to a private man's door, and utter their complaints at his elbow! I cannot take up a newspaper but I find that some wretched government or other, hard pushed and on its last legs, is interceding with me, the reader, to vote for it, — more importunate than an Italian beggar; and if I have a mind to look at its certificate, made, perchance, by some benevolent merchant's clerk, or the skipper

---

[4] A passage, dealing largely with the slavery issue, is omitted here for the sake of brevity.

that brought it over, for it cannot speak a word of English itself, I shall probably read of the eruption of some Vesuvius, or the overflowing of some Po, true or forged, which brought it into this condition. I do not hestitate, in such a case, to suggest work, or the almshouse; or why not keep its castle in silence, as I do commonly? The poor President, what with preserving his popularity and doing his duty, is completely bewildered. The newspapers are the ruling power. Any other government is reduced to a few marines at Fort Independence. If a man neglects to read the Daily Times, Government will go down on its knees to him, for this is the only treason in these days.

Those things which now most engage the attention of men, as politics and the daily routine, are, it is true, vital functions of human society, but should be unconsciously performed, like the corresponding functions of the physical body. They are *infra*-human, a kind of vegetation. I sometimes awake to a half-consciousness of them going on about me, as a man may become conscious of some of the processes of digestion in a morbid state, and so have the dyspepsia, as it is called. It is as if a thinker submitted himself to be rasped by the great gizzard of creation. Politics is, as it were, the gizzard of society, full of grit and gravel, and the two political parties are its two opposite halves, — sometimes split into quarters, it may be, which grind on each other. Not only individuals, but States, have thus a confirmed dyspepsia, which expresses itself, you can imagine by what sort of eloquence. Thus our life is not altogether a forgetting, but also, alas! to a great extent, a remembering of that which we should never have been conscious of, certainly not in our waking hours. Why should we not meet, not always as dyspeptics, to tell our bad dreams, but sometimes as *eu*-peptics, to congratulate each other on the ever glorious morning? I do not make an exorbitant demand, surely.

THE CROWN OF WILD OLIVE[1]

Introduction

JOHN RUSKIN (1819–1900)

TWENTY years ago, there was no lovelier piece of lowland scenery in South England, nor any more pathetic, in the world, by its expression of sweet human character and life, than that immediately bordering on the sources of the Wandel, and including the lower moors of Addington, and the villages of Beddington and Carshalton, with all their pools and streams. No clearer or diviner waters ever sang with constant lips of the hand which "giveth rain from heaven"; no pastures ever lightened in springtime with more passionate blossoming; no sweeter homes ever hallowed the heart of the passer-by with their pride of peaceful gladness, — fain-hidden — yet full-confessed. The place remains nearly unchanged in its larger features; but with deliberate mind I say, that I have never seen anything so ghastly in its inner tragic meaning, — not in Pisan Maremma, — not by Campagna tomb, — not by the sand-isles of the Torcellan shores, — as the slow stealing of aspects of reckless, indolent, animal neglect. over the delicate sweetness of that English scene: nor is any blasphemy or impiety, and frantic saying, or god-

---

[1] published as a preface to *Three Lectures on Work, Traffic and War*, 1866

less thought, more appalling to me, using the best power of judgment I have to discern its sense and scope, than the insolent defiling of those springs by the human herds that drink of them. Just where the welling of stainless water, trembling and pure, like a body of light, enters the pool at Carshalton, cutting itself a radiant channel down to the gravel, through warp of feathery weeds, all waving, which it traverses with its deep threads of clearness, like the chalcedony in moss-agate, starred here and there with white grenouillette; just in the very rush and murmur of the first spreading currents, the human wretches of the place cast their street and house foulness; heaps of dust and slime, and broken shreds of old metal, and rags of putrid clothes; which having neither energy to cart away, nor decency enough to dig into the ground, they thus shed into the stream, to diffuse what venom of it will float and melt, far away, in all places where God meant those waters to bring joy and health. And, in a little pool behind some houses farther in the village, where another spring rises, the shattered stones of the well, and of the little fretted channel which was long ago built and traced for it by gentler hands, lie scattered, each from each, under a ragged bank of mortar, and scoria, and bricklayer's refuse, on one side, which the clean water nevertheless chastises to purity; but it cannot conquer the dead earth beyond: and there, circled and coiled under festering scum, the stagnant edge of the pool effaces itself into a slope of black slime, the accumulation of indolent years. Half-a-dozen men, with one day's work, could cleanse those pools, and trim the flowers about their banks, and make every breath of summer air above them rich with cool balm; and every glittering wave medicinal, as if it ran, troubled of angels, from the porch of Bethesda.[2] But that day's work is never given, nor will be; nor will any joy be possible to heart of man, for evermore, about those wells of English waters.

When I last left them, I walked up slowly through the back streets of Croydon, from the old church to the hospital; and, just on the left, before coming up to the crossing of the High Street, there was a new public-house built. And the front of it was built in so wise manner, that a recess of two feet was left below its front windows, between them and the street-pavement; a recess too narrow for any possible use, (for even if it had been occupied by a seat, as in old time it might have been, everybody walking along the street would have fallen over the legs of the reposing wayfarers). But, by way of making this two feet depth of freehold land more expressive of the dignity of an establishment for the sale of spirituous liquors, it was fenced from the pavement by an imposing iron railing, having four or five spearheads to the yard of it, and six feet high; containing as much iron and ironwork, indeed, as could well be put into the space; and by this stately arrangement, the little piece of dead ground within, between wall and street, became a protective receptacle of refuse; cigar ends, and oyster shells, and the like, such as an open-handed English street-populace habitually scatters; and was thus left, unsweepable by any ordinary methods. Now the iron bars which, uselessly (or in great degree worse than uselessly) enclosed this bit of ground, and made it pestilent, represented a quantity of work which would have cleansed the Carshalton pools three times over: of work, partly cramped and deadly in the mine; partly

[2] John v. 2.

fierce and exhaustive, at the furnace: partly foolish and sedentary, of ill-taught students making bad designs: work from the beginning to the last fruits of it, and in all the branches of it, venomous, deathful, and miserable.

Now, how did it come to pass that this work was done instead of the other; that the strength and life of the English operative were spent in defiling ground, instead of redeeming it, and in producing an entirely (in that place) valueless, piece of metal, which can neither be eaten nor breathed, instead of medicinal fresh air and pure water?

There is but one reason for it, and at present a conclusive one,—that the capitalist can charge percentage on the work in the one case, and cannot in the other. If, having certain funds for supporting labour at my disposal, I pay men merely to keep my ground in order, my money is, in that function, spent once for all; but if I pay them to dig iron out of my ground, and work it, and sell it, I can charge rent for the ground, and percentage both on the manufacture and the sale, and make my capital profitable in these three by-ways. The greater part of the profitable investment of capital, in the present day, is in operations of this kind, in which the public is persuaded to buy something of no use to it, on production or sale of which the capitalist may charge percentage; the said public remaining all the while under the persuasion that the percentages thus obtained are real national gains, whereas, they are merely filchings out of light pockets, to swell heavy ones.

Thus, the Croydon publican buys the iron railing, to make himself more conspicuous to drunkards. The public-house keeper on the other side of the way presently buys another railing, to out-rail him with. Both are, as to their *relative* attractiveness, just where they were before; but they have both lost the price of the railings; which they must either themselves finally lose, or make their aforesaid customers, the amateurs of railings, pay, by raising the price of their beer, or adulterating it. Either the publicans, or their customers, are thus poorer by *precisely what the capitalist has gained;* and the value of the industry itself, meantime, has been lost to the nation; the iron bars, in that form and place, being wholly useless.

It is this mode of taxation of the poor by the rich which is referred to in the text, in comparing the modern acquisitive power of capital with that of the lance and sword; the only difference being that the levy of black mail in the old times was by force, and is now by cozening. The older rider and reiver frankly quartered himself on the publican for the night;— the modern one merely makes his lance into an iron spike, and persuades his host to buy it. One comes as an open robber, the other as a cheating peddler; but the result, to the injured person's pocket, is absolutely the same. Of course many useful industries mingle with, and disguise the useless ones; and in the habits of energy aroused by the struggle, there is a certain direct good. It is better to spend four thousand pounds in making a gun, and then blow it to pieces, than to pass life in idleness. Only do not let the proceeding be called "political economy."

There is also a confused notion in the minds of many persons, that the gathering of the property of the poor into the hands of the rich does no ultimate harm; since, in whosoever hands it may be, it must be spent at last, and thus, they think, return to the poor again. This fallacy has been again and again exposed; but granting the plea true, the same apology may, of course, be made for black mail, or any other form of robbery. It might be (though practically it never is) as advantageous for the nation that the robber should have the spending of the money he extorts, as that the person robbed should have spent it. But this is no excuse for the theft. If I were to put a turnpike on the road where it passes my own gate, and endeavour to exact a shilling from every passenger, the public would soon do away with my gate, without listening to any plea on my part that "it was as advantageous to them, in the end, that I should spend their shillings, as that they themselves should." But if, instead of outfacing them with a turnpike, I can only persuade them to come in and buy stones, or old iron, or any such useless thing, out of my ground, I may rob them to the same extent, and be, moreover, thanked as a public benefactor, and promoter of commercial prosperity. And this main question for the poor of England — for the poor of all countries — is wholly omitted in every common treatise on the subject of wealth. Even by the labourers themselves, the operation of capital is regarded only in its effect on their immediate interests; never in the far more terrific power of its appointment of the kind and the object of labour. It matters little, ultimately, how much a labourer is paid for making anything; but it matters fearfully what the thing is, which he is compelled to make. If his labour is so ordered as to produce food, and fresh air, and fresh water, no matter that his wages are low; — the food and fresh air and water will be at last there; and he will at last get them. But if he is paid to *destroy* food and fresh air, or to produce iron bars instead of them, — the food and air will finally *not* be there, and he will *not* get them, to his great and final inconvenience.

I have been long accustomed, as all men engaged in work of investigation must be, to hear my statements laughed at for years, before they are examined or believed; and I am generally content to wait the public's time. But it has not been without displeased surprise that I have found myself totally unable, as yet, by any repetition, or illustration, to force this plain thought into my readers' heads, — that the wealth of nations, as of men, consists in substance, not in ciphers; and that the real good of all work, and of all commerce, depends on the final intrinsic worth of the thing you make or get by it. This is a "practical" enough statement, one would think: but the English public has been so possessed by its modern school of economists with the notion that Business is always good, whether it be busy in mischief or in benefit; and that buying and selling are always salutary, whatever the intrinsic worth of what you buy or sell, that it seems impossible to gain so much as a patient hearing for any inquiry respecting the substantial result of our eager modern labour.

I have never felt more checked by the sense of this impossibility than in arranging the heads of the following lectures, which, though delivered at considerable intervals of time, and in different places, were not prepared without reference to each other. Their connection would, however, have been made far more distinct if I had not been prevented, by what I feel to be another great difficulty in addressing English audiences, from enforcing, with any decision, the common, and to me the most important, part of their subjects. I chiefly desired to question my hearers — operatives, merchants, and soldiers — as to the ultimate meaning of the *business* they had in hand; and to know from them what they expected or intended their manufacture to come to, their selling to come to, and their killing to come to. That appeared the first point needing determination before I could speak to them with any real utility or effect. "You craftsmen — salesmen — swordsmen, — do but tell me clearly what you want; then, if I can say anything to help you, I will; and if not, I will account to you as I best may for my inability."

But in order to put this question into any terms, one has first of all to face a difficulty — to me for the present insuperable, — the difficulty of knowing whether to address one's audience as believing, or not believing, in any other world than this. For if you address any average modern English company as believing in an Eternal life; and then endeavour to draw any conclusions from this assumed belief, as to their present business, they will forthwith tell you that "what you say is very beautiful, but it is not practical." If, on the contrary, you frankly address them as *un*believers in Eternal life, and try to draw any consequences from that unbelief, — they immediately hold you for an accursed person, and shake off the dust from their feet at you.

And the more I thought over what I had got to say, the less I found I could say it, without some reference to this intangible or intractable question. It made all the difference, in asserting any principle of war, whether one assumed that a discharge of artillery would merely knead down a certain quantity of once living clay into a level line, as in a brickfield; or whether, out of every separately Christian-named portion of the ruinous heap, there went out, into the smoke and dead-fallen air of battle, some astonished condition of soul, unwillingly released. It made all the difference, in speaking of the possible range of commerce, whether one assumed that all bargains related only to visible property — or whether property, for the present invisible, but nevertheless real, was elsewhere purchasable on other terms. It made all the difference, in addressing a body of men subject to considerable hardship and having to find some way out of it — whether one could confidently say to them, "My friends, — you have only to die, and all will be right"; or whether one had any secret misgiving that such advice was more blessed to him that gave than to him that took it.

And therefore the deliberate reader will find, throughout these lectures, a hesitation in driving points home, and a pausing short of conclusions which he will feel I would fain have come to; — hesitation which arises wholly from this uncertainty of my hearers' temper. For I do not speak, nor have I ever spoken, since the time of first forward youth, in any proselytizing temper, as desiring to persuade any one to believe anything; but whomsoever I venture to address, I take for the time, his creed as I find it; and endeavour to push it into such vital fruit as it seems capable of. Thus, it is a creed with a great part of the existing English people, that they are in possession of a book which tells them, straight from the lips of God, all they ought to do, and need to know. I have read that book, with as much care as most of them, for some forty years; and am thankful that, on those who trust it, I can press its pleadings. My endeavour has been uniformly to make them trust it more deeply than they do; trust it, not in their own favourite verses only, but in the sum of all; trust it, not as a fetish or talisman, which they are to be saved by daily repetitions of; but as a Captain's order, to be heard and obeyed at their peril. I was always encouraged by supposing my hearers to hold such belief. To these, if to any, I once had hope of addressing, with acceptance, words which insisted on the guilt of pride, and the futility of avarice; from these, if from any, I once expected ratification of a political economy, which asserted that the life was more than the meat, and the body than raiment; and these, it once seemed to me, I might ask, without being accused of fanaticism, not merely in doctrine of the lips, but in the bestowal of their heart's treasure, to separate themselves from the crowd of whom it is written, "After all these things do the Gentiles seek."

It cannot, however, be assumed, with any semblance of reason, that a general audience is now wholly, or even in majority, composed of these religious persons. A large portion must always consist of men who admit no such creed; or who, at least, are inaccessible to appeals founded on it. And as, with the so-called Christian, I desired to plead for honest declaration and fulfilment of his belief in life, — with the so-called Infidel, I desired to plead for an honest declaration and fulfilment of his belief in death. The dilemma is inevitable. Men must either hereafter live, or hereafter die; fate may be bravely met, and conduct wisely ordered, on either expectation; but never in hesitation between ungrasped hope and unconfronted fear. We usually believe in immortality, so far as to avoid preparation for death; and in mortality, so far as to avoid preparation for anything after death. Whereas, a wise man will at least hold himself ready for one or other of two events, of which one or other is inevitable;

and will have all things ended in order, for his sleep, or left in order, for his awakening.

Nor have we any right to call it an ignoble judgment, if he determine to end them in order, as for sleep. A brave belief in life is indeed an enviable state of mind, but as far as I can discern, an unusual one. I know few Christians so convinced of the splendour of the rooms in their Father's house, as to be happier when their friends are called to those mansions, than they would have been if the Queen had sent for them to live at Court: nor has the Church's most ardent "desire to depart, and be with Christ," ever cured it of the singular habit of putting on mourning for every person summoned to such departure. On the contrary, a brave belief in death has been assuredly held by many not ignoble persons; and it is a sign of the last depravity in the Church itself, when it assumes that such a belief is inconsistent with either purity of character, or energy of hand. The shortness of life is not, to any rational person, a conclusive reason for wasting the space of it which may be granted him; nor does the anticipation of death, to-morrow, suggest, to any one but a drunkard, the expediency of drunkenness to-day. To teach that there is no device in the grave,[3] may indeed make the deviceless person more contented in his dulness: but it will make the deviser only more earnest in devising: nor is human conduct likely, in every case, to be purer, under the conviction that all its evil may in a moment be pardoned, and all its wrongdoing in a moment redeemed; and that the sigh of repentance, which purges the guilt of the past, will waft the soul into a felicity which forgets its pain, — that it may be under the sterner, and to many not unwise

[3] Ecclesiastes ix. 10.

minds, more probable, apprehension, that "what a man soweth that shall he also reap" — or others reap, — when he, the living seed of pestilence, walketh no more in darkness, but lies down therein.

But to men for whom feebleness of sight, or bitterness of soul, or the offence given by the conduct of those who claim higher hope, may have rendered this painful creed the only possible one, there is an appeal to be made, more secure than any which can be addressed to happier persons. Might not a preacher, in comfortless, but faithful, zeal — from the poor height of a grave-hillock for his Hill of Mars,[4] and with the Cave of the Eumenides at his side — say to them thus: Hear me, you dying men, who will soon be deaf for ever. For these others, at your right hand and your left, who look forward to a state of infinite existence, in which all their errors will be overruled, and all their faults forgiven; — for these, who, stained and blackened in the battle smoke of mortality, have but to dip themselves for an instant in the font of death, and to rise renewed of plumage, as a dove that is covered with silver, and her feathers like gold: — for these, indeed, it may be permissible to waste their numbered moments, through faith in a future of innumerable hours; to these, in their weakness it may be conceded that they should tamper with sin which can only bring forth fruit of righteousness, and profit by the iniquity which, one day, will be remembered no more. In them, it may be no sign of hardness of heart to neglect the poor, over whom they know their Master is watching; and to leave those to perish temporarily, who cannot perish eternally. But, for *you* there is no such hope,

[4] Acts xvii. 22. The Eumenides were the spirits of vengeance in Greek mythology.

and therefore no such excuse. This fate, which you ordain for the wretched, you believe to be all their inheritance; you may crush them, before the moth, and they will never rise to rebuke you; — their breath, which fails for lack of food, once expiring, will never be recalled to whisper against you a word of accusing; — they and you, as you think, shall lie down together in the dust, and the worms cover you; and for them there shall be no consolation, and on you no vengeance, — only the question murmured above your grave: "Who shall repay him what he hath done?" Is it therefore easier for you, in your heart, to inflict the sorrow for which there is no remedy? Will you take, wantonly, this little all of his life from your poor brother, and make his brief hours long to him with pain? Will you be more prompt to the injustice which can never be redressed; and more niggardly of the mercy which you can bestow but once, and which, refusing, you refuse for ever?

I think better of you, even of the most selfish, than that you would act thus, well understanding your act. And for yourselves, it seems to me, the question becomes not less grave when brought into these curt limits. If your life were but a fever fit, — the madness of a night, whose follies were all to be forgotten in the dawn, it might matter little how you fretted away the sickly hours, — what toys you snatched at or let fall, — what visions you followed, wistfully, with the deceived eyes of sleepless phrenzy. Is the earth only an hospital? are health and heaven to come? *Then* play, if you care to play, on the floor of the hospital dens. Knit its straw into what crowns please you; gather the dust of it for treasure, and die rich in that, though clutching at the black motes in the air with your dying hands; — and yet, it may be well with you. But if this life be *no* dream, and the world no hospital, but your palace-inheritance; — if all the peace and power and joy you can ever win, must be won now, and all fruit of victory gathered here, or never; — will you still, throughout the puny totality of your life, weary yourselves in the fire for vanity? If there is no rest which remaineth for you, is there none you might presently take? was this grass of the earth made green for your shroud only, not for your bed? and can you never lie down *upon* it, but only *under* it? The heathen, in their saddest hours, thought not so. They knew that life brought its contest, but they expected from it also the crown of all contest: No proud one! no jewelled circlet flaming through Heaven above the height of the unmerited throne; only some few leaves of wild olive, cool to the tired brow, through a few years of peace. It should have been of gold, they thought; but Jupiter was poor; this was the best the god could give them. Seeking a better than this, they had known it a mockery. Not in war, not in wealth, not in tyranny, was there any happiness to be found for them — only in kindly peace, fruitful and free. The wreath was to be of *wild* olive, mark you: — the tree that grows carelessly, tufting the rocks with no vivid bloom, no verdure of branch; only with soft snow of blossom, and scarcely fulfilled fruit, mixed with grey leaf and thorn-set stem; no fastening of diadem for you but with such sharp embroidery! But this, such as it is, you may win, while yet you live; type of grey honour, and sweet rest. Freeheartedness, and graciousness, and undisturbed trust, and requited love, and the sight of the peace of others, and the ministry to their pain; these, — and the blue sky above you, and the sweet waters and flowers of the earth beneath; and mysteries and presences, innumerable, of living things; — may yet be here your riches; untormenting and divine: serviceable for the life that now is; nor, it may be, without promise of that which is to come.

SWEETNESS AND LIGHT[1]

MATTHEW ARNOLD (1822–1888)

THE disparagers of culture make its motive curiosity; sometimes, indeed, they make its motive mere exclusiveness and vanity. The culture which is supposed to plume itself on a smattering of Greek and Latin is a culture which is begotten by nothing so intellectual as curiosity; it is valued either out of sheer vanity and ignorance or else as an engine of social and class distinction, separating its holder, like a badge or title, from other people who have not got it. No serious man would call this *culture,* or attach any value to it, as culture, at all. To find the real ground for the very different estimate which serious people will set upon culture, we must find some motive for culture in the terms of which may lie a real ambiguity; and such a motive the word *curiosity* gives us.

I have before now pointed out that we English do not, like the foreigners, use this word in a good sense as well as in a bad sense. With us the word is always used in a somewhat disapproving sense. A liberal and intelligent eagerness about the things of the mind may be meant by a foreigner when he speaks of curiosity, but with us the word always conveys a certain notion of frivolous and unedifying activity. In the *Quarterly*

[1] From *Culture and Anarchy.*

Review, some little time ago, was an estimate of the celebrated French critic, M. Sainte-Beuve, and a very inadequate estimate it in my judgment was. And its inadequacy consisted chiefly in this: that in our English way it left out of sight the double sense really involved in the word *curiosity*, thinking enough was said to stamp M. Sainte-Beuve with blame if it was said that he was impelled in his operations as a critic by curiosity, and omitting either to perceive that M. Sainte-Beuve himself, and many other people with him, would consider that this was praiseworthy and not blameworthy, or to point out why it ought really to be accounted worthy of blame and not of praise. For as there is a curiosity about intellectual matters which is futile, and merely a disease, so there is certainly a curiosity, — a desire after the things of the mind simply for their own sakes and for the pleasure of seeing them as they are, — which is, in an intelligent being, natural and laudable. Nay, and the very desire to see things as they are implies a balance and regulation of mind which is not often attained without fruitful effort, and which is the very opposite of the blind and diseased impulse of mind which is what we mean to blame when we blame curiosity. Montesquieu says: "The first motive which ought to impel us to study is the desire to augment the excellence of our nature, and to render an intelligent being yet more intelligent." This is the true ground to assign for the genuine scientific passion, however manifested, and for culture, viewed simply as a fruit of this passion; and it is a worthy ground, even though we let the term *curiosity* stand to describe it.

But there is of culture another view, in which not solely the scientific passion, the sheer desire to see things as they are, natural and proper in an intelligent being, appears as the ground of it. There is a view in which all the love of our neighbour, the impulses towards action, help, and beneficence, the desire for removing human error, clearing human confusion, and diminishing human misery, the noble aspiration to leave the world better and happier than we found it, — motives eminently such as are called social, — come in as part of the grounds of culture, and the main and pre-eminent part. Culture is then properly described not as having its origin in curiosity, but as having its origin in the love of perfection; it is *a study of perfection.* It moves by the force, not merely or primarily of the scientific passion for pure knowledge, but also of the moral and social passion for doing good. As, in the first view of it, we took for its worthy motto Montesquieu's words: "To render an intelligent being yet more intelligent!" so, in the second view of it, there is no better motto which it can have than these words of Bishop Wilson: "To make reason and the will of God prevail!"

Only, whereas the passion for doing good is apt to be overhasty in determining what reason and the will of God say, because its turn is for acting rather than thinking and it wants to be beginning to act; and whereas it is apt to take its own conceptions, which proceed from its own state of development and share in all the imperfections and immaturities of this, for a basis of action; what distinguishes culture is, that it is possessed by the scientific passion as well as by the passion of doing good; that it demands worthy notions of reason and the will of God, and does not readily suffer its own crude conceptions to substitute themselves for them. And knowing that no action or institution can be salutary and stable which is not based on reason and the will of God, it is not so bent on acting and instituting, even with the great aim of diminishing human error and misery ever before its thoughts, but that it can remember that acting and instituting are of little use, unless we know how and what we ought to act and to institute.

This culture is more interesting and more far-reaching than that other, which is founded solely on the scientific passion for knowing. But it needs times of faith and ardour, times when the intellectual horizon is opening and widening all round us, to flourish in. And is not the close and bounded intellectual horizon within which we have long lived and moved now lifting up, and are not new lights finding free passage to shine in upon us? For a long time there was no passage for them to make their way in upon us, and then it was of no use to think of adapting the world's action to them. Where was the hope of making reason and the will of God prevail among people who had a routine which they had christened reason and the will of God, in which they were inextricably bound, and beyond which they had no power of looking? But now the iron force of adhesion to the old routine, — social, political, religious, — has wonderfully yielded; the iron force of exclusion of all which is new has wonderfully yielded. The danger now is, not that people should obstinately refuse to allow anything but their old routine to pass for reason and the will of God, but either that they should allow some novelty or other to pass for these too easily, or else that they should underrate the importance of them altogether, and think it enough to follow action for its own sake, without troubling themselves to make reason and the will of

God prevail therein. Now, then, is the moment for culture to be of service, culture which believes in making reason and the will of God prevail, believes in perfection, and is the study and pursuit of perfection, and is no longer debarred, by rigid invincible exclusion of whatever is new, from getting acceptance for its ideas, simply because they are new.

The moment this view of culture is seized, the moment it is regarded not solely as the endeavour to see things as they are, to draw towards a knowledge of the universal order which seems to be intended and aimed at in the world, and which it is a man's happiness to go along with or his misery to go counter to, — to learn, in short, the will of God, — the moment, I say, culture is considered not merely as the endeavour to *see* and *learn* this, but as the endeavour, also, to make it *prevail*, the moral, social, and beneficent character of culture becomes manifest. The mere endeavour to see and learn the truth for our own personal satisfaction is indeed a commencement for making it prevail, a preparing the way for this, which always serves this, and is wrongly, therefore, stamped with blame absolutely in itself and not only in its caricature and degeneration. But perhaps it has got stamped with blame, and disparaged with the dubious title of curiosity, because in comparison with this wider endeavour of such great and plain utility it looks selfish, petty, and unprofitable.

And religion, the greatest and most important of the efforts by which the human race has manifested its impulse to perfect itself, — religion, that voice of the deepest human experience, — does not only enjoin and sanction the aim which is the great aim of culture, the aim of setting ourselves to ascertain what perfection is and to make it prevail; but also, in determining generally in what human perfection consists, religion comes to a conclusion identical with that which culture, — culture seeking the determination of this question through *all* the voices of human experience which have been heard upon it, of art, science, poetry, philosophy, history, as well as of religion, in order to give a greater fulness and certainty to its solution, — likewise reaches. Religion says: *The kingdom of God is within you;* and culture, in like manner, places human perfection in an *internal* condition, in the growth and predominance of our humanity proper, as distinguished from our animality. It places it in the ever-increasing efficacy and in the general harmonious expansion of those gifts of thought and feeling, which make the peculiar dignity, wealth, and happiness of human nature. As I have said on a former occasion: "It is in making endless additions to itself, in the endless expansion of its powers, in endless growth in wisdom and beauty, that the spirit of the human race finds its ideal. To reach this ideal, culture is an indispensable aid, and that is the true value of culture." Not a having and a resting, but a growing and a becoming, is the character of perfection as culture conceives it; and here, too, it coincides with religion.

And because men are all members of one great whole, and the sympathy which is in human nature will not allow one member to be indifferent to the rest or to have a perfect welfare independent of the rest, the expansion of our humanity, to suit the idea of perfection which culture forms, must be a *general* expansion. Perfection, as culture conceives it, is not possible while the individual remains isolated. The individual is required, under pain of being stunted and enfeebled in his own development if he disobeys, to carry others along with him in his march towards perfection, to be continually doing all he can to enlarge and increase the volume of the human stream sweeping thitherward. And here, once more, culture lays on us the same obligation as religion which says, as Bishop Wilson has admirably put it, that "to promote the kingdom of God is to increase and hasten one's own happiness."

But, finally, perfection, — as culture from a thorough disinterested study of human nature and human experience learns to conceive it, — is a harmonious expansion of *all* the powers which make the beauty and worth of human nature, and is not consistent with the over-development of any one power at the expense of the rest. Here culture goes beyond religion, as religion is generally conceived by us.

If culture, then, is a study of perfection, and of harmonious perfection, general perfection, and perfection which consists in becoming something rather than in having something, in an inward condition of the mind and spirit, not in an outward set of circumstances, — it is clear that culture, instead of being the frivolous and useless thing which Mr. Bright, and Mr. Frederic Harrison, and many other Liberals are apt to call it, has a very important function to fulfil for mankind. And this function is particularly important in our modern world, of which the whole civilisation is, to a much greater degree than the civilisation of Greece and Rome, mechanical and external, and tends constantly to become more so. But above all in our own country has culture a weighty part to perform, because here that mechanical character, which civilisation tends to take everywhere, is shown in the most eminent degree. Indeed nearly all the characters of perfection, as culture teaches us to fix them, meet in this country with some powerful tendency which thwarts them and sets them at defiance. The idea of perfection as an *inward* condition of the mind and spirit is at variance with the mechanical and material civilisation in esteem with us, and nowhere, as I have said, so much in esteem as with us. The idea of perfection as a *general* expansion of the human family is at variance with our strong individualism, our hatred of all limits to the unrestrained swing of the individual's personality, our maxim of "every man for himself." Above all, the idea of perfection as a *harmonious* expansion of human nature is at variance with our want of flexibility, with our inaptitude for seeing more than one side of a thing, with our intense energetic absorption in the particular pursuit we happen to be following. So culture has a rough task to achieve in this country. Its preachers have, and are likely long to have, a hard time of it, and they will much oftener be regarded, for a great while to come, as elegant or spurious Jeremiahs than as friends and benefactors. That, however, will not prevent their doing in the end good service if they persevere. And, meanwhile, the mode of action they have to pursue, and the sort of habits they must fight against, ought to be made quite clear for every one to see, who may be willing to look at the matter attentively and dispassionately.

Faith in machinery, is, I said, our besetting danger; often in machinery most absurdly disproportioned to the end which this machinery, if it is to do any good at all, is to serve; but always in machinery, as if it had a value in and for itself. What is freedom but machinery? what is population but machinery? what is coal but machinery? what are railroads but machinery? what is wealth but machinery? what are, even, religious organisations but machinery? Now almost every voice in England is accustomed to speak of these things as if they were precious ends in themselves, and therefore had some of the characters of perfection indisputably joined to them. I have before now noticed Mr. Roebuck's stock argument for proving the greatness and happiness of England as she is, and for quite stopping the mouths of all gain-sayers. Mr. Roebuck is never weary of reiterating this argument of his, so I do not know why I should be weary of noticing it. "May not every man in England say what he likes?" — Mr. Roebuck perpetually asks; and that, he thinks, is quite sufficient, and when every man may say what he likes, our aspirations ought to be satisfied. But the aspirations of culture, which is the study of perfection, are not satisfied, unless what men say, when they may say what they like, is worth saying, — has good in it, and more good than bad. In the same way the *Times*, replying to some foreign strictures on the dress, looks, and behaviour of the English abroad, urges that the English ideal is that every one should be free to do and to look just as he likes. But culture indefatigably tries, not to make what each raw person may like the rule by which he fashions himself; but to draw ever nearer to a sense of what is indeed beautiful, graceful, and becoming, and to get the raw person to like that.

And in the same way with respect to railroads and coal. Every one must have observed the strange language current during the late discussions as to the possible failures of our supplies of coal. Our coal, thousands of people were saying, is the real basis of our national greatness; if our coal runs short, there is an end of the greatness of England. But what *is* greatness?

— culture makes us ask. Greatness is a spiritual condition worthy to excite love, interest, and admiration; and the outward proof of possessing greatness is that we excite love, interest, and admiration. If England were swallowed up by the sea to-morrow, which of the two, a hundred years hence, would most excite the love, interest, and admiration of mankind, — would most, therefore, show the evidences of having possessed greatness, — the England of the last twenty years, or the England of Elizabeth, of a time of splendid spiritual effort, but when our coal, and our industrial operations depending on coal, were very little developed? Well, then, what an unsound habit of mind it must be which makes us talk of things like coal or iron as constituting the greatness of England, and how salutary a friend is culture, bent on seeing things as they are, and thus dissipating delusions of this kind and fixing standards of perfection that are real!

Wealth, again, that end to which our prodigious works for material advantage are directed, — the commonest of commonplaces tells us how men are always apt to regard wealth as a precious end in itself; and certainly they have never been so apt thus to regard it as they are in England at the present time. Never did people believe anything more firmly than nine Englishmen out of ten at the present day believe that our greatness and welfare are proved by our being so very rich. Now, the use of culture is that it helps us, by means of its spiritual standard of perfection, to regard wealth as but machinery, and not only to say as a matter of words that we regard wealth as but machinery, but really to perceive and feel that it is so. If it were not for this purging effect wrought upon our minds by culture, the whole world, the future as well as the present, would inevitably belong to the Philistines.² The people who believe most that our greatness and welfare are proved by our being very rich, and who most give their lives and thoughts to becoming rich, are just the very people whom we call Philistines. Culture says: "Consider these people, then, their way of life, their habits, their manners, the very tones of their voice; look at them attentively; observe the literature they read, the things which give them pleasure, the words which come forth out of their mouths, the thoughts which make the furniture of their minds; would any amount of wealth be worth having with the condition that one was to become just like these people by having it?" And thus culture begets a dissatisfaction which is of the highest possible value in stemming the common tide of men's thoughts in a wealthy and industrial community, and which saves the future, as one may hope, from being vulgarised, even if it cannot save the present.

Population, again, and bodily health and vigour, are things which are nowhere treated in such an unintelligent, misleading, exaggerated way as in England. Both are really machinery; yet how many people all around us do we see rest in them and fail to look beyond them! Why, one has heard people, fresh from reading certain articles of the *Times* on the Register-General's returns of marriages and births in this country, who would talk of our large English families in quite a solemn strain, as if they had something in itself beautiful, elevating, and meritorious in them; as if the British Philistine would have only to present

---

² The Philistines were the chief enemies of the chosen people. Arnold uses it as a name for the militant champions of "the dismal and illiberal" life of the middle classes.

himself before the Great Judge with his twelve children, in order to be received among the sheep as a matter of right!

But bodily health and vigour, it may be said, are not to be classed with wealth and population as mere machinery; they have a more real and essential value. True; but only as they are more intimately connected with a perfect spiritual condition than wealth or population are. The moment we disjoin them from the idea of a perfect spiritual condition, and pursue them, as we do pursue them, for their own sake and as ends in themselves, our worship of them becomes as mere worship of machinery, as our worship of wealth or population, and as unintelligent and vulgarising a worship as that is. Every one with anything like an adequate idea of human perfection has distinctly marked this subordination to higher and spiritual ends of the cultivation of bodily vigour and activity. "Bodily exercise profiteth little; but godliness is profitable unto all things," says the author of the Epistle to Timothy. And the utilitarian Franklin says just as explicitly: — "Eat and drink such an exact quantity as suits the constitution of thy body, *in reference to the services of the mind.*" But the point of view of culture, keeping the mark of human perfection simply and broadly in view, and not assigning to this perfection, as religion or utilitarianism assigns to it, a special and limited character, this point of view, I say, of culture is best given by these words of Epictetus: — "It is a sign of ἀφυΐα," says he, — that is, of a nature not finely tempered, — "to give yourselves up to things which relate to the body; to make, for instance, a great fuss about exercise, a great fuss about eating, a great fuss about drinking, a great fuss about walking, a great fuss about riding. All these things ought to be done merely by the way: the formation of the spirit and character must be our real concern." This is admirable; and, indeed, the Greek word εὐφυΐα, a finely tempered nature, gives exactly the notion of perfection as culture brings us to conceive it: a harmonious perfection in which the characters of beauty and intelligence are both present, which unites "the noblest of things," — as Swift, who of one of the two, at any rate, had himself all too little, most happily calls them in his *Battle of the Books,* — "the two noblest things, *sweetness and light.*" The εὐφυής is the man who tends towards sweetness and light; the ἀφυής, on the other hand, is our Philistine. The immense spiritual significance of the Greeks is due to their having been inspired with this central and happy idea of the essential character of human perfection; and Mr. Bright's misconception of culture, as a smattering of Greek and Latin, comes itself, after all, from this wonderful significance of the Greeks having affected the very machinery of our education, and is in itself a kind of homage to it.

In thus making sweetness and light to be characters of perfection, culture is of like spirit with poetry, follows one law with poetry. Far more than on our freedom, our population, and our industrialism, many amongst us rely upon our religious organisations to save us. I have called religion a yet more important manifestation of human nature than poetry, because it has worked on a broader scale for perfection, and with greater masses of men. But the idea of beauty and of a human nature perfect on all its sides, which is the dominant idea of poetry, is a true and invaluable idea, though it has not yet had the success that the idea of conquering the obvious faults of our animality, and of a human nature perfect on the moral side, — which is the dominant idea of religion, — has been enabled to have; and it is destined, adding to itself the religious idea of a devout energy, to transform and govern the other.

The best art and poetry of the Greeks, in which religion and poetry are one, in which the idea of beauty and of a human nature perfect on all sides adds to itself a religious and devout energy, and works in the strength of that, is on this account of such surpassing interest and instructiveness for us, though it was, — as, having regard to the human race in general, and, indeed, having regard to the Greeks themselves, we must own, — a premature attempt, an attempt which for success needed the moral and religious fibre in humanity to be more braced and developed than it had yet been. But Greece did not err in having the idea of beauty, harmony, and complete human perfection, so present and paramount. It is impossible to have this idea too present and paramount; only, the moral fibre must be braced too. And we, because we have braced the moral fibre, are not on that account in the right way, if at the same time the idea of beauty, harmony, and complete human perfection, is wanting or misapprehended amongst us; and evidently it *is* wanting or misapprehended at present. And when we rely as we do on our religious organisations, which in themselves do not and cannot give us this idea, and think we have done enough if we make them spread and prevail, then, I say, we fall into our common fault of overvaluing machinery. . . .[3]

---

[3] A passage is omitted here, for the sake of brevity, which deals largely with illustrations from Arnold's own times of some of the problems he has stated.

Culture, however, shows its single-minded love of perfection, its desire simply to make reason and the will of God prevail, its freedom from fanaticism, by its attitude towards all this machinery, even while it insists that it *is* machinery. Fanatics, seeing this mischief men do themselves by their blind belief in some machinery or other, — whether it is wealth and industrialism, or whether it is the cultivation of bodily strength and activity, or whether it is a political organisation, — or whether it is a religious organisation, — oppose with might and main the tendency to this or that political and religious organisation, or to games and athletic exercises, or to wealth and industrialism and try violently to stop it. But the flexibility which sweetness and light give, and which is one of the rewards of culture pursued in good faith, enables a man to see that a tendency may be necessary, and even, as a preparation for something in the future, salutary, and yet that the generations or individuals who obey this tendency are sacrificed to it, that they fall short of the hope of perfection by following it; and that its mischiefs are to be criticised, lest it should take too firm a hold and last after it has served its purpose.

Mr. Gladstone well pointed out, in a speech at Paris, — and others have pointed out the same thing, — how necessary is the present great movement towards wealth and industrialism, in order to lay broad foundations of material well-being for the society of the future. The worst of these justifications is, that they are generally addressed to the very people engaged, body and soul, in the movement in question; at all events, that they are always seized with the greatest avidity by these people, and taken by them as quite justifying their life; and that thus they tend to harden them in their sins. Now, culture admits the necessity of the movement towards fortune-making and exaggerated industrialism, readily allows that the future may derive benefit from it; but insists, at the same time, that the passing generations of industrialists, — forming, for the most part, the stout main body of Philistinism, — are sacrificed to it. . . .[4]

The pursuit of perfection, then, is the pursuit of sweetness and light. He who works for sweetness and light, works to make reason and the will of God prevail. He who works for machinery, he who works for hatred, works only for confusion. Culture looks beyond machinery, culture hates hatred; culture has one great passion, the passion for sweetness and light. It has one even yet greater! — the passion for making them *prevail*. It is not satisfied till we *all* come to a perfect man; it knows that the sweetness and light of the few must be imperfect until the raw and unkindled masses of humanity are touched with sweetness and light. If I have not shrunk from saying that we must work for sweetness and light, so neither have I shrunk from saying that we must have a broad basis, must have sweetness and light for as many as possible. Again and again I have insisted how those are the happy moments of humanity, how those are the marking epochs of a people's life, how those are the flowering times for literature and art and all the creative power of genius, when there is a *national* glow of life and thought, when the whole society is in the fullest measure permeated by thought, sensible to beauty, intelligent and alive. Only it must be *real* thought and *real* beauty; *real* sweetness and *real* light.

Plenty of people will try to give the masses, as they

---

[4] Another discussion of purely temporary and local issues is here omitted.

call them, an intellectual food prepared and adapted in the way they think proper for the actual condition of the masses. The ordinary popular literature is an example of this way of working on the masses. Plenty of people will try to indoctrinate the masses with the set of ideas and judgments constituting the creed of their own profession or party. Our religious and political organisations give an example of this way of working on the masses. I condemn neither way; but culture works differently. It does not try to teach down to the level of inferior classes; it does not try to win them for this or that sect of its own, with ready-made judgments and watchwords. It seeks to do away with classes; to make the best that has been thought and known in the world current everywhere; to make all men live in an atmosphere of sweetness and light, where they may use ideas, as it uses them itself, freely, — nourished, and not bound by them.

This is the *social idea;* and the men of culture are the true apostles of equality. The great men of culture are those who have had a passion for diffusing, for making prevail, for carrying from one end of society to the other, the best knowledge, the best ideas of their time; who have laboured to divest knowledge of all that was harsh, uncouth, difficult, abstract, professional, exclusive; to humanise it, to make it efficient outside the clique of the cultivated and learned, yet still remaining the *best* knowledge and thought of the time, and a true source, therefore, of sweetness and light. Such a man was Abelard in the Middle Ages, in spite of all his imperfections; and thence the boundless emotion and enthusiasm which Abelard excited. Such were Lessing and Herder in Germany, at the end of the last century; and their services to Germany were in this way inestimably precious. Generations will pass, and literary monuments will accumulate, and works far more perfect than the works of Lessing and Herder will be produced in Germany; and yet the names of these two men will fill a German with a reverence and enthusiasm such as the names of the most gifted masters will hardly awaken. And why? Because they *humanised* knowledge; because they broadened the basis of life and intelligence; because they worked powerfully to diffuse sweetness and light, to make reason and the will of God prevail. With Saint Augustine they said: "Let us not leave thee alone to make in the secret of thy knowledge, as thou didst before the creation of the firmament, the division of light from darkness; let the children of thy spirit, placed in their firmament, make their light shine upon the earth, mark the division of night and day, and announce the revolution of the times; for the old order is passed, and the new arises; the night is spent, the day is come forth; and thou shalt crown the year with thy blessing, when thou shalt send forth labourers into thy harvest sown by other hands than theirs; when thou shalt send forth new labourers to new seed-times, whereof the harvest shall be not yet."

ON A PIECE OF CHALK [1]

THOMAS HENRY HUXLEY (1825–1895)

IF a well were sunk at our feet in the midst of the city of Norwich, the diggers would very soon find themselves at work in that white substance almost too soft to be called rock, with which we are all familiar as "chalk."

Not only here, but over the whole county of Norfolk, the well-sinker might carry his shaft down many hundred feet without coming to the end of the chalk; and, on the sea-coast, where the waves have pared away the face of the land which breasts them, the scarped faces of the high cliffs are often wholly formed of the same material. Northward, the chalk may be followed as far as Yorkshire; on the south coast it appears abruptly in the picturesque western bays of Dorset, and breaks into the Needles of the Isle of Wight; while on the shores of Kent it supplies that long line of white cliffs to which England owes her name of Albion.

Were the thin soil which covers it all washed away, a curved band of white chalk, here broader, and there narrower, might be followed diagonally across England from Lulworth in Dorset, to Flamborough Head in Yorkshire — a distance of over 280 miles as the crow flies. From this band to the North Sea, on the east, and the Channel, on the south, the chalk is largely

[1] a lecture given before the workingmen of Norwich in 1868

hidden by other deposits; but, except in the Weald of Kent and Sussex, it enters into the very foundation of all the southeastern counties.

Attaining, as it does in some places, a thickness of more than a thousand feet, the English chalk must be admitted to be a mass of considerable magnitude. Nevertheless, it covers but an insignificant portion of the whole area occupied by the chalk formation of the globe, much of which has the same general characters as ours, and is found in detached patches, some less, and others more extensive, than the English. Chalk occurs in north-west Ireland; it stretches over a large part of France, — the chalk which underlies Paris being, in fact, a continuation of that of the London basin; it runs through Denmark and Central Europe, and extends southward to North Africa; while eastward, it appears in the Crimea and in Syria, and may be traced as far as the shores of the sea of Aral, in Central Asia. If all the points at which true chalk occurs were circumscribed, they would lie within an irregular oval about 3,000 miles in long diameter — the area of which would be as great as that of Europe, and would many times exceed that of the largest existing inland sea — the Mediterranean.

Thus the chalk is no unimportant element in the masonry of the earth's crust, and it impresses a peculiar stamp, varying with the conditions to which it is exposed, on the scenery of the districts in which it occurs. The undulating downs and rounded coombs, covered with sweet-grassed turf, of our inland chalk country, have a peaceful domestic and mutton-suggesting prettiness, but can hardly be called either grand or beautiful. But on our southern coasts, the wall-sided cliffs, many hundred feet high, with vast needles and pinnacles

ON A PIECE OF CHALK

standing out in the sea, sharp and solitary enough to serve as perches for the wary cormorant, confer a wonderful beauty and grandeur upon the chalk headlands. And, in the East, chalk has its share in the formation of some of the most venerable of mountain ranges, such as the Lebanon.

What is this wide-spread component of the surface of the earth? and whence did it come?

You may think this no very hopeful inquiry. You may not unnaturally suppose that the attempt to solve such problems as these can lead to no result, save that of entangling the inquirer in vague speculations, incapable of refutation and of verification. If such were really the case, I should have selected some other subject than a "piece of chalk" for my discourse. But, in truth, after much deliberation, I have been unable to think of any topic which would so well enable me to lead you to see how solid is the foundation upon which some of the most startling conclusions of physical science rest.

A great chapter of the history of the world is written in the chalk. Few passages in the history of man can be supported by such an overwhelming mass of direct and indirect evidence as that which testifies to the truth of the fragment of the history of the globe, which I hope to enable you to read, with your own eyes, tonight. Let me add, that few chapters of human history have a more profound significance for ourselves. I weigh my words well when I assert, that the man who should know the true history of the bit of chalk which every carpenter carries about in his breeches-pocket, though ignorant of all other history, is likely, if he will think his knowledge out to its ultimate results, to have a truer, and therefore a better, conception of this wonderful universe, and of man's relation to it, than the most learned student who is deep-read in the records of humanity and ignorant of those of Nature.

The language of the chalk is not hard to learn, not nearly so hard as Latin, if you only want to get at the broad features of the story it has to tell; and I propose that we now set to work to spell that story out together.

We all know that if we "burn" chalk the result is quick-lime. Chalk, in fact, is a compound of carbonic acid gas, and lime, and when you make it very hot the carbonic acid flies away and the lime is left. By this method of procedure we see the lime, but we do not see the carbonic acid. If, on the other hand, you were to powder a little chalk and drop it into a good deal of strong vinegar, there would be a great bubbling and fizzing, and, finally, a clear liquid, in which no sign of chalk would appear. Here you see the carbonic acid in the bubbles; the lime, dissolved in the vinegar, vanishes from sight. There are a great many other ways of showing that chalk is essentially nothing but carbonic acid and quick-lime. Chemists enunciate the result of all the experiments which prove this, by stating that chalk is almost wholly composed of "carbonate of lime."

It is desirable for us to start from the knowledge of this fact, though it may not seem to help us very far towards what we seek. For carbonate of lime is a widely-spread substance, and is met with under very various conditions. All sorts of limestones are composed of more or less pure carbonate of lime. The crust which is often deposited by waters which have drained through limestone rocks, in the form of what

ON A PIECE OF CHALK

are called stalagmites and stalactites, is carbonate of lime. Or, to take a more familiar example, the fur on the inside of a tea-kettle is carbonate of lime; and, for anything chemistry tells us to the contrary, the chalk might be a kind of gigantic fur upon the bottom of the earth-kettle, which is kept pretty hot below.

Let us try another method of making the chalk tell us its own history. To the unassisted eye chalk looks simply like a very loose and open kind of stone. But it is possible to grind a slice of chalk down so thin that you can see through it — until it is thin enough, in fact, to be examined with any magnifying power that may be thought desirable. A thin slice of the fur of a kettle might be made in the same way. If it were examined microscopically, it would show itself to be a more or less distinctly laminated mineral substance, and nothing more.

But the slice of chalk presents a totally different appearance when placed under the microscope. The general mass of it is made up of very minute granules; but, imbedded in this matrix, are innumerable bodies, some smaller and some larger, but, on a rough average, not more than a hundredth of an inch in diameter, having a well defined shape and structure. A cubic inch of some specimens of chalk may contain hundreds of thousands of these bodies, compacted together with incalculable millions of the granules.

The examination of a transparent slice gives a good notion of the manner in which the components of the chalk are arranged, and of their relative proportions. But, by rubbing up some chalk with a brush in water and then pouring off the milky fluid, so as to obtain sediments of different degrees of fineness, the granules and the minute rounded bodies may be pretty well separated from one another, and submitted to microscopic examination, either as opaque or as transparent objects. By combining the views obtained in these various methods, each of the rounded bodies may be proved to be a beautifully-constructed calcareous fabric, made up of a number of chambers, communicating freely with one another. The chambered bodies are of various forms. One of the commonest is something like a badly-grown raspberry, being formed of a number of nearly globular chambers of different sizes congregated together. It is called *Globigerina,* and some specimens of chalk consist of little else than *Globigerinae* and granules. Let us fix our attention upon the *Globigerina*. It is the spoor of the game we are tracking. If we can learn what it is and what are the conditions of its existence, we shall see our way to the origin and past history of the chalk.

A suggestion which may naturally enough present itself is, that these curious bodies are the result of some process of aggregation which has taken place in the carbonate of lime; that, just as in winter, the rime on our windows simulates the most delicate and elegantly arborescent foliage — proving that the mere mineral water may, under certain conditions, assume the outward form of organic bodies — so this mineral substance, carbonate of lime, hidden away in the bowels of the earth, has taken the shape of these chambered bodies. I am not raising a merely fanciful and unreal objection. Very learned men, in former days, have even entertained the notion that all the formed things found in rocks are of this nature; and if no such conception is at present held to be admissible, it is because long and varied experience has now shown

ON A PIECE OF CHALK

that mineral matter never does assume the form and structure we find in fossils. If any one were to try to persuade you that an oyster-shell (which is also chiefly composed of carbonate of lime) had crystallized out of sea-water I suppose you would laugh at the absurdity. Your laughter would be justified by the fact that all experience tends to show that oyster-shells are formed by the agency of oysters, and in no other way. And if there were no better reasons, we should be justified, on like grounds, in believing that *Globigerina* is not the product of anything but vital activity.

Happily, however, better evidence in proof of the organic nature of the *Globigerinae* than that of analogy is forthcoming. It so happens that calcareous skeletons, exactly similar to the *Globigerinae* of the chalk, are being formed, at the present moment, by minute living creatures, which flourish in multitudes, literally more numerous than the sands of the sea-shore, over a large extent of that part of the earth's surface which is covered by the ocean.

The history of the discovery of these living *Globigerinae,* and of the part which they play in rock building, is singular enough. It is a discovery which, like others of no less scientific importance, has arisen, incidentally, out of work devoted to very different and exceedingly practical interests. When men first took to the sea, they speedily learned to look out for shoals and rocks; and the more the burthen of their ships increased, the more imperatively necessary it became for sailors to ascertain with precision the depth of the waters they traversed. Out of this necessity grew the use of the lead and sounding line; and, ultimately, marine-surveying, which is the recording of the form of coasts and of the depth of the sea, as ascertained by the sounding lead, upon charts.

At the same time, it became desirable to ascertain and to indicate the nature of the sea-bottom, since this circumstance greatly affects its goodness as holding ground for anchors. Some ingenious tar, whose name deserves a better fate than the oblivion into which it has fallen, attained this object by "arming" the bottom of the lead with a lump of grease, to which more or less of the sand or mud, or broken shells, as the case might be, adhered, and was brought to the surface. But, however well adapted such an apparatus might be for rough nautical purposes, scientific accuracy could not be expected from the armed lead, and to remedy its defects (especially when applied to sounding in great depths) Lieut. Brooke, of the American Navy, some years ago invented a most ingenious machine, by which a considerable portion of the superficial layer of the sea-bottom can be scooped out and brought up from any depth to which the lead descends. In 1853, Lieut. Brooke obtained mud from the bottom of the North Atlantic, between Newfoundland and the Azores, at a depth of more than 10,000 feet, or two miles, by the help of this sounding apparatus. The specimens were sent for examination to Ehrenberg of Berlin, and to Bailey of West Point, and those able microscopists found that this deep-sea mud was almost entirely composed of the skeletons of living organisms — the greater proportion of these being just like the *Globigerinae* already known to occur in the chalk.

Thus far, the work had been carried on simply in the interest of science, but Lieut. Brooke's method of sounding acquired a high commercial value, when the

ON A PIECE OF CHALK

enterprise of laying down the telegraph-cable between this country and the United States was undertaken. For it became a matter of immense importance to know, not only the depth of the sea over the whole line along which the cable was to be laid, but the exact nature of the bottom, so as to guard against chances of cutting or fraying the strands of that costly rope. The Admiralty consequently ordered Captain Dayman, an old friend and ship-mate of mine, to ascertain the depth over the whole line of the cable, and to bring back specimens of the bottom. In former days, such a command as this might have sounded very much like one of the impossible things which the young Prince in the Fairy Tales is ordered to do before he can obtain the hand of the Princess. However, in the months of June and July, 1857, my friend performed the task assigned to him with great expedition and precision, without, so far as I know, having met with any reward of that kind. The specimens of Atlantic mud which he procured were sent to me to be examined and reported upon.

The result of all these operations is, that we know the contours and the nature of the surface-soil covered by the North Atlantic for a distance of 1,700 miles from east to west, as well as we know that of any part of the dry land. It is a prodigious plain — one of the widest and most even plains in the world. If the sea were drained off, you might drive a waggon all the way from Valentia, on the west coast of Ireland, to Trinity Bay, in Newfoundland. And, except upon one sharp incline about 200 miles from Valentia, I am not quite sure that it would even be necessary to put the skid on, so gentle are the ascents and descents upon that long route. From Valentia the road would lie downhill for about 200 miles to the point at which the bottom is now covered by 1,700 fathoms of seawater. Then would come the central plain, more than a thousand miles wide, the inequalities of the surface of which would be hardly perceptible, though the depth of water upon it now varies from 10,000 to 15,000 feet; and there are places in which Mont Blanc might be sunk without showing its peak above water. Beyond this, the ascent on the American side commences, and gradually leads, for about 300 miles, to the Newfoundland shore.

Almost the whole of the bottom of this central plain (which extends for many hundred miles in a north and south direction) is covered by a fine mud, which, when brought to the surface, dries into a greyish white friable substance. You can write with this on a blackboard, if you are so inclined; and, to the eye, it is quite like very soft, greyish chalk. Examined chemically, it proves to be composed almost wholly of carbonate of lime; and if you make a section of it, in the same way as that of the piece of chalk was made, and view it with the microscope, it presents innumerable *Globigerinae* imbedded in a granular matrix. Thus this deep-sea mud is substantially chalk. I say substantially, because there are a good many minor differences; but as these have no bearing on the question immediately before us, — which is the nature of the *Globigerinae* of the chalk, — it is unnecessary to speak of them.

Globigerinae of every size, from the smallest to the largest, are associated together in the Atlantic mud, and the chambers of many are filled by a soft animal matter. This soft substance is, in fact, the remains of the creature to which the *Globigerina* shell, or rather

ON A PIECE OF CHALK

skeleton, owes its existence — and which is an animal of the simplest imaginable description. It is, in fact, a mere particle of living jelly, without defined parts of any kind — without a mouth, nerves, muscles, or distinct organs, and only manifesting its vitality to ordinary observation by thrusting out and retracting from all parts of its surface, long filamentous processes, which serve for arms and legs. Yet this amorphous particle, devoid of everything which, in the higher animals, we call organs, is capable of feeding, growing, and multiplying; of separating from the ocean the small proportion of carbonate of lime which is dissolved in sea-water; and of building up that substance into a skeleton for itself, according to a pattern which can be imitated by no other known agency.

The notion that animals can live and flourish in the sea, at the vast depths from which apparently living *Globigerinae* have been brought up, does not agree very well with our usual conceptions respecting the conditions of animal life; and it is not so absolutely impossible as it might at first sight appear to be, that the *Globigerinae* of the Atlantic sea-bottom do not live and die where they are found.

As I have mentioned, the soundings from the great Atlantic plain are almost entirely made up of *Globigerinae,* with the granules which have been mentioned, and some few other calcareous shells; but a small percentage of the chalky mud — perhaps at most some five per cent. of it — is of a different nature, and consists of shells and skeletons composed of silex, or pure flint. These silicious bodies belong partly to the lowly vegetable organisms which are called *Diatomaceae,* and partly to the minute, and extremely simple, animals, termed *Radiolaria.* It is quite certain that these creatures do not live at the bottom of the ocean, but at its surface — where they may be obtained in prodigious numbers by the use of a properly constructed net. Hence it follows that these silicious organisms, though they are not heavier than the lightest dust, must have fallen, in some cases through fifteen thousand feet of water, before they reached their final resting-place on the ocean floor. And considering how large a surface these bodies expose in proportion to their weight, it is probable that they occupy a great length of time in making their burial journey from the surface of the Atlantic to the bottom.

But if the *Radiolaria* and Diatoms are thus rained upon the bottom of the sea, from the superficial layer of its waters in which they pass their lives, it is obviously possible that the *Globigerinae* may be similarly derived; and if they were so, it would be much more easy to understand how they obtain their supply of food than it is at present. Nevertheless, the positive and negative evidence all points the other way. The skeletons of the full-grown, deep-sea *Globigerinae* are so remarkably solid and heavy in proportion to their surface as to seem little fitted for floating; and, as a matter of fact, they are not to be found along with the Diatoms and *Radiolaria* in the uppermost stratum of the open ocean. It has been observed, again, that the abundance of *Globigerinae,* in proportion to other organisms, of like kind, increases with the depth of the sea; and that deep-water *Globigerinae* are larger than those which live in shallower parts of the sea; and such facts negative the supposition that these organisms have been swept by currents from the shallows into the deeps of the Atlantic. It therefore seems to be

ON A PIECE OF CHALK

hardly doubtful that these wonderful creatures live and die at the depths in which they are found.[2]

However, the important points for us are, that the living *Globigerinae* are exclusively marine animals, the skeletons of which abound at the bottom of deep seas; and that there is not a shadow of reason for believing that the habits of the *Globigerinae* of the chalk differed from those of the existing species. But if this be true, there is no escaping the conclusion that the chalk itself is the dried mud of an ancient deep sea.

In working over the soundings collected by Captain Dayman, I was surprised to find that many of what I have called the "granules" of that mud were not, as one might have been tempted to think at first, the mere powder and waste of *Globigerinae,* but that they had a definite form and size. I termed these bodies *"coccoliths,"* and doubted their organic nature.[3] Dr. Wallich verified my observation, and added the interesting discovery that, not unfrequently, bodies similar to these "coccoliths" were aggregated together into spheroids, which he termed *"coccospheres."* So far as we knew,

[2] During the cruise of *H.M.S. Bulldog,* commanded by Sir Leopold M'Clintock, in 1860, living starfish were brought up, clinging to the lowest part of the sounding line, from a depth of 1260 fathoms, midway between Cape Farewell, in Greenland, and the Rockall banks. Dr. Wallich ascertained that the sea bottom at this point consisted of the ordinary *Globigerinae* ooze, and that the stomachs of the starfishes were full of *Globigerinae.* This discovery removes all objections to the existence of living *Globigerinae* at great depths, which are based upon the supposed difficulty of maintaining animal life under such conditions; and it throws the burden of proof upon those who object to the supposition that the *Globigerinae* live and die where they are found — HUXLEY

[3] I have recently traced out the development of the "coccoliths" from a diameter of 1/7000th of an inch up to their largest size (which is about 1/1600th), and no longer doubt that they are produced by independent organisms, which, like the *Globigerinae,* live and die at the bottom of the sea — HUXLEY

these bodies, the nature of which is extremely puzzling and problematical, were peculiar to the Atlantic soundings. But, a few years ago, Mr. Sorby, in making a careful examination of the chalk by means of thin sections and otherwise, observed, as Ehrenberg had done before him, that much of its granular basis possesses a definite form. Comparing these formed particles with those in the Atlantic soundings, he found the two to be identical; and thus proved that the chalk, like the surroundings, contains these mysterious coccoliths and coccospheres. Here was a further and most interesting confirmation, from internal evidence, of the essential identity of the chalk with modern deep-sea mud. *Globigerinae,* coccoliths, and coccospheres are found as the chief constituents of both, and testify to the general similarity of the conditions under which both have been formed.

The evidence furnished by the hewing, facing, and superposition of the stones of the Pyramids, that these structures were built by men, has no greater weight than the evidence that the chalk was built by *Globigerinae* and the belief that those ancient pyramid-builders were terrestrial and air-breathing creatures like ourselves, is not better based than the conviction that the chalk-makers lived in the sea. But as our belief in the building of the Pyramids by men is not only grounded on the internal evidence afforded by these structures, but gathers strength from multitudinous collateral proofs and is clinched by the total absence of any reason for a contrary belief; so the evidence drawn from the *Globigerinae* that the chalk is an ancient sea-bottom is fortified by innumerable independent lines of evidence; and our belief in the truth of the conclusion to which all positive testimony tends, receives the like negative justification from the fact that no other hypothesis has a shadow of foundation.

It may be worth while briefly to consider a few of these collateral proofs that the chalk was deposited at the bottom of the sea. The great mass of the chalk is composed, as we have seen, of the skeletons of *Globigerinae,* and other simple organisms, imbedded in granular matter. Here and there, however, this hardened mud of the ancient sea reveals the remains of higher animals which have lived and died, and left their hard parts in the mud, just as the oysters die and leave their shells behind them, in the mud of the present seas.

There are, at the present day, certain groups of animals which are never found in fresh waters, being unable to live anywhere but in the sea. Such are the corals; those corallines which are called *Polyzoa;* those creatures which fabricate the lampshells, and are called *Brachiopoda;* the pearly *Nautilus,* and all animals allied to it; and all the forms of sea-urchins and starfishes. Not only are all these creatures confined to salt water at the present day; but, so far as our records of the past go, the conditions of their existence have been the same: hence, their occurrence in any deposit is as strong evidence as can be obtained, that that deposit was formed in the sea. Now the remains of animals of all the kinds which have been enumerated, occur in the chalk, in greater or less abundance; while not one of those forms of shell-fish which are characteristic of fresh water has yet been observed in it.

When we consider that the remains of more than three thousand distinct species of aquatic animals have been discovered among the fossils of the chalk, that the great majority of them are of such forms as are now met with only in the sea, and that there is no reason to believe that any one of them inhabited fresh water — the collateral evidence that the chalk represents an ancient sea-bottom acquires as great force as the proof derived from the nature of the chalk itself. I think you will now allow that I did not overstate my case when I asserted that we have as strong grounds for believing that all the vast area of dry land, at present occupied by the chalk, was once at the bottom of the sea, as we have for any matter of history whatever; while there is no justification for any other belief.

No less certain it is that the time during which the countries we now call south-east England, France, Germany, Poland, Russia, Egypt, Arabia, Syria, were more or less completely covered by a deep sea, was of considerable duration. We have already seen that the chalk is, in places, more than a thousand feet thick. I think you will agree with me, that it must have taken some time for the skeletons of animalcules of a hundredth of an inch in diameter to heap up such a mass as that. I have said that throughout the thickness of the chalk the remains of other animals are scattered. These remains are often in the most exquisite state of preservation. The valves of the shell-fishes are commonly adherent; the long spines of some of the sea-urchins, which would be detached by the smallest jar, often remain in their places. In a word, it is certain that these animals have lived and died when the place which they now occupy was the surface of as much of the chalk as had then been deposited; and that each has been covered by the layer of *Globigerina* mud, upon which the creatures imbedded a little higher up have, in like manner, lived and died. But some of

ON A PIECE OF CHALK

these remains prove the existence of reptiles of vast size in the chalk sea. These lived their time, and had their ancestors and descendants, which assuredly implies time, reptiles being of slow growth.

There is more curious evidence, again, that the process of covering up, or, in other words, the deposit of *Globigerina* skeletons, did not go on very fast. It is demonstrable that an animal of the cretaceous sea might die, that its skeleton might lie uncovered upon the sea-bottom long enough to lose all its outward coverings and appendages by putrefaction; and that, after this had happened, another animal might attach itself to the dead and naked skeleton, might grow to maturity, and might itself die before the calcareous mud had buried the whole.

Cases of this kind are admirably described by Sir Charles Lyell. He speaks of the frequency with which geologists find in the chalk a fossilized sea-urchin, to which is attached the lower valve of a *Crania*. This is a kind of shell-fish, with a shell composed of two pieces, of which, as in the oyster, one is fixed and the other free.

"The upper valve is almost invariably wanting, though occasionally found in a perfect state of preservation in the white chalk at some distance. In this case, we see clearly that the sea-urchin first lived from youth to age, then died and lost its spines, which were carried away. Then the young *Crania* adhered to the bared shell, grew and perished in its turn; after which, the upper valve was separated from the lower, before the Echinus became enveloped in chalky mud." [4]

A specimen in the Museum of Practical Geology,

[4] *Elements of Geology*, by Sir Charles Lyell, Bart., F.R.S., p. 23 (Huxley).

in London, still further prolongs the period which must have elapsed between the death of the sea-urchin, and its burial by the *Globigerinae*. For the outward face of the valve of the *Crania,* which is attached to a sea-urchin (*Micraster*), is itself overrun by an incrusting coralline, which spreads thence over more or less of the surface of the sea-urchin. It follows that, after the upper valve of the *Crania* fell off, the surface of the attached valve must have remained exposed long enough to allow of the growth of the whole coralline, since corallines do not live imbedded in mud.

The progress of knowledge may, one day, enable us to deduce from such facts as these the maximum rate at which the chalk can have accumulated, and thus to arrive at the minimum duration of the chalk period. Suppose that the valve of the *Crania* upon which a coralline has fixed itself in the way just described, is so attached to the sea-urchin that no part of it is more than an inch above the face upon which the sea-urchin rests. Then, as the coralline could not have fixed itself, if the *Crania* had been covered up with chalk mud, and could not have lived had itself been so covered, it follows, that an inch of chalk mud could not have accumulated within the time between the death and decay of the soft parts of the sea-urchin and the growth of the coralline to the full size which it has attained. If the decay of the soft parts of the sea-urchin; the attachment, growth to maturity, and decay of the *Crania;* and the subsequent attachment and growth of the coralline, took a year (which is a low estimate enough), the accumulation of the inch of chalk must have taken more than a year: and the deposit of a thousand feet of chalk must, consequently, have taken more than twelve thousand years.

The foundation of all this calculation is, of course, a knowledge of the length of time the *Crania* and the coralline needed to attain their full size; and, on this head, precise knowledge is at present wanting. But there are circumstances which tend to show, that nothing like an inch of chalk has accumulated during the life of a *Crania;* and, on any probable estimate of the length of that life, the chalk period must have had a much longer duration than that thus roughly assigned to it.

Thus, not only is it certain that the chalk is the mud of an ancient sea-bottom; but it is no less certain, that the chalk sea existed during an extremely long period, though we may not be prepared to give a precise estimate of the length of that period in years. The relative duration is clear, though the absolute duration may not be definable. The attempt to affix any precise date to the period at which the chalk sea began, or ended, its existence, is baffled by difficulties of the same kind. But the relative age of the cretaceous epoch may be determined with as great ease and certainty as the long duration of that epoch.

You will have heard of the interesting discoveries recently made, in various parts of Western Europe, of flint implements, obviously worked into shape by human hands, under circumstances which show conclusively that man is a very ancient denizen of these regions. It has been proved that the whole populations of Europe, whose existence has been revealed to us in this way, consisted of savages, such as the Esquimaux are now; that, in the country which is now France, they hunted the reindeer, and were familiar with the ways of the mammoth and the bison. The physical geography of France was in those days different from what it is now — the river Somme, for instance, having cut its bed a hundred feet deeper between that time and this; and, it is probable, that the climate was more like that of Canada or Siberia, than that of Western Europe.

The existence of these people is forgotten even in the traditions of the oldest historical nations. The name and fame of them had utterly vanished until a few years back; and the amount of physical change which has been effected since their day renders it more than probable that, venerable as are some of the historical nations, the workers of the chipped flints of Hoxne or of Amiens are to them, as they are to us, in point of antiquity. But, if we assign to these hoar relics of long-vanished generations of men the greatest age that can possibly be claimed for them, they are not older than the drift, or boulder clay, which, in comparison with the chalk, is but a very juvenile deposit. You need go no further than your own sea-board for evidence of this fact. At one of the most charming spots on the coast of Norfolk, Cromer, you will see the boulder clay forming a vast mass, which lies upon the chalk, and must consequently have come into existence after it. Huge boulders of chalk are, in fact included in the clay, and have evidently been brought to the position they now occupy by the same agency as that which has planted blocks of syenite from Norway side by side with them.

The chalk, then, is certainly older than the boulder clay. If you ask how much, I will again take you no further than the same spot upon your own coasts for evidence. I have spoken of the boulder clay and drift as resting upon the chalk. That is not strictly true. Interposed between the chalk and the drift is a comparatively insignificant layer, containing vegetable matter. But that layer tells a wonderful history. It is full of stumps of trees standing as they grew. Fir-trees are there with their cones, and hazel-bushes with their nuts; there stand the stools of oak and yew trees, beeches and alders. Hence this stratum is appropriately called the "forest-bed."

It is obvious that the chalk must have been upheaved and converted into dry land, before the timber trees could grow upon it. As the bolls of some of these trees are from two to three feet in diameter, it is no less clear that the dry land thus formed remained in the same condition for long ages. And not only do the remains of stately oaks and well-grown firs testify to the duration of this condition of things, but additional evidence to the same effect is afforded by the abundant remains of elephants, rhinoceroses, hippopotamuses, and other great wild beasts, which it has yielded to the zealous search of such men as the Rev. Mr. Gunn. When you look at such a collection as he has formed, and bethink you that these elephantine bones did veritably carry their owners about, and these great grinders crunch, in the dark woods of which the forest-bed is now the only trace, it is impossible not to feel that they are as good evidence of the lapse of time as the annual rings of the tree stumps.

Thus there is a writing upon the wall of the cliffs of Cromer, and whoso runs may read it. It tells us, with an authority which cannot be impeached, that the ancient sea-bed of the chalk sea was raised up, and remained dry land, until it was covered with forest, stocked with the great game the spoils of which have rejoiced your geologists. How long it remained in that condition cannot be said; but, "the whirligig of time brought its revenges" in those days as in these. That dry land, with the bones and teeth of generations of long-lived elephants, hidden away among the gnarled roots and dry leaves of its ancient trees, sank gradually to the bottom of the icy sea, which covered it with huge masses of drift and boulder clay. Sea-beasts, such as the walrus now restricted to the extreme north, paddled about where birds had twittered among the topmost twigs of the fir-trees. How long this state of things endured we know not, but at length it came to an end. The upheaved glacial mud hardened into the soil of modern Norfolk. Forests grew once more, the wolf and the beaver replaced the reindeer and the elephant; and at length what we call the history of England dawned.

Thus you have, within the limits of your own country, proof that the chalk can justly claim a very much greater antiquity than even the oldest physical traces of mankind. But we may go further and demonstrate, by evidence of the same authority as that which testifies to the existence of the father of men, that the chalk is vastly older than Adam himself. The Book of Genesis informs us that Adam, immediately upon his creation, and before the appearance of Eve, was placed in the Garden of Eden. The problem of the geographical position of Eden has greatly vexed the spirits of the learned in such matters, but there is one point respecting which, so far as I know, no commentator has ever raised a doubt. This is, that of the four rivers which are said to run out of it, Euphrates and Hiddekel are identical with the rivers now known by the names of Euphrates and Tigris. But the whole country in which these mighty rivers take their origin, and through which they run, is composed of rocks which are either of the same age as the chalk, or of later date. So that the chalk must not only have been formed, but, after its formation, the time required for the deposit of these later rocks, and for their upheaval into dry land, must have elapsed, before the smallest brook which feeds the swift stream of "the great river, the river of Babylon" began to flow.

Thus, evidence which cannot be rebutted, and which need not be strengthened, though if time permitted I might indefinitely increase its quantity, compels you to believe that the earth, from the time of the chalk to the present day, has been the theatre of a series of changes as vast in their amount, as they were slow in their progress. The area on which we stand has been first sea and then land, for at least four alternations; and has remained in each of these conditions for a period of great length.

Nor have these wonderful metamorphoses of sea into land, and of land into sea, been confined to one corner of England. During the chalk period, or "cretaceous epoch," not one of the present great physical features of the globe was in existence. Our great mountain ranges, Pyrenees, Alps, Himalayas, Andes, have all been upheaved since the chalk was deposited, and the cretaceous sea flowed over the sites of Sinai and Ararat. All this is certain, because rocks of cretaceous, or still later, date have shared in the elevatory movements which gave rise to these mountain chains; and may be found perched up, in some cases, many thousand feet high upon their flanks. And evidence of equal cogency demonstrates that, though, in Norfolk, the forest-bed rests directly upon the chalk, yet it does so, not because the period at which the forest grew immediately followed that at which the chalk was formed, but because an immense lapse of time, represented elsewhere by thousands of feet of rock, is not indicated at Cromer.

I must ask you to believe that there is no less conclusive proof that a still more prolonged succession of similar changes occurred, before the chalk was deposited. Nor have we any reason to think that the first term in the series of these changes is known. The oldest seabeds preserved to us are sands, and mud, and pebbles, the wear and tear of rocks which were formed in still older oceans.

But, great as is the magnitude of these physical changes of the world, they have been accompanied by a no less striking series of modifications in its living inhabitants. All the great classes of animals, beasts of the field, fowls of the air, creeping things, and things which dwell in the waters, flourished upon the globe long ages before the chalk was deposited. Very few, however, if any, of these ancient forms of animal life were identical with those which now live. Certainly not one of the higher animals was of the same species as any of those now in existence. The beasts of the field, in the days before the chalk, were not our beasts of the field, nor the fowls of the air such as those which the eye of man has seen flying, unless his antiquity dates infinitely further back than we at present surmise. If we could be carried back into those times, we should be as one suddenly set down in Australia before it was colonized. We should see mammals, birds, reptiles, fishes, insects, snails, and the like, clearly recognizable as such, and yet not one of them would be just the same as those with which we are familiar, and many would be extremely different.

From that time to the present, the population of the world has undergone slow and gradual, but incessant, changes. There has been no grand catastrophe — no destroyer has swept away the forms of life of one period, and replaced them by a totally new creation: but one species has vanished and another has taken its place; creatures of one type of structure have diminished, those of another have increased, as time has passed on. And thus, while the differences between the living creatures of the time before the chalk and those of the present day appear startling, if placed side by side, we are led from one to the other by the most gradual progress, if we follow the course of Nature through the whole series of those relics of her operations which she had left behind. It is by the population of the chalk sea that the ancient and the modern inhabitants of the world are most completely connected. The groups which are dying out flourish, side by side, with the groups which are now the dominant forms of life. Thus the chalk contains remains of those strange flying and swimming reptiles, the pterodactyl, the ichthyosaurus and the plesiosaurus, which are found in no later deposits, but abounded in preceding ages. The chambered shells called ammonites and belemnites, which are so characteristic of the period preceding the cretaceous, in like manner die with it.

But, amongst these fading remainders of a previous state of things, are some very modern forms of life, looking like Yankee pedlars among a tribe of Red Indians. Crocodiles of modern type appear, bony fishes, many of them very similar to existing species, almost supplant the forms of fish which predominate in more ancient seas; and many kinds of living shell-fish first become known to us in the chalk. The vegetation acquires a modern aspect. A few living animals are not even distinguishable as species, from those which existed at that remote epoch. The *Globigerina* of the present day, for example, is not different specifically from that of the chalk; and the same may be said of many other *Foraminifera*. I think it probable that critical and unprejudiced examination will show that more than one species of much higher animals have had a similar longevity; but the only example which I can at present give confidently is the snake's-head lamp-shell (*Terebratulina caput serpentis*), which lives in our English seas and abounded (as *Terebratulina striata* of authors) in the chalk.

The longest line of human ancestry must hide its diminished head before the pedigree of this insignificant shell-fish. We Englishmen are proud to have an ancestor who was present at the Battle of Hastings. The ancestors of *Terebratulina caput serpentis* may have been present at a battle of *Ichthyosauria* in that part of the sea which, when the chalk was forming, flowed over the site of Hastings. While all around has changed, this *Terebratulina* has peacefully propagated its species from generation to generation, and stands to this day, as a living testimony to the continuity of the present with the past history of the globe.

Up to this moment I have stated, so far as I know, nothing but well-authenticated facts, and the immediate conclusions which they force upon the mind. But the mind is so constituted that it does not willingly rest in facts and immediate causes, but seeks always after a knowledge of the remoter links in the chain of causation.

Taking the many changes of any given spot of the

earth's surface, from sea to land and from land to sea, as an established fact, we cannot refrain from asking ourselves how these changes have occurred. And when we have explained them — as they must be explained — by the alternate slow movements of elevation and depression which have affected the crust of the earth, we go still further back, and ask, Why these movements?

I am not certain that any one can give you a satisfactory answer to that question. Assuredly I cannot. All that can be said, for certain, is, that such movements are part of the ordinary course of nature, inasmuch as they are going on at the present time. Direct proof may be given, that some parts of the land of the northern hemisphere are at this moment insensibly rising and others insensibly sinking; and there is indirect, but perfectly satisfactory, proof, that an enormous area now covered by the Pacific has been deepened thousands of feet, since the present inhabitants of that sea came into existence. Thus there is not a shadow of a reason for believing that the physical changes of the globe, in past times, have been affected by other than natural causes. Is there any more reason for believing that the concomitant modifications in the forms of the living inhabitants of the globe have been brought about in other ways?

Before attempting to answer this question, let us try to form a distinct mental picture of what has happened in some special case. The crocodiles are animals which, as a group, have a very vast antiquity. They abounded ages before the chalk was deposited; they throng the rivers in warm climates, at the present day. There is a difference in the form of the joints of the back-bone, and in some minor particulars, between crocodiles of the present epoch and those which lived before the chalk; but, in the cretaceous epoch, as I have already mentioned, the crocodiles had assumed the modern type of structure. Notwithstanding this, the crocodiles of the chalk are not identically the same as those which lived in the times called "older tertiary," which succeeded the cretaceous epoch; and the crocodiles of the older tertiaries are not identical with those of the newer tertiaries, nor are these identical with existing forms. I leave open the question whether particular species may have lived on from epoch to epoch. But each epoch has had its peculiar crocodiles; though all, since the chalk, have belonged to the modern type, and differ simply in their proportions, and in such structural particulars as are discernible only to trained eyes.

How is the existence of this long succession of different species of crocodiles to be accounted for? Only two suppositions seem to be open to us — Either each species of crocodile has been specially created, or it has arisen out of some pre-existing form by the operation of natural causes. Choose your hypothesis; I have chosen mine. I can find no warranty for believing in the distinct creation of a score of successive species of crocodiles in the course of countless ages of time. Science gives no countenance to such a wild fancy; nor can even the perverse ingenuity of a commentator pretend to discover this sense, in the simple words in which the writer of Genesis records the proceedings of the fifth and sixth days of the Creation.

On the other hand, I see no good reason for doubting the necessary alternative, that all these varied species have been evolved from pre-existing crocodilian forms, by the operation of causes as completely a part of the common order of nature as those which have effected the changes of the inorganic world. Few will venture to affirm that the reasoning which applies to crocodiles loses its force among other animals, or among plants. If one series of species has come into existence by the operation of natural causes, it seems folly to deny that all may have arisen in the same way.

A small beginning has led us to a great ending. If I were to put the bit of chalk with which we started into the hot but obscure flame of burning hydrogen, it would presently shine like the sun. It seems to me that this physical metamorphosis is no false image of what has been the result of our subjecting it to a jet of fervent, though nowise brilliant, thought to-night. It has become luminous, and its clear rays, penetrating the abyss of the remote past, have brought within our ken some stages of the evolution of the earth. And in the shifting "without haste, but without rest" of the land and sea, as in the endless variation of the forms assumed by living beings, we have observed nothing but the natural product of the forces originally possessed by the substance of the universe.

AES TRIPLEX

ROBERT LOUIS STEVENSON (1850–1894)

THE changes wrought by death are in themselves so sharp and final, and so terrible and melancholy in their consequences, that the thing stands alone in man's experience, and has no parallel upon earth. It outdoes all other accidents because it is the last of them. Sometimes it leaps suddenly upon its victims like a Thug; sometimes it lays a regular siege and creeps upon their citadel during a score of years. And when the business is done, there is sore havoc made in other people's lives, and a pin knocked out by which many subsidiary friendships hung together. There are empty chairs, solitary walks, and single beds at night. Again, in taking away our friends, death does not take them away utterly, but leaves behind a mocking, tragical, and soon intolerable residue, which must be hurriedly concealed. Hence a whole chapter of sights and customs striking to the mind, from the pyramids of Egypt to the gibbets and dule trees of medieval Europe. The poorest persons have a bit of pageant going toward the tomb; memorial stones are set up over the least memorable; and, in order to preserve some show of respect for what remains of our old loves and friendships, we must accompany it with much grimly ludicrous ceremonial, and the hired undertaker parades before the door. All this, and much more of the same sort, accompanied by the eloquence of poets, has gone a great way to put humanity in error; nay, in many philosophies the error has been embodied and laid down with every circumstance of logic; although in real life the bustle and swiftness, in leaving people little time to think, have not left them time enough to go dangerously wrong in practice.

As a matter of fact, although few things are spoken of with more fearful whisperings than this prospect of death, few have less influence on conduct under healthy circumstances. We have all heard of cities in South America built upon the side of fiery mountains, and how, even in this tremendous neighborhood, the inhabitants are not a jot more impressed by the solemnity of mortal conditions than if they were delving gardens in the greenest corner of England. There are serenades and suppers and much gallantry among the myrtles overhead; and meanwhile the foundation shudders underfoot, the bowels of the mountain growl, and at any moment living ruin may leap sky-high into the moonlight, and tumble man and his merry-making in the dust. In the eyes of very young people, and very dull old ones, there is something indescribably reckless and desperate in such a picture. It seems not credible that respectable married people, with umbrellas, should find appetite for a bit of supper within quite a long distance of a fiery mountain; ordinary life begins to smell of high-handed debauch when it is carried on so close to a catastrophe; and even cheese and salad, it seems, could hardly be relished in such circumstances without something like a defiance of the Creator. It should be a place for nobody but hermits dwelling in prayer and maceration, or mere borndevils drowning care in a perpetual carouse.

And yet, when one comes to think upon it calmly, the situation of these South American citizens forms only a very pale figure for the state of ordinary mankind. This world itself, travelling blindly and swiftly in overcrowded space, among a million other worlds travelling blindly and swiftly in contrary directions, may very well come by a knock that would set it into explosion like a penny squib. And what, pathologically looked at, is the human body with all its organs, but a mere bagful of petards? The least of these is as dangerous to the whole economy as the ship's powder-magazine to the ship; and with every breath we breathe, and every meal we eat, we are putting one or more of them in peril. If we clung as devotedly as some philosophers pretend we do to the abstract idea of life, or were half as frightened as they make out we are, for the subversive accident that ends it all, the trumpets might sound by the hour and no one would follow them into battle — the blue peter [2] might fly at the truck, but who would climb into a sea-going ship? Think (if these philosophers were right) with what a preparation of spirit we should affront the daily peril of the dinner-table: a deadlier spot than any battlefield in history, where the far greater proportion of our ancestors have miserably left their bones! What woman would ever be lured into marriage, so much more dangerous than the wildest sea? And what would it be to grow old? For, after a certain distance, every step we take in life we find the ice growing thinner below our feet, and all around us and behind us we see our contemporaries going through. By the time

[2] the blue flag which, when flying at the masthead (the truck), was a signal to set sail

a man gets well into the seventies, his continued existence is a mere miracle; and when he lays his old bones in bed for the night, there is an overwhelming probability that he will never see the day. Do the old men mind it, as a matter of fact? Why, no. They were never merrier; they have their grog at night, and tell the raciest stories; they hear of the death of people about their own age, or even younger, not as if it was a grisly warning, but with a simple childlike pleasure at having outlived some one else; and when a draught might puff them out like a guttering candle, or a bit of a stumble shatter them like so much glass, their old hearts keep sound and unaffrighted, and they go on, bubbling with laughter, through years of man's age compared to which the valley of Balaclava [3] was as safe and peaceful as a village cricket-green on Sunday. It may fairly be questioned (if we look to the peril only) whether it was a much more daring feat for Curtius [4] to plunge into the gulf, than for any old gentleman of ninety to doff his clothes and clamber into bed.

Indeed, it is a memorable subject for consideration, with what unconcern and gaiety mankind pricks on along the Valley of the Shadow of Death. The whole way is one wilderness of snares, and the end of it, for those who fear the last pinch, is irrevocable ruin. And yet we go spinning through it all, like a party for the Derby. Perhaps the reader remembers one of the humorous devices of the deified Caligula: [5] how he encouraged a vast concourse of holiday-makers on to

[3] the valley across which the Light Brigade made its famous charge
[4] a heroic youth who threw himself into an earthquake fissure to pacify the angry gods who had caused it
[5] the Roman Emperor from 37–41 A.D. The Praetorians were the Emperor's special guards.

his bridge over Baiae bay; and when they were in the height of their enjoyment, turned loose the Praetorian guards among the company, and had them tossed into the sea. This is no bad miniature of the dealings of nature with the transitory race of men. Only, what a checkered picnic we have of it, even while it lasts! and into what great waters, not to be crossed by any swimmer, God's pale Praetorian throws us over in the end!

We live the time that a match flickers; we pop the cork of a gingerbeer bottle, and the earthquake swallows us on the instant. Is it not odd, is it not incongruous, is it not, in the highest sense of human speech, incredible, that we should think so highly of the gingerbeer, and regard so little the devouring earthquake? The love of Life and the fear of Death are two famous phrases that grow harder to understand the more we think about them. It is a well-known fact that an immense proportion of boat accidents would never happen if people held the sheet in their hands instead of making it fast; and yet, unless it be some martinet of a professional mariner or some landsman with shattered nerves, every one of God's creatures makes it fast. A strange instance of man's unconcern and brazen boldness in the face of death!

We confound ourselves with metaphysical phrases, which we import into daily talk with noble inappropriateness. We have no idea of what death is, apart from its circumstances and some of its consequences to others; and although we have some experience of living, there is not a man on earth who has flown so high into abstraction as to have any practical guess at the meaning of the word life. All literature, from Job and Omar Khayyam to Thomas Carlyle or Walt

Whitman, is but an attempt to look upon the human state with such largeness of view as shall enable us to rise from the consideration of living to the Definition of Life. And our sages give us about the best satisfaction in their power when they say that it is a vapor, or a show, or made of the same stuff with dreams. Philosophy, in its more rigid sense, has been at the same work for ages; and after a myriad bald heads have wagged over the problem, and piles of words have been heaped one upon another into dry and cloudy volumes without end, philosophy has the honor of laying before us, with modest pride, her contribution toward the subject: that life is a Permanent Possibility of Sensation. Truly a fine result! A man may very well love beef, or hunting, or a woman; but surely, surely, not a Permanent Possibility of Sensation! He may be afraid of a precipice, or a dentist, or a large enemy with a club, or even an undertaker's man; but not certainly of abstract death. We may trick with the word life in its dozen senses until we are weary of tricking; we may argue in terms of all the philosophies on earth, but one fact remains true throughout — that we do not love life, in the sense that we are greatly preoccupied about its conservation — that we do not, properly speaking, love life at all, but living. Into the views of the least careful there will enter some degree of providence; no man's eyes are fixed entirely on the passing hour; but although we have some anticipation of good health, good weather, wine, active employment, love, and self-approval, the sum of these anticipations does not amount to anything like a general view of life's possibilities and issues; nor are those who cherish them most vividly, at all the most scrupulous of their personal safety. To be deeply interested in the acccidents of our existence, to enjoy keenly the mixed texture of human experience, rather leads a man to disregard precautions, and risk his neck against a straw. For surely the love of living is stronger in an Alpine climber roping over a peril, or a hunter riding merrily at a stiff fence, than in a creature who lives upon a diet and walks a measured distance in the interest of his constitution.

There is a great deal of very vile nonsense talked upon both sides of the matter: tearing divines reducing life to the dimensions of a mere funeral procession, so short as to be hardly decent; and melancholy unbelievers yearning for the tomb as if it were a world too far away. Both sides must feel a little ashamed of their performances now and again when they draw in their chairs to dinner. Indeed, a good meal and a bottle of wine is an answer to most standard works upon the question. When a man's heart warms to his viands, he forgets a great deal of sophistry, and soars into a rosy zone of contemplation. Death may be knocking at the door, like the Commander's statue; we have something else in hand, thank God, and let him knock. Passing bells are ringing all the world over. All the world over, and every hour, some one is parting company with all his aches and ecstasies. For us also the trap is laid. But we are so fond of life that we have no leisure to entertain the terror of death. It is a honeymoon with us all through, and none of the longest. Small blame to us if we give our whole hearts to this glowing bride of ours, to the appetites, to honor, to the hungry curiosity of the mind, to the pleasure of the eyes in nature, and the pride of our own nimble bodies.

We all of us appreciate the sensations; but as for caring about the Permanence of the Possibility, a man's head is generally very bald, and his senses very dull, before he comes to that. Whether we regard life as a lane leading to a dead wall — a mere bag's end, as the French say — or whether we think of it as a vestibule or gymnasium, where we wait our turn and prepare our faculties for some more noble destiny; whether we thunder in a pulpit, or pule in little atheistic poetry-books, about its vanity and brevity; whether we look justly for years of health and vigor, or are about to mount into a Bath chair, as a step toward the hearse; in each and all of these views and situations there is but one conclusion possible: that a man should stop his ears against paralyzing terror, and run the race that is set before him with a single mind. No one surely could have recoiled with more heartache and terror from the thought of death than our respected lexicographer;[6] and yet we know how little it affected his conduct, how wisely and boldly he walked, and in what a fresh and lively vein he spoke of life. Already an old man, he ventured on his Highland tour; and his heart, bound with triple brass, did not recoil before twenty-seven individual cups of tea. As courage and intelligence are the two qualities best worth a good man's cultivation, so it is the first part of intelligence to recognize our precarious estate in life, and the first part of courage to be not at all abashed before the fact. A frank and somewhat headlong carriage, not looking too anxiously before, not dallying in maudlin regret over the past, stamps the man who is well armored for this world.

And not only well armored for himself, but a good

[6] Dr. Samuel Johnson, 1709–1784

friend and a good citizen to boot. We do not go to cowards for tender dealing; there is nothing so cruel as panic; the man who has least fear for his own carcass, has most time to consider others. That eminent chemist who took his walks abroad in tin shoes, and subsisted wholly upon tepid milk, had all his work cut out for him in considerate dealings with his own digestion. So soon as prudence has begun to grow up in the brain, like a dismal fungus, it finds its first expression in a paralysis of generous acts. The victim begins to shrink spiritually; he develops a fancy for parlors with a regulated temperature, and takes his morality on the principle of tin shoes and tepid milk. The care of one important body or soul becomes so engrossing, that all the noises of the outer world begin to come thin and faint into the parlor with the regulated temperature; and the tin shoes go equably forward over blood and rain. To be overwise is to ossify; and the scruple-monger ends by standing stock-still. Now the man who has his heart on his sleeve, and a good whirling weathercock of a brain, who reckons his life as a thing to be dashingly used and cheerfully hazarded, makes a very different acquaintance of the world, keeps all his pulses going true and fast, and gathers impetus as he runs, until, if he be running toward anything better than wildfire, he may shoot up and become a constellation in the end. Lord, look after his health; Lord, have a care of his soul, says he; and he has at the key of the position, and swashes through incongruity and peril toward his aim. Death is on all sides of him with pointed batteries, as he is on all sides of all of us; unfortunate surprises gird him round; mimmouthed friends and relations hold up their hands in quite a little elegiacal synod about his path: and what cares he for all this? Being a true lover of living, a fellow with something pushing and spontaneous in his inside, he must, like any other soldier, in any other stirring, deadly warfare, push on at his best pace until he touch the goal. "A peerage or Westminster Abbey!" cried Nelson in his bright, boyish, heroic manner. These are great incentives; not for any of these, but for the plain satisfaction of living, of being about their business in some sort or other, do the brave, serviceable men of every nation tread down the nettle danger, and pass flyingly over all the stumbling-blocks of prudence. Think of the heroism of Johnson, think of that superb indifference to mortal limitation that set him upon his dictionary, and carried him through triumphantly until the end! Who, if he were wisely considerate of things at large, would ever embark upon any work much more considerable than a half penny post card? Who would project a serial novel, after Thackeray and Dickens had each fallen in mid-course? Who would find heart enough to begin to live, if he dallied with the consideration of death?

And, after all, what sorry and pitiful quibbling all this is! To forego all the issues of living in a parlor with the regulated temperature — as if that were not to die a hundred times over, and for ten years at a stretch! As if it were not to die in one's own lifetime, and without even the sad immunities of death! As if it were not to die, and yet be the patient spectators of our own pitiable change! The Permanent Possibility is preserved, but the sensations carefully held at arm's length, as if one kept a photographic plate in a dark chamber. It is better to lose health like a spendthrift than to waste it like a miser. It is better to live and be done with it, than to die daily in the sickroom. By all means begin your folio; even if the doctor does not give you a year, even if he hesitates about a month, make one brave push and see what can be accomplished in a week. It is not only in finished undertakings that we ought to honor useful labor. A spirit goes out of the man who means execution, which outlives the most untimely ending. All who have meant good work with their whole hearts, have done good work, although they may die before they have the time to sign it. Every heart that has beat strong and cheerfully has left a hopeful impulse behind it in the world, and bettered the tradition of mankind. And even if death catch people, like an open pitfall, and in mid-career, laying out vast projects, and planning monstrous foundations, flushed with hope, and their mouths full of boastful language, they should be at once tripped up and silenced; is there not something brave and spirited in such a termination? and does not life go down with a better grace, foaming in full body over a precipice, than miserably straggling to an end in sandy deltas? When the Greeks made their fine saying that those whom the gods love die young, I cannot help believing they had this sort of death also in their eye. For surely, at whatever age it overtake the man, this is to die young. Death has not been suffered to take so much as an illusion from his heart. In the hot-fit of life, a-tiptoe on the highest point of being, he passes at a bound on to the other side. The noise of the mallet and chisel is scarcely quenched, the trumpets are hardly done blowing, when, trailing with him clouds of glory, this happy-starred, full-blooded spirit shoots into the spiritual land.

THE LANTERN-BEARERS[1]

I

THESE boys congregated every autumn about a certain easterly fisher-village, where they tasted in a high degree the glory of existence. The place was created seemingly on purpose for the diversion of young gentlemen. A street or two of houses, mostly red and many of them tiled; a number of fine trees clustered about the manse and the kirkyard, and turning the chief street into a shady alley; many little gardens more than usually bright with flowers; nets a-drying, and fisher-wives scolding in the backward parts; a smell of fish, a genial smell of seaweed; whiffs of blowing sand at the street-corners; shops with golf-balls and bottled lollipops; another shop with penny pickwicks (that remarkable cigar) and the *London Journal,* dear to me for its startling pictures, and a few novels, dear for their suggestive names: such, as well as memory serves me, were the ingredients of the town. These, you are to conceive posted on a spit between two sandy bays, and sparsely flanked with villas — enough for the boys to lodge in with their subsidiary parents, not enough (not yet enough) to cocknify the scene; a haven in the rocks in front: in front of that, a file of gray islets: to the left, endless links and sand wreaths, a wilderness of hiding-holes, alive with rabbits and soaring gulls: to the right, a range of seaward crags, one rugged brow beyond another; the ruins of a mighty and ancient fortress on the brink of one; coves between — now charmed into sunshine quiet, now whistling with

[1] From *Across the Plains.*

wind and clamorous with bursting surges; the dens and sheltered hollows redolent of thyme and southernwood, the air at the cliff's edge brisk and clean and pungent of the sea — in front of all, the Bass Rock, tilted seaward like a doubtful bather, the surf ringing it with white, the solan-geese hanging round its summit like a great and glittering smoke. This choice piece of seaboard was sacred, besides, to the wrecker; and the Bass, in the eye of fancy, still flew the colours of King James; and in the ear of fancy the arches of Tantallon still rang with horse-shoe iron, and echoed to the commands of Bell-the-Cat.

There was nothing to mar your days, if you were a boy summering in that part, but the embarrassment of pleasure. You might golf if you wanted; but I seem to have been better employed. You might secrete yourself in the Lady's Walk, a certain sunless dingle of elders, all mossed over by the damp as green as grass, and dotted here and there by the streamside with roofless walls, the cold homes of anchorites. To fit themselves for life, and with a special eye to acquire the art of smoking, it was even common for the boys to harbour there; and you might have seen a single penny pickwick, honestly shared in lengths with a blunt knife, bestrew the glen with these apprentices. Again, you might join our fishing parties, where we sat perched as thick as solan-geese, a covey of little anglers, boy and girl, angling over each other's heads, to the much entanglement of lines and loss of podleys and consequent shrill recrimination — shrill as the geese themselves. Indeed, had that been all, you might have done this often; but though fishing be a fine pastime, the podley is scarce to be regarded as a dainty for the table; and it was a point of honour that a boy should eat all that he had taken. Or again, you might climb the Law, where the whale's jawbone stood landmark in the buzzing wind, and behold the face of many counties, and the smoke and spires of many towns, and the sails of distant ships. You might bathe, now in the flaws of fine weather, that we pathetically call our summer, now in a gale of wind, with the sand scourging your bare hide, your clothes thrashing abroad from underneath their guardian stone, the froth of the great breakers casting you headlong ere it had drowned your knees. Or you might explore the tidal rocks, above all in the ebb of springs, when the very roots of the hills were for the nonce discovered; following my leader from one group to another, groping in slippery tangle for the wreck of ships, wading in pools after the abominable creatures of the sea, and ever with an eye cast backward on the march of the tide and the menaced line of our retreat. And then you might go Crusoeing, a word that covers all extempore eating in the open air: digging perhaps a house under the margin of the links, kindling a fire of the seaware, and cooking apples there — if they were truly apples, for I sometimes suppose the merchant must have played us off with some inferior and quite local fruit, capable of resolving, in the neighbourhood of fire, into mere sand and smoke and iodine; or perhaps pushing to Tantallon, you might lunch on sandwiches and visions in the grassy court, while the wind hummed in the crumbling turrets; or clambering along the coast, eat geans [2] (the worst, I must suppose in Christendom) from an adventurous gean tree that had taken root under a cliff, where it was shaken with an ague of east wind, and silvered after gales with salt, and grew so foreign among its bleak

[2] wild cherries

surroundings that to eat of its produce was an adventure in itself.

There are mingled some dismal memories with so many that were joyous. Of the fisher-wife, for instance, who had cut her throat at Canty Bay; and of how I ran with the other children to the top of the Quandrant, and beheld a posse of silent people escorting a cart, and on the cart, bound in a chair, her throat bandaged, and the bandage all bloody — horror! — the fisher-wife herself, who continued henceforth to hag-ride my thoughts, and even today (as I recall the scene) darkens daylight. She was lodged in the little old jail in the chief street; but whether or no she died there, with a wise terror of the worst, I never inquired. She had been tippled; it was but a dingy tragedy; and it seems strange and hard that, after all these years, the poor crazy sinner should be still pilloried on her cart in the scrap-book of my memory. Nor shall I readily forget a certain house in the Quandrant where a visitor died, and a dark old woman continued to dwell alone with the dead body; nor how this old woman conceived a hatred to myself and one of my cousins, and in the dread hour of the dusk, as we were clambering on the garden-walls, opened a window in that house of mortality and cursed us in a shrill voice and with a marrowy choice of language. It was a pair of very colourless urchins that fled down the lane from this remarkable experience! But I recall with a more doubtful sentiment, compounded out of fear and exultation, the coil of equinoctial tempests; trumpeting squalls, scouring flaws of rain; the boats with their reefed lugsails scudding for the harbour mouth, where danger lay, for it was hard to make when the wind had any east in it; the wives clustered with blowing shawls at the pierhead, where (if fate was against them) they might see boat and husbands and sons — their whole wealth and their whole family — engulfed under their eyes; and (what I saw but once) a troop of neighbours forcing such an unfortunate homeward, and she squalling and battling in their midst, a figure scarcely human, a tragic Maenad.

These are things that I recall with interest; but what my memory dwells upon the most, I have been all this while withholding. It was a sport peculiar to the place, and indeed to a week or so of our two months' holiday there. Maybe it still flourishes in its native spot; for boys and their pastimes are swayed by periodic forces inscrutable to man; so that tops and marbles reappear in their due season, regular like the sun and moon, and the harmless art of kuncklebones has seen the fall of the Roman empire and the rise of the United States. It may still flourish in its native spot, but nowhere else, I am persuaded; for I tried myself to introduce it on Tweedside, and was defeated lamentably, its charm being quite local, like a country wine that cannot be exported.

The idle manner of it was this: —

Toward the end of September, when school-time was drawing near and the nights were already black, we would begin to sally from our respective villas, each equipped with a tin bull's-eye lantern. The thing was so well known that it had worn a rut in the commerce of Great Britain; and the grocers, about the due time, began to garnish their windows with our particular brand of luminary. We wore them buckled to the waist upon a cricket belt, and over them, such was the rigour of the game, a buttoned top-coat. They smelled noisomely of glistered tin; they never burned aright, though they would always burn our fingers; their use was naught; the pleasure of them merely fanciful; and yet a boy with a bull's-eye under his top-coat asked for nothing more. The fishermen used lanterns about their boats, and it was from them, I suppose, that we had got the hint; but theirs were not bull's-eyes, nor did we ever play at being fishermen. The police carried them at their belts, and we had plainly copied them in that; yet we did not pretend to be policemen. Burglars, indeed, we may have had some haunting thoughts of; and we had certainly an eye to past ages when lanterns were more common, and to certain story-books in which we had found them to figure very largely. But take it for all in all, the pleasure of the thing was substantive; and to be a boy with a bull's-eye under his top-coat was good enough for us.

When two of these asses met, there would be an anxious "Have you got your lantern?" and a gratified "Yes!" That was the shibboleth, and very needful too; as it was the rule to keep our glory contained, none could recognize a lantern-bearer, unless (like the polecat) by the smell. Four or five would sometime climb into the belly of a ten-man lugger, with nothing but the thwarts above them — for the cabin was usually locked, or choose out some hollow of the links where the wind might whistle overhead. There the coats would be unbuttoned and the bull's-eye discovered; and in the chequering glimmer under the huge windy hall of the night, and cheered by a rich steam of toasting tinware, these fortunate young gentleman would crouch together in the cold sand of the links or on the scaly bilges of the fishing-boat, and delight themselves with inappropriate talk. Woe is me that I may not give some specimens — some of their foresights of life, or deep inquiries into the rudiments of man and nature, these were so fiery and so innocent, they were so richly silly, so romantically young. But the talk, at any rate, was but a condiment; and these gatherings themselves only accidents in the career of the lantern-bearer. The essence of this bliss was to walk by yourself in the black night; the slide shut, the top-coat buttoned; not a ray escaping, whether to conduct your footsteps or to make your glory public: a mere pillar of darkness in the dark; and all the while, deep down in the privacy of your fool's heart, to know you had a bull's-eye at your belt, and to exult and sing over the knowledge.

II

It is said that a poet has died young in the breast of the most stolid. It may be contended, rather, that this (somewhat minor) bard in almost every case survives, and is the spice of life to his possessor. Justice is not done to the versatility and unplumbed childishness of man's imagination. His life from without may seem but a rude mound of mud; there will be some golden chamber at the heart of it, in which he dwells delighted; and for as dark as his pathway seems to the observer, he will have some kind of a bull's-eye at his belt.

It would be hard to pick out a career more cheerless than that of Dancer,[3] the miser, as he figures in the *Old Bailey Reports,* a prey to the most sordid persecutions, the butt of his neighbourhood, betrayed by his hired man, his house beleaguered by the impish school-

---

[3] Daniel Dancer (1716–1794), who denied himself fuel, wore rags on his feet for shoes, ate but one slender meal a day, and died worth 3000 pounds *per annum.* For all this, he had many admirable traits of character.

boy, and he himself grinding and fuming and impotently fleeing to the law against these pin-pricks. You marvel at first that any one should willingly prolong a life so destitute of charm and dignity; and then you call to memory that had he chosen, had he ceased to be a miser, he would have been freed at once from these trials, and might have built himself a castle and gone escorted by a squadron. For the love of more recondite joys, which we cannot estimate, which, it may be, we should envy, the man had willingly foregone both comfort and consideration. "His mind to him a kingdom was"; and sure enough, digging into that mind, which seems at first a dust-heap, we unearth some priceless jewels. For Dancer must have had the love of power and the disdain of using it, a noble character in itself; disdain of many pleasures, a chief part of what is commonly called wisdom; disdain of the inevitable end, that finest trait of mankind; scorn of men's opinions, another element of virtue; and at the back of all, a conscience just like yours and mine, whining like a cur, swindling like a thimble-rigger, but still pointing (there or there-about) to some conventional standard. Here were a cabinet portrait to which Hawthorne perhaps had done justice; and yet not Hawthorne either, for he was mildly minded, and it lay not in him to create for us that throb of the miser's pulse, his fretful energy of gusto, his vast arms of ambition clutching in he knows not what: insatiable, insane, a god with a muck-rake. Thus, at least, looking in the bosom of the miser, consideration detects the poet in the full tide of life, with more, indeed, of the poetic fire than usually goes to epics; and tracing that mean man about his cold hearth, and to and fro in his discomfortable house, spies within him a blazing bonfire of delight. And so with others, who do not live by bread alone, but by some cherished and perhaps fantastic pleasure; who are meat salesmen to the external eye, and possibly to themselves are Shakespeares, Napoleons, or Beethovens; who have not one virtue to rub against another in the field of active life, and yet perhaps, in the life of contemplation, sit with the saints. We see them on the street, and we can count their buttons; but heavens knows in what they pride themselves! heavens knows where they have set their treasure!

There is one fable that touches very near the quick of life: the fable of the monk who passed into the woods, heard a bird break into song, hearkened for a trill or two, and found himself on his return a stranger at his convent gates; for he had been absent fifty years, and of all his comrades there survived but one to recognise him. It is not only in the woods that this enchanter carols, though perhaps he is native there. He sings in the most doleful places. The miser hears him and chuckles, and the days are moments. With no more apparatus than an ill-smelling lantern I have evoked him on the naked links. All life that is not merely mechanical is spun out of two strands: seeking for that bird and hearing him. And it is just this that makes life so hard to value, and the delight of each so incommunicable. And just a knowledge of this, and a remembrance of those fortunate hours in which the bird has sung to us, that fills us with such wonder when we turn the pages of the realist. There, to be sure, we find a picture of life in so far as it consists of mud and of old iron, cheap desires and cheap fears, that which we are ashamed to remember and that which we are careless whether we forget; but of the note of that time-devouring nightingale we hear no news.

The case of these writers of romance is most obscure. They have been boys and youths; they have lingered outside the window of the beloved, who was then most probably writing to some one else; they have sat before a sheet of paper, and felt themselves mere continents of congested poetry, not one line of which would flow; they have walked alone in the woods, they have walked in cities under the countless lamps; they have been to sea, they have hated, they have feared, they have longed to knife a man, and maybe done it; the wild taste of life has stung their palate. Or, if you deny them all the rest, one pleasure at least they have tasted to the full — their books are there to prove it — the keen pleasure of successful literary composition. And yet they fill the globe with volumes, whose cleverness inspires me with despairing admiration, and whose consistent falsity to all I care to call existence, with despairing wrath. If I had no better hope than to continue to revolve among the dreary and petty businesses, and to be moved by the paltry hopes and fears with which they surround and animate their heroes, I declare I would die now. But there has never been an hour of mine gone quite so dully yet; if it were spent waiting at a railway junction, I would have some scattering thoughts, I could count some grains of memory, compared to which the whole of one of these romances seems but dross.

These writers would retort (if I take them properly) that this was very true; that it was the same with themselves and other persons of (what they call) the artistic temperament; that in this we were exceptional, and should apparently be ashamed of ourselves; but that our works must deal exclusively with (what they call) the average man, who was a prodigious dull fellow, and quite dead to all but the paltriest considerations. I accept the issue. We can only know others by ourselves. The artistic temperament (a plague on the expression) does not make us different from our fellow-men, or it would make us incapable of writing novels; and the average man (a murrain on the word!) is just like you and me, or he would not be average. It was Whitman who stamped a kind of Birmingham sacredness upon the latter phrase; but Whitman knew very well, and showed very nobly, that the average man was full of joys and full of a poetry of his own. And this harping on life's dulness and man's meanness is a loud profession of incompetence; it is one of two things: the cry of the blind eye, *I cannot see,* or the complaint of the dumb tongue, *I cannot utter.* To draw a life without delights is to prove I have not realized it. To picture a man without some sort of poetry — well, it goes near to prove my case, for it shows an author may have little enough. To see Dancer only as a dirty, old, small-minded, impotently fuming man, in a dirty house, besieged by Harrow boys, and probably beset by small attorneys, is to show myself as keen an observer as . . . the Harrow boys. But these young gentlemen (with a more becoming modesty) were content to pluck Dancer by the coat-tails; they did not suppose they had surprised his secret or could put him living in a book: and it is there my error would have lain. Or say that in the same romance — I continue to call these books romances, in the hope of giving pain — say that in the same romance, which now begins really to take shape, I should leave to speak of Dancer, and follow instead the Harrow boys; and say that I came on some such business as that of my lantern-bearers on the links; and describe the boys as very cold, spat upon by flurries of rain, and drearily surrounded, all of which they were; and their talk as silly and indecent, which it certainly was. I might upon these lines, and had I Zola's genius, turn out, in a page or so, a gem of literary art, render the lantern-light with the touches of a master, and lay on the indecency with the ungrudging hand of love; and when all was done, what a triumph would my picture be of shallowness and dulness! how it would have missed the point; how it would have belied the boys! To the ear of the stenographer, the talk is merely silly and indecent; but ask the boys themselves, and they are discussing (as it is highly proper they should) the possibilities of existence. To the eye of the observer they are wet and cold and drearily surrounded; but ask themselves, and they are in the heaven of a recondite pleasure, the ground of which is an ill-smelling lantern.

III

For, to repeat, the ground of a man's joy is often hard to hit. It may hinge at times upon a mere accessory, like a lantern; it may reside, like Dancer's, in the mysterious inwards of psychology. It may consist with perpetual failure, and find exercise in the continued chase. It has so little bond with externals (such as the observer scribbles in his note-book) that it may even touch them not; and the man's true life, for which he consents to live, lie altogether in the field of fancy. The clergyman, in his spare hours, may be winning battles, the farmer sailing ships, the banker reaping triumph in the arts: all leading another life, plying an-

THE LANTERN-BEARERS 317

other trade from that they chose; like the poet's house-builder, who, after all is cased in stone,

> By his fireside, as impotent fancy prompts,
> Rebuilds it to his liking.

In such a case the poetry runs underground. The observer (poor soul, with his documents!) is all abroad. For to look at the man is but to court deception. We shall see the trunk from which he draws his nourishment; but he himself is above and abroad in the green dome of foliage, hummed through by winds and nested in by nightingales. And the true realism were that of the poets, to climb up after him like a squirrel, and catch some glimpse of the heaven for which he lives. And the true realism, always and everywhere, is that of the poets: to find out where joy resides and give it a voice far beyond singing.

For to miss the joy is to miss all. In the joy of the actors lies the sense of any action. That is the explanation, that the excuse. To one who has not the secret of the lanterns, the scene upon the links is meaningless. And hence the haunting and truly spectral unreality of realistic books. Hence, when we read the English realists, the incredulous wonder with which we observe the hero's constancy under the submerging tide of dulness, and how he bears up with his jibbing sweetheart, and endures the chatter of idiot girls, and stands by his whole unfeatured wilderness of an existence, instead of seeking relief in drink or foreign travel. Hence, in the French, in that meat-market of middle-aged sensuality, the disgusted surprise with which we see the hero drift sidelong, and practically quite untempted, into every description of misconduct and dishonour. In each, we miss the personal poetry, the enchanted atmosphere, that rainbow work of fancy that clothes what is naked and seems to ennoble what is base; in each, life falls dead like dough, instead of soaring away like a balloon into the colours of the sunset; each is true, each inconceivable; for no man lives in the external truth, among salts and acids, but in the warm, phantasmagoric chamber of his brain, with the painted windows and the storied walls.

Of this falsity we have had a recent example from a man who knows far better — Tolstoi's *Power of Darkness*. Here is a piece full of force and truth, yet quite untrue. For before Mikita was led into so dire a situation he was tempted, and temptations are beautiful at least in part; and a work which dwells on the ugliness of crime and gives no hint of any loveliness in the temptation, sins against the modesty of life, and even when a Tolstoi writes it, sinks to melodrama. The peasants are not understood; they saw their life in fairer colours; even the deaf girl was clothed in poetry for Mikita, or he had never fallen. And so, once again, even an Old Bailey melodrama, without some brightness of poetry and lustre of existence, falls into the inconceivable and ranks with fairy tales.

IV

In nobler books we are moved with something like the emotions of life; and this emotion is very variously provoked. We are so moved when Levine labours in the field, when André sinks beyond emotion, when Richard Feverel and Lucy Desborough meet beside the river, when Antony, "not cowardly, puts off his helmet," when Kent has infinite pity on the dying Lear, when, in Dostoieffsky's *Despised and Rejected,* the uncomplaining hero drains his cup of suffering and virtue. These are notes that please the great heart of man. Not only love, and the fields, and the bright face of danger, but sacrifice and death and unmerited suffering humbly supported, touch in us the vein of the poetic. We love to think of them, we long to try them, we are humbly hopeful that we may prove heroes also.

We have heard, perhaps, too much of lesser matters. Here is the door, here is the open air. *Itur in antiquam silvam.*

A FREE MAN'S WORSHIP[1]

BERTRAND RUSSELL (1872-   )

To Dr. Faustus in his study Mephistopheles told the history of the Creation, saying: —

"The endless praises of the choirs of angels had begun to grow wearisome; for, after all, did he not deserve their praise? Had he not given them endless joy? Would it not be more amusing to obtain undeserved praise, to be worshiped by beings whom he tortured? He smiled inwardly, and resolved that the great drama should be performed.

"For countless ages the hot nebula whirled aimlessly through space. At length it began to take shape, the central mass threw off planets, the planets cooled, boiling seas and burning mountains heaved and tossed, from black masses of cloud hot sheets of rain deluged the barely solid crust. And now the first germ of life grew in the depths of the ocean, and developed rapidly in the fructifying warmth into vast forest trees, huge ferns springing from the damp mould, sea monsters breeding, fighting, devouring, and passing away. And from the monsters, as the play unfolded itself, Man was born, with the power of thought, the knowledge of good and evil, and the cruel thirst for worship. And Man saw that all is passing in this mad, monstrous

[1] From *Mysticism and Logic*.

world, that all is struggling to snatch, at any cost, a few brief moments of life before Death's inexorable decree. And Man said: 'There is a hidden purpose, could we but fathom it, and the purpose is good; for we must reverence something, and in the visible world there is nothing worthy of reverence.' And Man stood aside from the struggle, resolving that God intended harmony to come out of chaos by human efforts. And when he followed the instincts which God had transmitted to him from his ancestry of beasts of prey, he called it Sin, and asked God to forgive him. But he doubted whether he could be justly forgiven, until he invented a divine Plan by which God's wrath was to have been appeased. And seeing the present was bad, he made it yet worse that thereby the future might be better. And he gave God thanks for the strength that enabled him to forgo even the joys that were possible. And God smiled; and when he saw that Man had become perfect in renunciation and worship, he sent another sun through the sky, which crashed into Man's sun; and all returned again to nebula.

"'Yes,' he murmured, 'it was a good play; I will have it performed again.'"

Such, in outline, but even more purposeless, more void of meaning, is the world which Science presents for our belief. Amid such a world, if anywhere, our ideals henceforward must find a home. That Man is the product of causes which had no prevision of the end they were achieving; that his origin, his growth, his hopes and fears, his loves and his beliefs, are but the outcome of accidental collocations of atoms; that no fire, no heroism, no intensity of thought and feeling, can preserve an individual life beyond the grave; that all the labors of the ages, all the devotion, all the inspiration, all the noon-day brightness of human genius, are destined to extinction in the vast death of the solar system, and that the whole temple of Man's achievement must inevitably be buried beneath the débris of a universe in ruins — all these things, if not quite beyond dispute, are yet so nearly certain that no philosophy which rejects them can hope to stand. Only within the scaffolding of these truths, only on the firm foundation of unyielding despair, can the soul's habitation henceforth be safely built.

How, in such an alien and inhuman world, can so powerless a creature as Man preserve his aspirations untarnished? A strange mystery it is that Nature, omnipotent but blind, in the revolutions of her secular hurryings through the abysses of space, has brought forth at last a child, subject still to her power, but gifted with sight, with knowledge of good and evil, with the capacity of judging all the works of his unthinking mother. In spite of Death, the mark and seal of the parental control, Man is yet free, during his brief years, to examine, to criticize, to know, and in imagination to create. To him alone, in the world with which he is acquainted, this freedom belongs; and in this lies his superiority to the resistless forces that control his outward life.

The savage, like ourselves, feels the oppression of his impotence before the powers of Nature; but having in himself nothing that he respects more than Power, he is willing to prostrate himself before his gods, without inquiring whether they are worthy of his worship. Pathetic and very terrible is the long history of cruelty and torture, of degradation and human sacrifice, endured in the hope of placating the jealous gods; surely, the trembling believer thinks, when what is most precious has been freely given, their lust for blood must be appeased, and more will not be required. The religion of Moloch — as such creeds may be generically called — is in essence the cringing submission of the slave, who dares not, even in his heart, allow the thought that his master deserves no adulation. Since the independence of ideals is not yet acknowledged, Power may be freely worshiped and receive an unlimited respect, despite its wanton infliction of pain.

But gradually, as morality grows bolder, the claim of the ideal world begins to be felt; and worship, if it is not to cease, must be given to gods of another kind than those created by the savage. Some, though they feel the demands of the ideal, will still consciously reject them, still urging that naked Power is worthy of worship. Such is the attitude inculcated in God's answer to Job out of the whirlwind; the divine power and knowledge are paraded, but of the divine goodness there is no hint. Such also is the attitude of those who, in our own day, base their morality upon the struggle for survival, maintaining that the survivors are necessarily the fittest. But others, not content with an answer so repugnant to the moral sense, will adopt the position which we have become accustomed to regard as specially religious, maintaining that, in some hidden manner, the world of fact is really harmonious with the world of ideals. Thus Man creates God, all-powerful and all-good, the mystic unity of what is and what should be.

But the world of fact, after all, is not good; and, in submitting our judgment to it, there is an element of slavishness from which our thoughts must be purged. For in all things it is well to exalt the dignity of Man by freeing him as far as possible from the tyranny of non-human Power. When we have realized that Power is largely bad, that man, with his knowledge of good and evil, is but a helpless atom in a world which has no such knowledge, the choice is again presented to us: Shall we worship Force, or shall we worship Goodness? Shall our God exist and be evil, or shall he be recognized as the creation of our own conscience?

The answer to this question is very momentous, and affects profoundly our whole morality. The worship of Force, to which Carlyle and Nietzsche and the creed of Militarism have accustomed us, is the result of failure to maintain our own ideals against a hostile universe; it is itself a prostrate submission to evil, a sacrifice of our best to Moloch. If strength indeed is to be respected, let us respect rather the strength of those who refuse that false "recognition of facts" which fails to recognize that facts are often bad. Let us admit that, in the world we know, there are many things that would be better otherwise and that the ideals to which we do and must adhere are not realized in the realm of matter. Let us preserve our respect for truth, for beauty, for the ideal of perfection which life does not permit us to attain, though none of these things meets with the approval of the unconscious universe. If power is bad, as it seems to be, let us reject it from our hearts. In this lies Man's true freedom: in determination to worship only the God created by our own love of the good, to respect only the heaven which inspires the insight of our best moments. In action, in desire, we must submit perpetually to the tyranny of outside forces; but in thought, in aspiration, we are free, free from our fellow men, free from the petty planet on which our bodies impotently crawl, free even, while we live, from the tyranny of death. Let us learn, then, that energy of faith which enables us to live constantly in the vision of the good; and let us descend in action into the world of fact with that vision always before us.

When first the opposition of fact and ideal grows fully visible, a spirit of fiery revolt, of fierce hatred of the gods, seems necessary to the assertion of freedom. To defy with Promethean constancy a hostile universe, to keep its evil always in view, always actively hated, to refuse no pain that the malice of Power can invent, appear to be the duty of all who will not bow before the inevitable. But indignation is still a bondage, for it compels our thoughts to be occupied with an evil world; and in the fierceness of desire from which rebellion springs there is a kind of self-assertion which it is necessary for the wise to overcome. Indignation is a submission of our thoughts, but not of our desires; the Stoic freedom in which wisdom consists is found in the submission of our desires, but not of our thoughts. From the submission of our desires springs the virtue of resignation; from the freedom of our thoughts springs the whole world of art and philosophy and the vision of beauty by which at last we half reconquer the reluctant world. But the vision of beauty is possible only to unfettered contemplation, to thoughts not weighted by the load of eager wishes; and thus freedom comes only to those who no longer ask of life that it shall yield them any of those personal goods that are subject to the mutations of Time.

Although the necessity of renunciation is evidence of the existence of evil, yet Christianity, in preaching it, has shown a wisdom exceeding that of the Promethean philosophy of rebellion. It must be admitted that, of the things we desire, some, though they prove impossible, are yet real goods; others, however, as ardently longed for, do not form part of a fully purified ideal. The belief that what must be renounced is bad, though sometimes fake, is far less often false than untamed passion supposes; and the creed of religion, by providing a reason for proving that it is never false, has been the means of purifying our hopes by the discovery of many austere truths.

But there is in resignation a further good element; even real goods, when they are unattainable, ought not to be fretfully desired. To every man comes, sooner or later, the great renunciation. For the young, there is nothing unattainable; a good thing desired with the whole force of a passionate will, and yet impossible, is to them not credible. Yet, by Death, by illness, by poverty, or by the voice of duty, we must learn, each one of us, that the world was not made for us, and that, however beautiful may be the things we crave for, Fate may nevertheless forbid them. It is the part of courage, when misfortune comes, to bear without repining the ruin of our hopes, to turn away our thoughts from vain regrets. This degree of submission to Power is not only just and right; it is the very gate of wisdom.

But passive renunciation is not the whole wisdom; for not by renunciation alone can we build a temple for the worship of our own ideals. Haunting foreshadowings of the temple appear in the realm of imagination, in music, in architecture, in the untroubled kingdom of reason, and in the golden sunset of lyrics, where beauty shines and glows, remote from the touch of sorrow, remote from the fear of change, remote from the failures and the disenchantments of the world of fact. In the contemplation of these things the vision of heaven will shape itself in our hearts, giving at once a touchstone to judge the world about us, and an inspiration by which to fashion to our needs whatever is not incapable of serving as a stone in the sacred temple.

Except for those rare spirits that are born without sin, there is a cavern of darkness to be traversed before that temple can be entered. The gate of the cavern is despair, and its floor is paved with the gravestones of abandoned hopes. There Self must die; there the eagerness, the greed of untamed desire, must be slain, for only so can the soul be freed from the empire of Fate. But out of the cavern the Gate of Renunciation leads again to the daylight of wisdom, by whose radiance a new insight, a new joy, a new tenderness, shine forth to gladden the pilgrim's heart.

When, without the bitterness of impotent rebellion, we have learnt both to resign ourselves to the outward rule of Fate and to recognize that the non-human world is unworthy of our worship, it becomes possible at last so to transform and refashion the unconscious universe, so to transmute it in the crucible of imagination, that a new image of shining gold replaces the old idol of clay. In all the multiform facts of the world — in the visual shapes of trees and mountains and clouds, in the events of the life of Man, even in the very omnipotence of Death — the insight of creative idealism can find the reflection of a beauty which its own thought first made. In this way mind asserts its subtle mastery over the thoughtless forces of Nature. The more evil the material with which it deals, the more thwarting to untrained desire, the greater is its achievement in inducing the reluctant rock to yield up its hidden treasures, the prouder its victory in compelling the opposing forces to swell the pageant of its triumph. Of all the arts,

Tragedy is the proudest, the most triumphant; for it builds its shining citadel in the very center of the enemy's country, on the very summit of his highest mountain; from its impregnable watchtowers, his camps and arsenals, his columns and forts are all revealed; within its walls the free life continues, while the legions of Death and Pain and Despair, and all the servile captains of tyrant Fate, afford the burghers of that dauntless city new spectacles of beauty. Happy those sacred ramparts, thrice happy the dwellers on that all-seeing eminence. Honor to those brave warriors who, through countless ages of warfare, have preserved for us the priceless heritage of liberty and have kept undefiled by sacrilegious invaders the home of the unsubdued.

But the beauty of Tragedy does not make visible a quality which, in more or less obvious shapes, is present always and everywhere in life. In the spectacle of Death, in the endurance of intolerable pain, and in the irrevocableness of a vanished Past, there is a sacredness, an overpowering awe, a feeling of the vastness, the depth, the inexhaustible mystery of existence, in which, as by some strange marriage of pain, the sufferer is bound to the world by bonds of sorrow. In these moments of insight, we lose all eagerness of temporary desire, all struggling and striving for petty ends, all care for the little trivial things that, to a superficial view, make up the common life of day by day; we see, surrounding the narrow raft illumined by the flickering light of human comradeship, the dark ocean on whose rolling waves we toss for a brief hour; from the great night without, a chill blast breaks in upon our refuge; all the loneliness of humanity amid hostile forces is concentrated upon the individual soul, which must struggle alone, with what of courage it can command, against the whole weight of a universe that cares nothing for its hopes and fears. Victory, in this struggle with the powers of darkness, is the true baptism into the glorious company of heroes, the true initiation into the overmastering beauty of human existence. From that awful encounter of the soul with the outer world, renunciation, wisdom, and charity are born; and with their birth a new life begins. To take into the inmost shrine of the soul the irresistible forces whose puppets we seem to be — Death and change, the irrevocableness of the past, and the powerlessness of Man before the blind hurry of the universe from vanity to vanity — to feel these things and know them is to conquer them.

This is the reason why the Past has such magical power. The beauty of its motionless and silent pictures is like the enchanted purity of late autumn, when the leaves, though one breath would make them fall, still glow against the sky in golden glory. The Past does not change or strive; like Duncan, after life's fitful fever it sleeps well; what was eager and grasping, what was petty and transitory, has faded away; the things that were beautiful and eternal shine out of it like stars in the night. Its beauty to a soul not worthy of it is unendurable; but to a soul which has conquered Fate it is the key of religion.

The life of Man, viewed outwardly, is but a small thing in comparison with the forces of Nature. The slave is doomed to worship Time and Fate and Death, because they are greater than anything he finds in himself and because all his thoughts are of things which they devour. But, great as they are, to think of them greatly, to feel their passionless splendor, is greater still. And such thought makes us free men; we no longer bow before the inevitable in Oriental subjection, but we absorb it, and make it a part of ourselves. To abandon the struggle for private happiness, to expel all eagerness of temporary desire, to burn with passion for eternal things — this is emancipation, and this is the free man's worship. And this liberation is effected by a contemplation of Fate; for Fate itself is subdued by the mind which leaves nothing to be purged by the purifying fire of Time.

United with his fellow men by the strongest of all ties, the tie of a common doom, the free man finds that a new vision is with him always, shedding over every daily task the light of love. The life of Man is a long march through the night, surrounded by invisible foes, tortured by weariness and pain, toward a goal that few can hope to reach, and where none may tarry long. One by one, as they march, our comrades vanish from our sight, seized by the silent orders of omnipotent Death. Very brief is the time in which we can help them, in which their happiness or misery is decided. Be it ours to shed sunshine on their path, to lighten their sorrows by the balm of sympathy, to give them the pure joy of a never-tiring affection, to strengthen failing courage, to instill faith in hours of despair. Let us not weigh in grudging scales their merits and demerits, but let us think only of their need — of the sorrows, the difficulties, perhaps the blindnesses, that make the misery of their lives; let us remember that they are fellow sufferers in the same darkness, actors in the same tragedy with ourselves. And so, when their day is over, when their good and their evil have become eternal by the immortality of the Past, be it ours to feel that, where they suffered, where they failed, no deed of ours was the cause; but wherever a spark of the divine fire kindled in their hearts, we were ready with encouragement, with sympathy, with brave words in which high courage glowed.

Brief and powerless is Man's life; on him and all his race the slow, sure doom falls pitiless and dark. Blind to good and evil, reckless of destruction, omnipotent matter rolls on its relentless way; for Man, condemned to-day to lose his dearest, to-morrow himself to pass through the gate of darkness, it remains only to cherish, ere yet the blow falls, the lofty thoughts that ennoble his little day, disdaining the coward terrors of the slave of Fate; to worship at the shrine that his own hands have built, undismayed by the empire of chance, to preserve a mind free from the wanton tyranny that rules his outward life; proudly defiant of the irresistible forces that tolerate, for a moment, his knowledge and his condemnation, to sustain alone, a weary but unyielding Atlas, the world that his own ideals have fashioned despite the trampling march of unconscious power.

LAUGHTER [1]

MAX BEERBOHM (1872-   )

M. BERGSON, in his well-known essay on this theme, says . . . well, he says many things; but none of these, though I have just read them, do I clearly remember, nor am I sure that in the act of reading I understood any of them. That is the worst of these fashionable philosophers — or rather, the worst of me. Somehow I never manage to read them till they are just going out of fashion, and even then I don't seem able to cope with them. About twelve years ago, when everyone suddenly talked to me about Pragmatism and William James, I found myself moved by a dull but irresistible impulse to try Schopenhauer, of whom, years before that, I had heard that he was the easiest reading in the world, and the most exciting and amusing. I wrestled with Schopenhauer for a day or so, in vain. Time passed; M. Bergson appeared "and for his hour was lord of the ascendant"; I tardily tackled William James. I bore in mind, as I approached him, the testimonials that had been lavished on him by all my friends. Alas, I was insensible to his thrillingness. His gayety did not make me gay. His crystal clarity confused me dreadfully. I could make nothing of William

[1] From *And Even Now*.

James. And now, in the fullness of time, I have been floored by M. Bergson.

It distresses me, this failure to keep pace with the leaders of thought as they pass into oblivion. It makes me wonder whether I am, after all, an absolute fool. Yet surely I am not that. Tell me of a man or a woman, a place or an event, real or fictitious: surely you will find me a fairly intelligent listener. Any such narrative will present to me some image, and will stir me to not altogether fatuous thoughts. Come to me in some grievous difficulty: I will talk to you like a father, even like a lawyer. I'll be hanged if I have n't a certain mellow wisdom. But if you are by way of weaving theories as to the nature of things in general, and if you want to try those theories on someone who will luminously confirm them or powerfully rend them, I must, with a hangdog air, warn you that I am not your man. I suffer from a strong suspicion that things in general cannot be accounted for through any formula or set of formulae, and that any one philosophy, howsoever new, is no better than another. That is in itself a sort of philosophy, and I suspect it accordingly; but it has for me the merit of being the only one I can make head or tail of. If you try to expound any other philosophic system to me, you will find not merely that I can detect no flaw in it (except the one great flaw just suggested), but also that I have n't, after a minute or two, the vaguest notion of what you are driving at. "Very well," you say, "instead of trying to explain all things all at once, I will explain some little, simple, single thing." It was for sake of such shorn lambs as myself, doubtless, that M. Bergson sat down and wrote about — Laughter. But I have profited by his kindness no more than if he had been treating of the Cosmos. I cannot tread even a limited space of air. I have a gross satisfaction in the crude fact of being on hard ground again, and I utter a coarse peal of — Laughter.

At least, I say I do so. In point of fact, I have merely smiled. Twenty years ago, ten years ago, I should have laughed, and have professed to you that I had merely smiled. A very young man is not content to be very young, nor even a young man to be young: he wants to share the dignity of his elders. There is no dignity in laughter, there is much of it in smiles. Laughter is but a joyous surrender, smiles give token of mature criticism. It may be that in the early ages of this world there was far more laughter than is to be heard now, and that aeons hence laughter will be obsolete, and smiles universal — everyone, always, mildly, slightly, smiling. But it is less useful to speculate as to mankind's past and future than to observe men. And you will have observed with me in the club room that young men at most times look solemn, whereas old men or men of middle age mostly smile; and also that those young men do often laugh loud and long among themselves, while we others — the gayest and best of us in the most favorable circumstances — seldom achieve more than our habitual act of smiling. Does the sound of that laughter jar on us? Do we liken it to the crackling of thorns under a pot? Let us do so. There is no cheerier sound. But let us not assume it to be the laughter of fools because we sit quiet. It is absurd to disapprove of what one envies, or to wish a good thing were no more because it has passed out of our possession.

But (it seems that I must begin every paragraph by questioning the sincerity of what I have just said) *has* the gift of laughter been withdrawn from me? I protest that I do still, at the age of forty-seven, laugh often and loud and long. But not, I believe, so long and loud and often as in my less smiling youth. And I am proud, nowadays, of laughing, and grateful to anyone who makes me laugh. That is a bad sign. I no longer take laughter as a matter of course. I realize, even after reading M. Bergson on it, how good a thing it is. I am qualified to praise it.

As to what is most precious among the accessories to the world we live in, different men hold different opinions. There are people whom the sea depresses, whom mountains exhilarate. Personally, I want the sea always — some not populous edge of it for choice; and with it sunshine, and wine, and a little music. My friend on the mountain yonder is of tougher fibre and sterner outlook, disapproves of the sea's laxity and instability, has no ear for music and no palate for the grape, and regards the sun as a rather enervating institution, like central heating in a house. What he likes is a gray day and the wind in his face; crags at a great altitude; and a flask of whiskey. Yet I think that even he, if we were trying to determine from what inner sources mankind derives the greatest pleasure in life, would agree with me that only the emotion of love takes higher rank than the emotion of laughter. Both these emotions are partly mental, partly physical. It is said that the mental symptoms of love are wholly physical in origin. They are not the less ethereal for that. The physical sensations of laughter, on the other hand, are reached by a process whose starting point is in the mind. They are not the less "gloriously of our clay." There is laughter that goes so far as to lose all touch with its motive, and to exist only, grossly, in itself.

This is laughter at its best. A man to whom such laughter has often been granted may happen to die in a workhouse. No matter. I will not admit that he has failed in life. Another man, who has never laughed thus, may be buried in Westminster Abbey, leaving more than a million pounds overhead. What then? I regard him as a failure.

Nor does it seem to me to matter one jot how such laughter is achieved. Humor may rollick on high planes of fantasy or in depths of silliness. To many people it appeals only from those depths. If it appeal to them irresistibly, they are more enviable than those who are sensitive only to the finer kind of joke and not so sensitive as to be mastered and dissolved by it. Laughter is a thing to be rated according to its own intensity.

Many years ago I wrote an essay in which I poured scorn on the fun purveyed by the music halls, and on the great public for which that fun was quite good enough. I take that callow scorn back. I fancy that the fun itself was better than it seemed to me, and might not have displeased me if it had been wafted to me in private, in presence of a few friends. A public crowd, because of a lack of broad impersonal humanity in me, rather insulates than absorbs me. Amidst the guffaws of a thousand strangers I become unnaturally grave. If these people were the entertainment, and I the audience, I should be sympathetic enough. But to be one of them is a position that drives me spiritually aloof. Also, there is to me something rather dreary in the notion of going anywhere for the specific purpose of being amused. I prefer that laughter shall take me unawares. Only so can it master and dissolve me. And in this respect, at any rate, I am not peculiar.

In music halls and such places, you may hear loud laughter, but — not see silent laughter, not see strong men weak, helpless, suffering, gradually convalescent, dangerously relapsing. Laughter at its greatest and best is not there.

To such laughter nothing is more propitious than an occasion that demands gravity. To have a good reason for not laughing is one of the surest aids. Laughter rejoices in bonds. If music halls were schoolrooms for us, and the comedians were our schoolmasters, how much less talent would be needed for giving us how much more joy! Even in private and accidental intercourse, few are the men whose humor can reduce us, be we never so susceptible, to paroxysms of mirth. I will wager that nine tenths of the world's best laughter is laughter *at,* not *with.* And it is the people set in authority over us that touch most surely our sense of the ridiculous. Freedom is a good thing, but we lose through its golden moments. The schoolmaster to his pupils, the monarch to his courtiers, the editor to his staff — how priceless they are! Reverence is a good thing, and part of its value is that the more we revere a man, the more sharply are we struck by anything in him (and there is always much) that is incongruous with his greatness. And herein lies one of the reasons why, as we grow older, we laugh less. The men we esteemed so great are gathered to their fathers. Some of our coevals may, for aught we know, be very great, but, good heavens! we can't esteem *them* so.

Of extreme laughter I know not in any annals a more satisfying example than one that is to be found in Moore's *Life of Byron.* Both Byron and Moore were already in high spirits when, on an evening in the spring of 1813, they went "from some early assembly" to Mr. Rogers's house in St. James's Place and were regaled there with an impromptu meal. But not high spirits alone would have led the two young poets to such an excess of laughter as made the evening so very memorable. Luckily they both venerated Rogers (strange as it may seem to us) as the greatest of living poets. Luckily, too, Mr. Rogers was ever the kind of man, the coldly and quietly suave kind of man, with whom you don't take liberties if you can help it — with whom, if you *can't* help it, to take liberties is in itself a most exhilarating act. And he had just received a presentation copy of Lord Thurlow's latest book, *Poems on Several Occasions*. The two young poets found in this elder's Muse much that was so execrable as to be delightful. They were soon, as they turned the pages, held in throes of laughter, laughter that was but intensified by the endeavors of their correct and nettled host to point out the genuine merits of his friend's work. And then suddenly — oh joy! — "We lighted," Moore records, "on the discovery that our host, in addition to his sincere approbation of some of this book's contents, had also the motive of gratitude for standing by its author, as one of the poems was a warm and, I need not add, well-deserved panegyric on himself. We were, however" — the narrative has an added charm from Tom Moore's demure care not to offend or compromise the still-surviving Rogers — "too far gone in nonsense for even this eulogy, in which we both so heartily agreed, to stop us. The opening line of the poem was, as well as I can recollect, "When Rogers o'er this labour bent"; and Lord Byron undertook to read it aloud; — but he found it impossible to get beyond the first two words. Our laughter had now increased to such a pitch that nothing could restrain it. Two or three times he began; but no sooner had the words "When Rogers" passed his lips, than our fit burst out afresh, — till even Mr. Rogers himself, with all his feeling of our injustice, found it impossible not to join us; and we were, at last, all three in such a state of inextinguishable laughter that, had the author himself been of our party, I question much whether he could have resisted the infection." The final fall and dissolution of Rogers, Rogers behaving as badly as either of them, is all that was needed to give perfection to this heart-warming scene. I like to think that on a certain night in spring, year after year, three ghosts revisit that old room and (without, I hope, inconvenience to Lord Northcliffe, who may happen to be there) sit rocking and writhing in the grip of that old shared rapture. Uncanny? Well, not more so than would have seemed to Byron and Moore and Rogers the notion that more than a hundred years away from them was someone joining in their laughter — as *I* do.

Alas, I cannot join in it more than gently. To imagine a scene, however vividly, does not give us the sense of being, or even of having been, present at it. Indeed, the greater the glow of the scene reflected, the sharper is the pang of our realization that we were *not* there, and of our annoyance that we were n't. Such a pang comes to me with special force whenever my fancy posts itself outside the Temple's gate in Fleet Street, and there, at a late hour of the night of May 10, 1773, observes a gigantic old man laughing wildly, but having no one with him to share and aggrandize his emotion. Not that he is alone; but the young man beside him laughs only in politeness and is inwardly puzzled, even shocked. Boswell has a keen, an exquisitely keen, scent for comedy, for the fun that is latent in fine shades of character; but imaginative burlesque, anything that borders on lovely nonsense, he was not formed to savor. All the more does one revel in his account of what led up to the moment when Johnson, "to support himself, laid hold of one of the posts at the side of the foot pavement, and sent forth peals so loud that in the silence of the night his voice seemed to resound from Temple Bar to Fleet Ditch."

No evening ever had an unlikelier ending. The omens were all for gloom. Johnson had gone to dine at General Paoli's, but was so ill that he had to leave before the meal was over. Later he managed to go to Mr. Chambers's rooms in the Temple. "He continued to be very ill" there, but gradually felt better, and "talked with a noble enthusiasm of keeping up the representation of respectable families," and was great on "the dignity and propriety of male succession." Among his listeners, as it happened, was a gentleman for whom Mr. Chambers had that day drawn up a will devising his estate to his three sisters. The news of this might have been expected to make Johnson violent in wrath. But no, for some reason he grew violent only in laughter, and insisted thenceforth on calling that gentleman "The Testator" and chaffing him without mercy. "I daresay he thinks he has done a mighty thing. He won't stay till he gets home to his seat in the country, to produce this wonderful deed: he'll call up the landlord of the first inn on the road; and after a suitable preface upon mortality and the uncertainty of life, will tell him that he should not delay in making his will; and Here, Sir, will he say, is *my* will, which I have just made, with the assistance of one of the ablest lawyers in the kingdom; and he will read it to him. He believes he has made this will; but he did not make it; you, Chambers, made it for him. I hope you have more conscience than to make him say 'being of sound understanding!' ha, ha, ha! I hope he has left me a legacy. I'd have his will turned into verse, like a ballad." These flights annoyed Mr. Chambers, and are recorded by Boswell with the apology that he wishes his readers to be "acquainted with the slightest occasional characteristics of so eminent a man." Certainly, there is nothing ridiculous in the fact of a man making a will. But this is the measure of Johnson's achievement. He had created gloriously much out of nothing at all. There he sat, old and ailing and unencouraged by the company, but soaring higher and higher in absurdity, more and more rejoicing, and still soaring and rejoicing after he had gone out into the night with Boswell, till at last in Fleet Street his paroxysms were too much for him and he could no more. Echoes of that huge laughter come ringing down the ages. But is there also perhaps a note of sadness for us in them? Johnson's endless sociability came of his inherent melancholy: he could not bear to be alone; and his very mirth was but a mode of escape from the dark thoughts within him. Of these the thought of death was the most dreadful to him, and the most insistent. He was forever wondering how death would come to him, and how he would acquit himself in the extreme moment. A later but not less devoted Anglican, meditating on his own end, wrote in his diary that "to die in church appears to be a great euthanasia, but not," he quaintly and touchingly added, "at a time to disturb worshippers." Both the sentiment here expressed and the reservation drawn would have been as characteristic of Johnson as they were of Gladstone.

But to die of laughter — this, too, seems to me a great euthanasia; and I think that for Johnson to have died thus, that night in Fleet Street, would have been a grand ending to "a life radically wretched." Well, he was destined to outlive another decade; and, selfishly, who can wish such a life as his, or such a Life as Boswell's, one jot shorter?

Strange, when you come to think of it, that of all the countless folk who have lived before our time on this planet not one is known in history or in legend as having died of laughter. Strange, too, that not to one of all the characters in romance has such an end been allotted. Has it ever struck you what a chance Shakespeare missed when he was finishing the Second Part of *Henry the Fourth?* Falstaff was not the man to stand cowed and bowed while the new young king lectured him and cast him off. Little by little, as Hal proceeded in that portentous allocution, the humor of the situation would have mastered old Sir John. His face, blank with surprise at first, would presently have glowed and widened, and his whole bulk have begun to quiver. Lest he should miss one word, he would have mastered himself. But the final words would have been the signal for release of all the roars pent up in him; the welkin would have rung; the roars, belike, would have gradually subsided in dreadful rumblings of more than utterable or conquerable mirth. Thus and thus only might his life have been rounded off with dramatic fitness, *secundum ipsius naturam.* He never should have been left to babble of green fields and die "an it had been any christom child." [2]

Falstaff is a triumph of comedic creation because we are kept laughing equally at and with him. Neverthe-

[2] See *Henry V* II. iii.

less, if I had the choice of sitting with him at the Boar's Head or with Johnson at the Turk's, I should n't hesitate for an instant. The agility of Falstaff's mind gains much of its effect by contrast with the massiveness of his body; but in contrast with Johnson's equal agility is Johnson's moral as well as physical bulk. His sallies "tell" the more startlingly because of the noble weight of character behind them: they are the better because *he* makes them. In Falstaff there is n't this final incongruity and element of surprise. Falstaff is but a sublimated sample of "the funny man." We cannot, therefore, laugh so greatly with him as with Johnson. (Nor even *at* him; because we are not tickled so much by the weak points of a character whose points are all weak ones; also because we have no reverence trying to impose restraint upon us.) Still, Falstaff has indubitably the power to convulse us. I don't mean we ever are convulsed in reading *Henry the Fourth*. No printed page, alas, can thrill us to extremities of laughter. These are ours only if the mirthmaker be a living man whose jests we hear as they come fresh from his own lips. All I claim for Falstaff is that he would be able to convulse us if he were alive and accessible. Few, as I have said, are the humorists who can induce this state. To master and dissolve us, to give us the joy of being worn down and tired out with laughter, is a success to be won by no man save in virtue of a rare staying power. Laughter becomes extreme only if it be consecutive. There must be no pauses for recovery. Touch-and-go humor, however happy, is not enough. The jester must be able to grapple his theme and hang on to it, twisting it this way and that, and making it yield magically all manner of strange and precious things, one after another, without pause.

He must have invention keeping pace with utterance. He must be inexhaustible. Only so can he exhaust us.

I have a friend whom I would praise. There are many other of my friends to whom I am indebted for much laughter; but I do believe that if all of them sent in their bills to-morrow and all of them overcharged me not a little, the total of all those totals would be less appalling than that which looms in my own vague estimate of what I owe to Comus. Comus I call him here in observance of the line drawn between public and private virtue, and in full knowledge that he would of all men be the least glad to be quite personally thanked and laureled in the market place for the hours he has made memorable among his cronies. No one is so diffident as he, no one so self-postponing. Many people have met him again and again without faintly suspecting "anything much" in him. Many of his acquaintances — friends, too — relatives, even — have lived and died in the belief that he was quite ordinary. Thus is he the more greatly valued by his cronies. Thus do we pride ourselves on possessing some curious right quality to which alone he is responsive. But it would seem that either this asset of ours or its effect on him is intermittent. He can be dull and null enough with us sometimes — a mere asker of questions, or drawer of comparisons between this and that brand of cigarettes, or full expatiator on the merits of some new patent razor. A whole hour and more may be wasted in such humdrum and darkness. And then — something will have happened. There has come a spark in the murk; a flame now, presage of a radiance; Comus has begun. His face is a great part of his equipment. A cast of it might be somewhat akin to the comic mask of the ancients; but no cast could be worthy of it; mobility is the essence of it. It flickers and shifts in accord to the matter of his discourse; it contracts and it expands; is there anything its elastic can't express? Comus would be eloquent even were he dumb. And he is mellifluous. His voice, while he develops an idea or conjures up a scene, takes on a peculiar richness and unction. If he be describing an actual scene, voice and face are adaptable to those of the actual persons therein. But it is not in such mimicry that he excels. As a reporter he has rivals. For the most part, he moves on a higher plane than that of mere fact: he imagines, he creates, giving you not a person, but a type, a synthesis, and not what anywhere has been, but what anywhere might be — what, as one feels, for all the absurdity of it, just would be. He knows his world well, and nothing human is alien to him, but certain skeins of life have a special hold on him, and he on them. In his youth he wished to be a clergyman; and over the clergy of all grades and denominations his genius hovers and swoops and ranges with a special mastery. Lawyers he loves less; yet the legal mind seems to lie almost as wide-open to him as the sacerdotal; and the legal manner in all its phases he can unerringly burlesque. In the minds of journalists, diverse journalists, he is not less thoroughly at home, so that of the wild contingencies imagined by him there is none about which he cannot reel off an oral "leader" or "middle" in the likeliest style, and with as much ease as he can preach a High Church or Low Church sermon on it. Nor are his improvisations limited by prose. If a theme call for nobler treatment, he becomes an unflagging fountain of ludicrously adequate blank verse. Or, again, he may deliver himself in rhyme.

There is no form of utterance that comes amiss to him for interpreting the human comedy, or for broadening the farce into which that comedy is turned by him. Nothing can stop him when once he is in the vein. No appeals move him. He goes from strength to strength while his audience is more and more piteously debilitated.

What a gift to have been endowed with! What a power to wield! And how often have I envied Comus! But this envy of him has never taken root in me. His mind laughs, doubtless, at his own conceptions; but not his body. And if you tell him something that you have been sure will convulse him you are likely to be rewarded with no more than a smile betokening that he sees the point. Incomparable laughter-giver, he is not much a laugher. He is vintner, not toper. I would therefore not change places with him. I am well content to have been his beneficiary during thirty years, and to be so for as many more as may be given us.

SCIENCE AND THE SAVAGES [1]

G. K. CHESTERTON (1874–   )

A PERMANENT disadvantage of the study of folklore and kindred subjects is that the man of science can hardly be in the nature of things very frequently a man of the world. He is a student of nature; he is scarcely ever a student of human nature. And even where this difficulty is overcome, and he is in some sense a student of human nature, this is only a very faint beginning of the painful progress towards being human. For the study of primitive race and religion stands apart in one important respect from all, or nearly all, the ordinary scientific studies. A man can understand astronomy only by being an astronomer; he can understand entomology only by being an entomologist (or, perhaps, an insect); but he can understand a great deal of anthropology merely by being a man. He is himself the animal which he studies. Hence arises the fact which strikes the eye everywhere in the records of ethnology and folklore — the fact that the same frigid and detached spirit which leads to success in the study of astronomy or botany leads to disaster in the study of mythology or human origins. It is necessary to cease to be a man in order to do justice to a microbe; it is not necessary to cease to be a man in order to do justice to men. That same suppression of sympathies, that same waving away of intuitions or guesswork, which make a man preternaturally clever in dealing with the stomach of a spider will make him preternaturally stupid in dealing with the heart of man. He is making himself inhuman in order to understand humanity. An ignorance of the other world is boasted by many men of science; but in this matter their defect arises, not from ignorance of the other world, but from ignorance of this world. For the secrets about which anthropologists concern themselves can be best learnt, not from books or voyages, but from the ordinary commerce of man with man. The secret of why some savage tribe worships monkeys or the moon is not to be found even by traveling among those savages and taking down their answers in a notebook, although the cleverest man may pursue this course. The answer to the riddle is in England; it is in London; nay, it is in his own heart. When a man has discovered why men in Bond Street wear black hats he will at the same moment have discovered why men in Timbuctoo wear red feathers. The mystery in the heart of some savage war dance should not be studied in books of scientific travel; it should be studied at a subscription ball. If a man desires to find out the origins of religions, let him not go to the Sandwich Islands; let him go to church. If a man wishes to know the origin of human society, to know what society, philosophically speaking, really is, let him not go into the British Museum; let him go into society.

This total misunderstanding of the real nature of ceremonial gives rise to the most awkward and dehumanized versions of the conduct of men in rude lands and ages. The man of science, not realizing that ceremonial is essentially a thing which is done without a reason, has to find a reason for every sort of ceremonial, and, as might be supposed, the reason is generally a very absurd one — absurd because it originates not in the simple mind of the barbarian, but in the sophisticated mind of the professor. The learned man will say, for instance, "The natives of Mumbojumbo Land believe that the dead man can eat, and will require food upon his journey to the other world. This is attested by the fact that they place food in the grave, and that any family not complying with this rite is the object of the anger of the priests and the tribe." To anyone acquainted with humanity this way of talking is topsy-turvy. It is like saying, "The English in the twentieth century believed that a dead man could smell. This is attested by the fact that they always covered his grave with lilies, violets, or other flowers. Some priestly and tribal terrors were evidently attached to the neglect of this action, as we have records of several old ladies who were very much disturbed in mind because their wreaths had not arrived in time for the funeral." It may be of course that savages put food with a dead man because they think that a dead man can eat, or weapons with a dead man because they think that a dead man can fight. But personally I do not believe that they think anything of the kind. I believe they put food or weapons on the dead for the same reason that we put flowers, because it is an exceedingly natural and obvious thing to do. We do not understand, it is true, the emotion which makes us think it obvious and natural; but that is because, like all the important emotions of human existence, it is essentially irrational. We do not understand the savage for the same reason that the savage does not understand himself. And the savage does not understand himself for the same reason that we do not understand ourselves either.

The obvious truth is that the moment any matter has passed through the human mind it is finally and forever spoilt for all purposes of science. It has become a thing incurably mysterious and infinite; this mortal has put on immortality. Even what we call our material desires are spiritual, because they are human. Science can analyze a pork chop, and say how much of it is phosphorus and how much is protein; but science cannot analyze any man's wish for a pork chop, and say how much of it is hunger, how much custom, how much nervous fancy, how much a haunting love of the beautiful. The man's desire for the pork chop remains literally as mystical and ethereal as his desire for heaven. All attempts, therefore, at a science of any human things, at a science of history, a science of folklore, a science of sociology, are by their nature not merely hopeless, but crazy. You can no more be certain in economic history that a man's desire for money was merely a desire for money than you can be certain in hagiology that a saint's desire for God was merely a desire for God. And this kind of vagueness in the primary phenomena of the study is an absolutely final blow to anything in the nature of a science. Men can construct a science with very few instruments, or with very plain instruments; but no one on earth could construct a science with unreliable instruments. A man might work out the whole of mathematics with a handful of pebbles, but not with a handful of clay which was always falling apart into new fragments, and falling together into new combinations. A man might measure heaven and earth with a reed, but not with a growing reed.

SCIENCE AND THE SAVAGES

As one of the enormous follies of folklore, let us take the case of the transmigration of stories, and the alleged unity of their source. Story after story the scientific mythologists have cut out of its place in history, and pinned side by side with similar stories in their museum of fables. The process is industrious, it is fascinating, and the whole of it rests on one of the plainest fallacies in the world. That a story has been told all over the place at some time or other not only does not prove that it really never happened; it does not even faintly indicate or make slightly more probable that it never happened. That a large number of fishermen have falsely asserted that they have caught a pike two feet long does not in the least affect the question of whether anyone ever really did so. That numberless journalists announce a Franco-German war merely for money is no evidence one way or the other upon the dark question of whether such a war ever occurred. Doubtless in a few hundred years the innumerable Franco-German wars that did not happen will have cleared the scientific mind of any belief in the legendary war of '70 which did. But that will be because, if folklore students remain at all, their nature will be unchanged; and their services to folklore will be still as they are at present, greater than they know. For in truth these men do something far more godlike than studying legends; they create them.

There are two kinds of stories which the scientists say cannot be true, because everybody tells them. The first class consists of the stories which are told everywhere, because they are somewhat odd or clever; there is nothing in the world to prevent their having happened to somebody as an adventure any more than there is anything to prevent their having occurred, as they certainly did occur, to somebody as an idea. But they are not likely to have happened to many people. The second class of their "myths" consists of the stories that are told everywhere for the simple reason that they happen everywhere. Of the first class, for instance, we might take such an example as the story of William Tell, now generally ranked among legends upon the sole ground that it is found in the tales of other peoples. Now, it is obvious that this was told everywhere because, whether true or fictitious, it is what is called "a good story"; it is odd, exciting, and it has a climax. But to suggest that some such eccentric incident can never have happened in the whole history of archery, or that it did not happen to any particular person of whom it is told, is stark impudence. The idea of shooting at a mark attached to some valuable or beloved person is an idea doubtless that might easily have occurred to any inventive poet. But it is also an idea that might easily occur to any boastful archer. It might be one of the fantastic caprices of some story-teller. It might equally well be one of the fantastic caprices of some tyrant. It might occur first in real life and afterwards occur in legends. Or it might just as well occur first in legends and afterwards occur in real life. If no apple has ever been shot off a boy's head from the beginning of the world, it may be done to-morrow morning, and by somebody who has never heard of William Tell.

This type of tale, indeed, may be pretty fairly paralleled with the ordinary anecdote terminating in a repartee or an Irish bull. Such a retort as the famous *"Je ne vois pas la necessité"* [2] we have all seen attributed to Talleyrand, to Voltaire, to Henri Quatre, to an

[2] the answer given to one who attempted to justify having published some libels on the ground that he had to live somehow

anonymous judge, and so on. But this variety does not in any way make it more likely that the thing was never said at all. It is highly likely that it was really said by somebody unknown. It is highly likely that it was really said by Talleyrand. In any case, it is not any more difficult to believe that the *mot* might have occurred to a man in conversation than to a man writing memoirs. It might have occurred to any of the men I have mentioned. But there is this point of distinction about it, that it is not likely to have occurred to all of them. And this is where the first class of so-called myth differs from the second to which I have previously referred. For there is a second class of incident found to be common to the stories of five or six heroes, say to Sigurd, to Hercules, to Rustem, to the Cid, and so on. And the peculiarity of this myth is that not only is it highly reasonable to imagine that it really happened to one hero, but it is highly reasonable to imagine that it really happened to all of them. Such a story, for instance, is that of a great man having his strength swayed or thwarted by the mysterious weakness of a woman. The anecdotal story, the story of William Tell, is, as I have said, popular because it is peculiar. But this kind of story, the story of Samson and Delilah, of Arthur and Guinevere, is obviously popular because it is not peculiar. It is popular as good, quiet fiction is popular, because it tells the truth about people. If the ruin of Samson by a woman, and the ruin of Hercules by a woman, have a common legendary origin, it is gratifying to know that we can also explain, as a fable, the ruin of Nelson by a woman and the ruin of Parnell by a woman. And, indeed, I have no doubt whatever that, some centuries hence, the students of folklore will refuse altogether to believe that

Elizabeth Barrett eloped with Robert Browning, and will prove their point up to the hilt by the unquestionable fact that the whole fiction of the period was full of such elopements from end to end.

Possibly the most pathetic of all the delusions of the modern students of primitive belief is the notion they have about the thing they call anthropomorphism. They believe that primitive men attributed phenomena to a god in human form in order to explain them, because his mind in its sullen limitation could not reach any further than his own clownish existence. The thunder was called the voice of a man, the lightning the eyes of a man, because by this explanation they were made more reasonable and comfortable. The final cure for all this kind of philosophy is to walk down a lane at night. Anyone who does so will discover very quickly that men pictured something semihuman at the back of all things, not because such a thought was natural, but because it was supernatural; not because it made things more comprehensible, but because it made them a hundred times more incomprehensible and mysterious. For a man walking down a lane at night can see the conspicuous fact that as long as nature keeps to her own course, she has no power with us at all. As long as a tree is a tree, it is a top-heavy monster with a hundred arms, a thousand tongues, and only one leg. But so long as a tree is a tree, it does not frighten us at all. It begins to be something alien, to be something strange, only when it looks like ourselves. When a tree really looks like a man our knees knock under us. And when the whole universe looks like a man we fall on our faces.

ON BEING THE RIGHT SIZE [1]

J. B. S. HALDANE (1892-)

THE most obvious differences between different animals are differences of size, but for some reason the zoölogists have paid singularly little attention to them. In a large textbook of zoölogy before me I find no indication that the eagle is larger than the sparrow, or the hippopotamus bigger than the hare, though some grudging admissions are made in the case of the mouse and the whale. But yet it is easy to show that a hare could not be as large as a hippopotamus, or a whale as small as a herring. For every type of animal there is a most convenient size, and a large change in size inevitably carries with it a change of form.

Let us take the most obvious of possible cases, and consider a giant man sixty feet high — about the height of Giant Pope and Giant Pagan in the illustrated *Pilgrim's Progress* of my childhood. These monsters were not only ten times as high as Christian, but ten times as wide and ten times as thick, so that their total weight was a thousand times his, or about eighty to ninety tons. Unfortunately, the cross sections of their bones were only a hundred times those of Christian, so that every square inch of giant bone had to support ten times the weight borne by a square inch

[1] From *Possible Worlds*.

of human bone. As the human thigh bone breaks under about ten times the human weight, Pope and Pagan would have broken their thighs every time they took a step. This was doubtless why they were sitting down in the picture I remember. But it lessens one's respect for Christian and Jack the Giant Killer.

To turn to zoölogy, suppose that a gazelle, a graceful little creature with long thin legs, is to become large — it will break its bones unless it does one of two things. It may make its legs short and thick, like the rhinoceros, so that every pound of weight has still about the same area of bone to support it. Or it can compress its body and stretch out its legs obliquely to gain stability like the giraffe. I mention these two beasts because they happen to belong to the same order as the gazelle, and both are quite successful mechanically, being remarkably fast runners.

Gravity, a mere nuisance to Christian, was a terror to Pope, Pagan, and Despair. To the mouse and any smaller animal it presents practically no dangers. You can drop a mouse down a thousand-yard mine shaft and, on arriving at the bottom, it gets a slight shock and walks away, provided that the ground is fairly soft. A rat is killed, a man is broken, a horse splashes. For the resistance presented to movement by the air is proportional to the surface of the moving object. Divide an animal's length, breadth, and height each by ten; its weight is reduced to a thousandth, but its surface only to a hundredth. So the resistance to falling in the case of the small animal is relatively ten times the driving force.

An insect, therefore, is not afraid of gravity; it can fall without danger, and can cling to the ceiling with remarkably little trouble. It can go in for elegant

ON BEING THE RIGHT SIZE

fantastic forms of support like that of the daddy longlegs. But there is a force which is as formidable to an insect as gravitation to a mammal. This is surface tension. A man coming out of a bath carries with him a film of water of about one fiftieth of an inch in thickness. This weighs roughly a pound. A wet mouse has to carry about its own weight of water. A wet fly has to lift many times its own weight and, as everyone knows, a fly once wetted by water or any other liquid is in a very serious position indeed. An insect going for a drink is in as great danger as a man leaning out over a precipice in search of food. If it once falls into the grip of the surface tension of the water, — that is to say, gets wet, — it is likely to remain so until it drowns. A few insects, such as water beetles, contrive to be unwettable; the majority keep well away from their drink by means of a long proboscis.

Of course tall land animals have other difficulties. They have to pump their blood to greater heights than a man and, therefore, require a larger blood pressure and tougher blood vessels. A great many men die from burst arteries, especially in the brain, and this danger is presumably still greater for an elephant or a giraffe. But animals of all kinds find difficulties in size for the following reason: A typical small animal, say a microscopic worm or rotifer, has a smooth skin through which all the oxygen it requires can soak in, a straight gut with sufficient surface to absorb its food, and a simple kidney. Increase its dimensions tenfold in every direction, and its weight is increased a thousand times, so that if it is to use its muscles as efficiently as its miniature counterpart, it will need a thousand times as much food and oxygen per day and will excrete a thousand times as much of waste products.

Now if its shape is unaltered, its surface will be increased only a hundredfold, and ten times as much oxygen must enter per minute through each square millimetre of skin, ten times as much food through each square millimetre of intestine. When a limit is reached to their absorptive powers their surface has to be increased by some special device. For example, a part of the skin may be drawn out into tufts to make gills, or pushed in to make lungs, thus increasing the oxygen-absorbing surface in proportion to the animal's bulk. A man, for example, has a hundred square yards of lung. Similarly the gut, instead of being smooth and straight, becomes coiled and develops a velvety surface, and other organs increase in complication. The higher animals are not larger than the lower because they are more complicated. They are more complicated because they are larger. Just the same is true of plants. The simplest plants, such as the green algae growing in stagnant water or on the bark of trees, are mere round cells. The higher plants increase their surface by putting out leaves and roots. Comparative anatomy is largely the story of the struggle to increase surface in proportion to volume.

Some of the methods of increasing the surface are useful up to a point but not capable of a very wide adaptation. For example, while vertebrates carry the oxygen from the gills or lungs all over the body in the blood, insects take air directly to every part of their body by tiny blind tubes called tracheae which open to the surface at many different points. Now, although by their breathing movements they can renew the air in the outer part of the tracheal system, the oxygen has to penetrate the finer branches by means of diffusion. Gases can diffuse easily through very small

ON BEING THE RIGHT SIZE 359

distances, not many times larger than the average length traveled by a gas molecule between collisions with other molecules. But when such vast journeys — from the point of view of a molecule — as a quarter of an inch have to be made, the process becomes slow. So the portions of an insect's body more than a quarter of an inch from the air would always be short of oxygen. In consequence hardly any insects are much more than half an inch thick. Land crabs are built on the same general plan as insects, but are much clumsier. Yet, like ourselves, they carry oxygen around in their blood, and are therefore able to grow far larger than any insects. If the insects had hit on a plan for driving air through their tissues instead of letting it soak in, they might well have become as large as lobsters, though other considerations would have prevented them from becoming as large as man.

Exactly the same difficulties attach to flying. It is an elementary principle of aeronautics that the minimum speed needed to keep an airplane of a given shape in the air varies as the square root of its length. If its linear dimensions are increased four times, it must fly twice as fast. Now the power needed for the minimum speed increases more rapidly than the weight of the machine. So the larger airplane, which weighs sixty-four times as much as the smaller, needs one hundred and twenty-eight times its horsepower to keep up. Applying the same principles to the birds, we find that the limit to their size is soon reached. An angel whose muscles developed no more power, weight for weight, than those of an eagle or a pigeon would require a breast projecting for about four feet to house the muscles engaged in working its wings, while to economize in weight its legs would have to be reduced to mere stilts. Actually a large bird such as an eagle or kite does not keep in the air mainly by moving its wings. It is generally to be seen soaring, that is to say balanced on a rising column of air. But even soaring becomes more and more difficult with increasing size. Were this not the case eagles might be as large as tigers and as formidable to man as hostile airplanes.

But it is time that we passed to some of the advantages of size. One of the most obvious is that it enables one to keep warm. All warm-blooded animals at rest lose the same amount of heat from a unit area of skin, for which purpose they need a food supply proportional to their surface and not to their weight. Five thousand mice weigh as much as a man. Their combined surface and food, or oxygen consumption, are about seventeen times a man's. In fact a mouse eats about one quarter of its own weight of food every day, which is mainly used in keeping it warm. For the same reason small animals cannot live in cold countries. In the arctic regions there are no reptiles or amphibians, and no small mammals. The smallest mammal in Spitzbergen is the fox. The small birds fly away in the winter, while the insects die, though their eggs can survive six months or more of frost. The most successful mammals are bears, seals, and walruses.

Similarly, the eye is a rather inefficient organ until it reaches a large size. The back of the human eye on which an image of the outside world is thrown, and which corresponds to the film of a camera, is composed of a mosaic of "rods and cones" whose diameter is little more than a length of an average light wave. Each eye has about half a million, and for two objects

ON BEING THE RIGHT SIZE 361

to be distinguishable their images must fall on separate rods or cones. It is obvious that with fewer but larger rods and cones we should see less distinctly. If they were twice as broad, two points would have to be twice as far apart before we could distinguish them at a given distance. But if their size were diminished and their number increased, we should see no better. For it is impossible to form a definite image smaller than a wave length of light. Hence a mouse's eye is not a small-scale model of a human eye. Its rods and cones are not much smaller than ours, and therefore there are far fewer of them. A mouse could not distinguish one human face from another six feet away. In order that they should be of any use at all, the eyes of small animals have to be much larger in proportion to their bodies than our own. Large animals, on the other hand, only require relatively small eyes, and those of the whale and elephant are little larger than our own.

For rather more recondite reasons the same general principle holds true of the brain. If we compare the brain weights of a set of very similar animals such as the cat, cheetah, leopard, and tiger, we find that as we quadruple the body weight the brain weight is only doubled. The larger animal with proportionately larger bones can economize on brain, eyes, and certain other organs.

Such are a very few of the considerations which show that for every type of animal there is an optimum size. Yet although Galileo demonstrated the contrary more than three hundred years ago, people still believe that if a flea were as large as a man it could jump a thousand feet into the air. As a matter of fact the height to which an animal can jump is more nearly independent of its size than proportional to it. A flea can jump about two feet, a man about five. To jump a given height, if we neglect the resistance of air, requires an expenditure of energy proportional to the jumper's weight. But if the jumping muscles form a constant fraction of the animal's body, the energy developed per ounce of muscle is independent of the size, provided it can be developed quickly enough in the small animal. As a matter of fact an insect's muscles, although they can contract more quickly than our own, appear to be less efficient, as otherwise a flea or grasshopper could rise six feet into the air.

And just as there is a best size for every animal, so the same is true for every human institution. In the Greek type of democracy all the citizens could listen to a series of orators and vote directly on questions of legislation. Hence their philosophers held that a small city was the largest possible democratic state. The English invention of representative government made a democratic nation possible, and the possibility was first realized in the United States, and later elsewhere. With the development of broadcasting it has once more become possible for every citizen to listen to the political views of representative orators, and the future may perhaps see the return of the national state to the Greek form of democracy. Even the referendum has been made possible only by the institution of daily newspapers.

To the biologist the problem of socialism appears largely as a problem of size. The extreme socialists desire to run every nation as a single business concern. I do not suppose that Henry Ford would find much difficulty in running Andorra or Luxembourg on a socialistic basis. He has already more men on his pay roll than their population. It is conceivable that a syndicate of Fords, if we could find them, would make Belgium, Ltd., or Denmark, Inc., pay their way. But while nationalization of certain industries is an obvious possibility in the largest of states, I find it no easier to picture a completely socialized British Empire or United States than an elephant turning somersaults or a hippopotamus jumping a hedge.